Praise for *Capital Choices*

"*Capital Choices* breaks new ground, providing a convincing explanation for the wide variations we observe in the characteristics of sovereign wealth funds around the world. Clearly written and thoroughly researched, the book is a must read for anyone interested in the domestic politics of international finance."

—Benjamin Cohen, University of California, Santa Barbara

"This is a major work not just about the increasingly important sovereign wealth funds but also about how non-Western states pursue industrial policies. It combines theory, non-Western cases and new empirical material to tell a story of why states create sovereign wealth funds and their scope for choosing distinct paths of economic development."

—Mark Thatcher, London School of Economics and Political Science

"In *Capital Choices*, Juergen Braunstein provides an illuminating original account of the emergence and divergence of sovereign wealth funds. Explaining how different interests and coalitions shape varying SWF paths, this compelling argument finally places politics where it belongs—at the centre of analysis. A decisive intervention in the debate."

—Garry Rodan, Murdoch University

"Braunstein provides a fresh account for the creation of sovereign funds in particular but the state's relations with capital more broadly. This book shows that capital choices are not driven by a too-much-money problem, but through the dynamic interactions and competing interests of domestic policy networks."

—Adam Dixon, Maastricht University

"When the label 'Sovereign Wealth Funds' was applied to a set of government-owned asset funds, it fostered the impression that we were talking about a single well-defined animal. *Capital Choices* shows that SWFs in fact vary widely and explores the nature and origins of the differences."

—Jeffrey Frankel, Harvard University

Capital Choices

Sovereign wealth funds are state-controlled pools of capital that hold financial and real assets, including shares of state enterprises, and manage them to preserve and grow the nation's base of sovereign wealth. The dramatic rise of sovereign wealth funds (SWFs) in number and size—the funds are now larger than the combined size of global private equity and hedge funds—and that the majority of them are located in non-OECD countries have raised concerns about the future direction of capitalism. Yet SWFs are not a homogenous group of actors. Why do some countries with large current account surpluses, notably China, create SWFs while others, such as Switzerland and Germany, don't? Why do countries with no macroeconomic justification, such as Senegal and Turkey, create SWFs? And why do countries with similar macroeconomic features, such as Kuwait and Qatar or Singapore and Hong Kong, choose very different types of SWFs?

Capital Choices analyzes the struggles behind the creation of different SWFs from a comparative political economy perspective. Examining small open economies, the book argues that different state-society structures at the sectoral level are the core drivers responsible for SWF variation. Author Juergen Braunstein looks inside the "black box" of SWF creation, focusing on the early formation period of SWFs, a critical but little understood area in the current debate, given the high levels of political sensitivity and lack of transparency. Braunstein's novel analytical framework provides practical lessons for business and finance organizations, as well as for policymakers of countries that have created or are planning to create SWFs. This book illustrates the scope for domestic politics and the strategies of small states in economic policy despite strong transnational forces, notably international economic and diffusion pressures.

Dr. Juergen Braunstein is a research fellow at the Harvard Kennedy School's Belfer Center for Science and International Affairs.

CAPITAL CHOICES

*Sectoral Politics and the Variation
of Sovereign Wealth*

Revised Edition

Juergen Braunstein

University of Michigan Press
Ann Arbor

New and updated edition published 2022
Copyright © 2019, 2022 by Juergen Braunstein
All rights reserved

For questions or permissions, please contact um.press.perms@umich.edu.

Published in the United States of America by the
University of Michigan Press
Printed and bound by CPI Group (UK) Ltd, Croydon, CR0 4YY

A CIP catalog record for this book is available from the British Library.

First published February 2022

Library of Congress Cataloging-in-Publication Data

Names: Braunstein, Juergen, 1983– author.
Title: Capital choices : sectoral politics and the variation of sovereign wealth / Juergen
    Braunstein.
Description: Ann Arbor : University of Michigan Press, [2019] | Includes bibliographical
    references and index. |
Identifiers: LCCN 2019010281 (print) | LCCN 2019013707 (ebook) | ISBN
    9780472125180 (E-book) | ISBN 9780472131327 (hardcover : alk. paper)
Subjects: LCSH: Sovereign wealth funds—Political aspects. | Investment of public funds.
Classification: LCC HJ3801 (ebook) | LCC HJ3801 .B73 2019 (print) | DDC
    332.67/252—dc23
LC record available at https://lccn.loc.gov/2019010281

ISBN: 978-0-472-03886-2 (alk paper : paper)
ISBN: 978-0-472-12996-6 (ebook)

Contents

Digital materials related to this title can be found on
the Fulcrum platform via the following citable URL:
https://doi.org/10.3998/mpub.12110921

Contents

Abbreviations

ADIA	Abu Dhabi Investment Corporation
ADNOC	Abu Dhabi National Oil Corporation
APF	Alaska Permanent Fund
AUM	assets under management
BRIC	Brazil, Russia, India, China
CMA	Chinese Manufacturers' Association
CPF	Central Provident Fund
DBS	Development Board of Singapore
DPM	deputy prime minister's office
DPMO	Deputy Prime Ministers Office
EDB	Economic Development Board
ExCo	Executive Council
FHKI	Federation of Hong Kong Industries
GCC	Gulf Cooperation Council
GIC	Government Investment Corporation
HK$	Hong Kong dollar
HKGCC	Hong Kong General Chamber of Commerce
KIA	Kuwait Investment Authority
LAC	Labour Advisory Committee
LegCo	Legislative Council
MAS	Monetary Authority of Singapore
MFI	Minister for Finance Incorporated
MNCs	multinational corporations
OECD	Organisation of Economic Co-operation and Development

PAP	People's Action Party
PM	prime minister
PMO	Prime Minister's Office
POSB	Post Office Savings Bank
PN	policy network
PSDC	Public Sector Divestment Committee
QIA	Qatar Investment Authority
S$	Singapore dollar
SCCCI	Singapore Chinese Chamber of Commerce and Industry
SFCCI	Singapore Federation of Chambers of Commerce and Industry
SICCI	Singapore Indian Chamber of Commerce and Industry
SGS	Singapore Government Securities
SMA	Singapore Manufacturing Association
SMCCI	Singapore Malay Chamber of Commerce and Industry
SMEs	small and medium enterprises
SWAC	Social Welfare Advisory Committee
SWF	sovereign wealth fund
UNDP	United Nations Development Programme
$	US dollar

Foreword

Sovereign wealth funds (SWF) are at the heart of the contemporary global finance debate. The growth of SWFs in recent decades has been truly remarkable. Almost a third of all countries now have one or more such fund, most of them located in non-OECD countries. They have become key features of the global financial architecture and their sheer size makes them larger than the combined size of global private equity and hedge funds. They raise concerns about the future direction of capitalism, especially among Western policy makers. Some states create such funds for the purpose of self-insurance, against financial instability, or just to smooth out state revenues over time. Others establish SWFs to distribute current wealth across generations for future generations or to support development and industrial policy.

Capital Choices analyses the struggles behind the creation of different state finance institutions from a comparative political economy perspective. Choices in creating state financial institutions, such as sovereign wealth funds (SWFs), have massive impact on capital allocation within and across sectors of an economy. They have different distributional implications, potentially crowding out private asset managers, at least in the early stages of SWF creation. They structure the flow of capital with differential impact across different economic actors, beneficial to some and disadvantageous to others.

The monograph provides an overview of these choices across countries, comparing different SWF policies and explain why some countries with large reserves, notably Switzerland, have not created such a fund. It examines the paradox of why countries with similar macro-economic fundamentals, such as small open economies in the Gulf or Asia, make different choices regarding SWFs, and why states with very different characteristics, such as Malaysia and Kazakhstan, or Ireland and Senegal, opt for similar structures.

Ultimately, the book links the choices of state finance institutions to comparative politics. These choices are seen as neither mere outcomes of a set of macro-characteristics nor the product of cross-national learning or emulation, but they reflect the distribution of power among groups in a state. The framework developed offers mechanisms and hypotheses linking the variation in domestic structures to variation in SWFs, and provides practical lessons for business and finance organizations as well as for policy makers of countries who have or are planning to create SWFs.

The documented experience of SWF creation in small states offers insights into developments in larger countries (e.g., BRICS' economies) by illustrating the scope for domestic politics and strategies of small states in economic policy. The chapters offer an insightful and balanced analysis of the various responses of small open economies to common pressures. The cross country and sectoral comparisons offer an opportunity to look at how sectoral politics plays out to affect capital choices and who benefits from these choices.

Studying the politics of SWFs is challenging, due to lack of transparency and high political sensitivity. Although much has been written about SWFs, this book makes a unique contribution by offering a rich empirical and analytical picture of the domestic politics aspect behind SWF choices. Through extensive fieldwork in Asia and the Gulf, the author uses a combination of newly released archival documents as well as oral history, and interviews, allowing the author to unmask the underlying conflicts reflected in the shaping of SWFs. *Capital Choices* makes a valuable contribution to the study of this increasingly important aspect of the global financial architecture.

Erik Berglöf

Acknowledgments

The international finance architecture has changed dramatically over the last decade and at the heart of this are new actors, such as sovereign wealth funds (SWFs)—large state investment funds. The purpose of this book is to contribute to the practical and academic understanding of sovereign wealth funds in one of its defining elements, namely domestic politics. The resulting dynamics are shaping SWF mandates, their governance structures, and their investment practices.

Over the past few years, I have encountered many people who have been instrumental in the completion of this book. At the London School of Economics and Political Science (LSE), I was fortunate to have been surrounded by supportive colleagues. I would particularly like to express my profound gratitude to Mark Thatcher, Razeen Sally, Steffen Hertog, Henry Yeung, and Jeffrey Chwieroth for their encouragement, advice, and insight over the years. I would also like to thank Lynne Roberts, Marion Laboure, Adam Austerfield and Julius Sen from the LSE, Pat Schena and Paul Rose from SovereigNet as well as Adam Robbins and Kristian Flyvholm (then of the International Forum of Sovereign Wealth Funds) who provided me with unique access to the sovereign fund community.

A special word of thanks goes to Meghan O'Sullivan, who generously supported my book project at Harvard Kennedy School's Belfer Center. Additional thanks go to Nikoleta Sremac for her work as an editor. I would also like to thank the three anonymous reviewers who read the entire manuscript. Their useful comments have been key to the development of the book. Financial support for portions of this project was provided by the LSE Government Department, LSE's Centre for Analysis of Risk and Regulation, and Santander.

Part of this book is based on research conducted at the Lee Kuan Yew School of Public Policy in Singapore and the Department of Politics and Public Administration at the University of Hong Kong as a visiting research fellow during the two years from 2013 to 2014. During my stay in Hong Kong, I had the privilege of meeting Helmut Sohmen who provided me with key insights into Hong Kong's economic policymaking and became an important mentor. Masako Watanabe's feedback and comments were crucial in sharpening my perspective. I would also thank Anson Chan, Leo Goodstadt, David Akers-Jones, and John Nugée for their help with my research in Hong Kong. My stay at the Lee Kuan Yew School was enriched by Ajith Prasad, and Donald Low. Further thanks go to Jennifer Lewis, Freddy Orchard, J. Y. Pillay, and Ng Kok Song who provided me with unique insights into the early history of Singapore's Government Investment Corporation as well as Temasek. I am immensely grateful to all these individuals for their help.

The research on sectoral politics and the variation of sovereign wealth greatly relied on unpublished government documents, memos, and oral history recordings at the Hong Kong Public Records Office, the National Archives of Singapore, the National Archives (Kew, London), the archives at the British Library, and the Monetary Authority of Singapore Information and Resource Center.

The initial plan for this book was enthusiastically embraced by Meredith Norwich (then of University of Michigan Press) and then by Elizabeth Demers, Danielle Coty, and Mary Hashman. I am very grateful for their commitment and interest.

This book draws upon my PhD research at the LSE. Here I would like to acknowledge the permission of the publishers to use portions of two previously published papers: "Domestic Sources of Twenty-First-Century Geopolitics: Domestic Politics and Sovereign Wealth Funds in GCC Economies," *New Political Economy* (5 February 2018); and "The Domestic Drivers of State Finance Institutions: Evidence from Sovereign Wealth Funds," *Review of International Political Economy* 24, no. 6 (2017), 980–1003.

Finally, my thanks go to family and friends, whose unrelenting support and encouragement brought me to the end of this journey. However, this book could not have been completed without the sustained tolerance and all-round support of my parents, Franz and Monika. For these and many other reasons, it is to them that this book is lovingly dedicated.

ONE

Introduction

The proliferation of sovereign wealth funds (SWFs) lies at the heart of the emerging international finance architecture. Sovereign wealth funds are large state-owned funds that use national savings to acquire domestic and international assets. They have become a salient feature of twenty-first century capitalism, reflecting the shift of wealth from the West to the East and the continued role of state involvement in the economy (see Bremmer 2009; Kurlantzick 2016). While in 2007 SWFs held assets under management (AUM) of $1 trillion, this number increased to nearly $7 trillion by 2016—making SWF assets larger than those of global private equity and hedge funds combined. The dramatic rise of SWFs in number and size, combined with the fact that the majority are located in non-Organization of Economic Co-operation and Development (OECD) countries has raised concerns about the future direction of capitalism.[1]

It has been more than ten years since investment expert Andrew Rozanov coined the term "sovereign wealth fund." In his article "Who Holds the Wealth of Nations," Rozanov provided an initial description of SWFs as government-related pools of capital that are not state-owned enterprises nor traditional central bank reserves. He divided SWFs into commodity and non-commodity funds based on their funding source (Rozanov 2005). Although SWFs had been in existence for more than six decades, it was not until the 2000s that they were noticed by a larger audience. SWFs, together with large state-owned enterprises, have received much attention in the context of trade disputes between emerging economies, most notably China, and the United States, in the early 2000s (Rose 2014; Thatcher and Vlandas 2016). In 2005, the state-owned China National Offshore Oil Corporation attempted to acquire two strategic US oil companies, Chevron Texaco and Unocal Cooperation, and in 2006, state-owned Dubai Ports World made an offer to purchase port facilities located in the United States.[2] These offers were ultimately withdrawn because the host country had become increasingly suspicious of high-profile state-related foreign investments (Cohen 2009). These moves sparked a fear of capital account protectionism, which was aggravated by a sudden rise in the number and size of SWFs. SWF activities and projected growth have stirred a debate about the extent to which their size may allow them to affect financial markets.

SWFs and their variations were widely debated during the global financial crisis of 2007–08, attracting attention from economists such as Lawrence Summers (2007) and Ted Truman (2008, 2010a); finance experts, such as Bernstein, Lerner, and Schoar (2013); politicians, notably German chancellor Angela Merkel and former French president Nicolas Sarkozy (see Raphaeli and Gersten 2008, 2); and the international financial press, including the *Financial Times* and the *Economist*. One major concern was the investment motives of various SWFs—that is, whether they are driven by politics or economics (e.g., see Rose 2008). Their combination of size and "novelty" has led commentators to describe SWFs as potential sources of stability or instability in the international economy.[3] While there are those, most notably Summers (2007), who argue that SWF investments might be politically motivated and therefore destabilizing, others, such as Srinivasan et al. (2008), highlight the stabilizing effect of the long-term investments made by SWFs. These views are related to the characteristics and investment mandates of SWFs.[4]

Since the global financial crisis of 2007–8, SWFs experienced rapid growth in numbers and size.[5] Within a single decade, between 2005 and 2015, assets under SWF management increased by more than 600 percent, from $ 895 billion in 2005 to nearly $7 trillion in 2017 (Rozanov 2005; Sovereign Investor Institute, SovereigNet database). Even countries that do not have sufficient resources have begun creating these investment vehicles (Schena, Braunstein, and Ali 2018). For example, countries with account deficits, notably Turkey, have created SWFs (Milhench 2017). SWFs have become international symbols of economic strength and prosperity (Dixon 2017). Given the strong international appeal of SWFs, it seems even more paradoxical that a number of countries with massive reserves, notably Switzerland, have resisted domestic calls to create SWFs (Sornette 2015; Senner and Sornette 2017). This suggests that the decision to establish SWFs is not solely determined by reserve and surplus levels, but also by public debates, and that political decisions about the allocation of wealth are taken in particular contexts.

If surplus alone does not lead to the creation of SWFs, which other factors determines their creation? Why do some countries with large current account surpluses create SWFs while others do not? What drives these choices? Relatedly, why do countries with similar macroeconomic features, such as Kuwait, Bahrain, Qatar, and Abu Dhabi or Singapore and Hong Kong, choose very different types of SWFs? Based on their similar economic profiles, established macroeconomic theories would expect them to establish similar types of SWFs. SWFs differ in terms of their mandates, ranging from savings and stabilization to industrial and development mandates. Related to these different mandates—but often neglected in the debate—are different distributional implications. Choices about SWF creation are choices about massive capital allocation on the sectoral or macro level. What are the implications of SWF choices for other economic actors? And how do the features of actors in a particular institutional environment affect their SWF choices?

Capital Choices looks inside the "black box" of SWF creation. It shows how the characteristics of socioeconomic actors—including business/finance organizations, bureaucrats, and politicians—influence policy processes and choices regarding SWFs. Drawing on extensive fieldwork, this book reveals how socioeconomic actors contest and negotiate the creation of various state finance vehicles. It focuses mostly on the early formation period of SWFs. This is a critical but little-understood area in the current debate, given high levels of political sensitivity and lack of transparency. Through its historical perspective, the book provides a window into the underlying politics of SWF creation. This is crucial in understanding the contemporary manifestations of SWFs, as well as the countries planning to create such funds.

Capital Choices is one of the first books to analyze the struggles behind the creation of different SWFs from a comparative political economy perspective. This book investigates cross-country as well as cross-sector variation in state finance institutions. It relates this to the variance in the formal and informal linkages that structure economic policy. The book presents a detailed empirical analysis in the form of a guided narrative. Drawing on recently released archival material, it examines systematically how domestic structures have affected policy processes about state finance institutions in small open economies.

Standard theories expect the capital choices of small open economies to be the least driven by domestic politics. International economic forces, such as capital mobility, put powerful constraints on the policy choices available for small open economies, especially in the financial sector. Unlike large countries with their large domestic markets small open economies are fully exposed to international market forces and have less room to maneuver in their economic policy. As such, if domestic structures are critical for explaining capital choices in small open economies then this strengthens confidence about the role of domestic structures in explaining the capital choices of large emerging economies (e.g., Brazil, Russia, India, and China—the "BRIC" countries) and OECD countries.

This analysis is consequential given the number of countries that have publicly announced their intention to create SWFs over the next five years (e.g., the United Kingdom, Indonesia, Israel, the Philippines, Bolivia, Morocco, Uganda, Cyprus, and Uruguay).

Capital Choices offers an explanation for the divergent paths followed by various countries. The puzzle of varying SWFs within small open economies offers an opportunity to explore the underlying political economy of state finance institutions and particularly the impact of sectoral differences among countries with similar macroeconomic characteristics. Most of the existing studies on the politics behind SWFs focus on individual case studies, regression analysis, or modeling.[6] But what is the impact of politics on cross-country and within-country variation in SWFs? Only few studies have looked at this comparatively but at the macro level.[7] None of the studies have addressed the question of intra-state variation and variation among countries with similar macro-level characteristics. Yet empirical evidence shows striking variation in SWF types across and within countries that is inconsistent with macro-political explanations, calling for a further disaggregated analysis of politics. This work is distinctive in that it brings sectoral-level politics into its explanation for the creation of different SWFs through cross-country and cross-sectoral comparisons.

By analyzing small, open economies, I argue that various state-society structures at the sectoral level are the core drivers of SWF variations. The notion of state-society structures refers to the organizational context of policymaking (Atkinson and Coleman 1989). It describes the organizational features of actors—both private and state—in the policymaking processes. These features including the level of state autonomy, degree of business mobilization, and level of state concentration. Peter Katzenstein introduced the concept of policy networks (PNs) as a shorthand to capture these features, which shape the interactions among actors, thereby influencing consultation, negotiation, and bargaining in formal and informal institutional arrangements (Atkinson and Coleman 1989). In turn these organizational differences of actors in the policymaking processes give rise to different capital choices.

More broadly, this tells us that meso-level structures play a more significant role in affecting macro-level phenomena such as SWFs than is assumed in the contemporary literature. The relevant literature on SWFs neglects the role of subnational politics, as well as the implications of SWF creation for socioeconomic actors. That is due to the fact that standard theories focus on institutions and economic variables at the macro level. This book shows that SWFs are critical for resource mobilization and economic development, but also have redistributive consequences. In engaging with the literature on SWFs and on policy networks, this book also has a bearing on recent theoretical debates on state-business relations, state capitalism, and the resurgence of state finance institutions more broadly.[8]

This book analyzes the role of formal and informal linkages between public and private actors in policymaking processes. Acknowledging particular regional and historical contexts helps to account for the varying effects of these structural linkages within countries and across sectors. These linkages refer to official political bodies, advisory committees/boards, and informal policy review panels. These possess a critical influence on economic policy decisions. Particular emphasis is placed on decisions concerning SWFs with savings mandates and with development mandates. Using a new qualitative dataset, the research identifies key actors and interests involved in policy processes. It offers insights into the mechanisms that connect state-society structures at the meso-level to decisions about the creation of SWFs. Although its focus is on SWFs, this book also offers new insights about state finance institutions more broadly. It discovers that various types of SWFs have close links to other state finance vehicles, such as pension funds and development banks. These are novel insights because the existing literature has not explicated these connections.

Capital Choices pertains to a number of literatures in the field of comparative political economy. First, it develops the SWF literature through concrete hypotheses regarding the inner workings of political processes and the decisions to create SWFs, and, if so, what type. By showing how formal and informal linkages between public and private actors shape conflicts about state finance institutions, this book closes an empirical gap in the burgeoning literature on SWFs that looks at the effects of domestic politics. The first study of its kind, this monograph provides a critique of the existing literature and develops out of it a policy network analysis of SWFs, which helps explain their variation. This framework advances mechanisms and hypotheses linking variation in domestic structures to that of SWFs, and provides practical lessons for business and finance organizations as well as for policymakers of countries that have created or are planning to create SWFs. The experience of SWF creation in small states offers important insights about developments in larger countries (e.g., the BRIC economies). It illustrates how small states navigate strong transnational forces and highlights the central role of domestic politics.

This book fills an important gap in the existing SWF literature. Its goal is to explain and elaborate on individual countries' choices to create or not create SWFs. It offers systematic insights into the effects of domestic structures on SWF creation and accounts for the implications of SWF creation for private economic actors (i.e., the winners and losers of SWF creation). Cross-national comparison allows for analysis of the effects of structures across countries, whereas cross-sectoral comparison permits an investigation of the effects of structures across sectors. This generates new insights in this evolving space, as covered in chapters 4–7. This book is a valuable contribution to the existing literature, because it analyzes the effects of state-society structures on the kinds of financial institutions generated in policy domain.

Research Design and Case Studies

The book adopts an inductive research design. It examines whether domestic politics, and particularly PNs, can explain the puzzle of why different types of SWFs are established, especially across and within countries. It uses a PN analysis of the puzzle of SWF variation in small open economies to develop hypotheses about why and how organizational characteristics of socioeconomic actors affect the forms of financial institutions established. Running counter to the expectations of the two dominant analyses, small open economies within similar peer groupings in comparable regions have established different types of SWFs. Furthermore, varying SWF types exist not only across but also within countries.

Standard explanations predict that countries similar in economic profile as well as in their exposure to powerful transnational pressures should make similar choices concerning SWFs. Hence, similar SWF choices should be observable, especially in small open economies, because they are uniformly exposed to these pressures. As such, small open economies are the most likely cases for efficiency-based explanations. Likewise, they are the most likely cases for constructivist explanations highlighting the role of economic fads and fashions (Chwieroth 2014) among countries with similar structural profiles located in comparable regions. Countries are expected to create particular types of SWFs if countries in similar peer groupings created that type of SWF when confronted with an analogous but distinct challenge, such as windfall oil revenues.

Standard explanations highlight macro-national variables, which are surprisingly alike across Asian city-states (e.g., Hong Kong and Singapore) and small open economies in the Gulf (e.g., Bahrain, Abu Dhabi, Kuwait, and Qatar). These economies share similar developmental starting points with comparable exposures to efficiency pressures. They are regional/international financial centers with immense domestic private and public savings levels, and are extremely open and exposed to inflation, currency volatility, and competition. Furthermore, given their geographic proximity, they were highly susceptible to the influence of fads and fashions. For example, Hong Kong and Singapore were both exposed to international organizations, such as the World Bank and the United Nations Conference on Trade and Development (UNCTAD), promoting the adaptation of similar policies. However, even small open economies within similar peer groupings (e.g., the city-states of East Asia, small open oil- and gas-exporting economies of the Middle East, or phosphate-exporting island economies of the Pacific) exhibit significant variation in their SWF choices.

This book looks at the kinds of financial institutions discussed, PNs in place, financial institutions set up, and the beneficiaries and those harmed by particular SWF choices. By using the tool of process-tracing on a new set of largely primary empirical material, *Capital Choices* develops hypotheses through a number of case studies: SWF variation within and across Asian city-states and Gulf Cooperation Council (GCC) economies. This material comprised official state documents (e.g., statistical information, acts of parliament, decrees, and other textual material), and publicly available official documents from the private sector, such as company documents and annual reports. To make sense of the private sector's stance vis-à-vis the creation of different types of SWFs, it is necessary to analyze material that reveals its interests in relation to SWFs, such as mission statements, lobbying reports, and local newspapers. Furthermore, an analysis of the academic literature and press releases reveals how private commercial and industrial sectors have related to policy processes in the form of business associations. This dataset is complemented by semi-structured elite interviews. These targeted individuals who have been directly or indirectly involved in decisions surrounding the creation of state finance institutions.

These interviews shed light on the manner in which PNs operate and the sequence in which actors are included or excluded.

Chapter 1 outlines the analytical and policy background of state finance institutions in the twenty-first century. Chapter 2 provides a global review of SWFs and the variations that pose a puzzle to standard explanations, highlighting economic efficiency and international diffusion. Chapter 3 introduces domestic politics explanations to advance a critique out of which it develops an analytical framework, which is refined in subsequent chapters. Chapters 4–6 apply the themes of Chapters 2 and 3 to the empirical cases. Chapter 4, on commodity-poor city-state economies in Asia (i.e., Hong Kong and Singapore), demonstrates the effects of domestic politics on the choices of state finance institutions in the industrial domain. Chapter 5 reveals the effects of politics on the choices of state finance institutions within the savings domain. Chapter 6 examines the politics of SWF choices in commodity-rich small open economies in the Middle East (i.e., the GCC countries). Chapter 7 applies the findings of the previous chapters to the BRIC and OECD economies. Chapter 8 interprets the patterns of SWF variation and relates them to contemporary debates, in order to project a fuller picture of the future of state finance institutions and economic statecraft in the twenty-first century.

TWO

Global Review

Since the Global Financial Crisis of 2008 the shift of wealth from the West to the East has been a salient feature of the international financial system. Academics and investors alike have been interested in the changing distribution of wealth, exemplified by the rise of BRICS (e.g., Jim O'Neill), the rise of Asia (e.g., Mahbubani 2008) and the shift in global foreign exchange reserves (e.g., Truman 2007). While in the 1980s the global economic center of gravity—in terms of GDP produced—was located in the mid-Atlantic, it shifted further east and in 2050 will be located somewhere between India and China (Quah 2010, 2011).

SWFs are central to this wealth shift. Through SWFs, states have been acquiring stakes in companies that were once purely private. Following the Global Financial Crisis of 2007-8, a number of SWFs purchased large stakes in international banks. For example, the Abu Dhabi Investment Authority, the Government Investment Corporation of Singapore, and the Kuwait Investment Authority each acquired more than 5 percent in Citigroup, while Temasek (Singapore) bought a 3 percent stake in Merrill Lynch and the China Investment Corporation bought a 6 percent stake in Blackstone (Fleischer 2008, 29). SWFs have also expanded into technology, the media, and the life science sectors, increasingly through unconventional means—notably venture capital. For example, Singapore's SWF, Temasek, has its own venture arms, notably Vertex. Vertex plays an important role for Temasek in gaining exposure to growth sectors across countries. It has a total deployed capital in excess of $1.2 billion and a presence in Singapore, Beijing, Shanghai, Taipei, Bangalore, and the Silicon Valley.

9

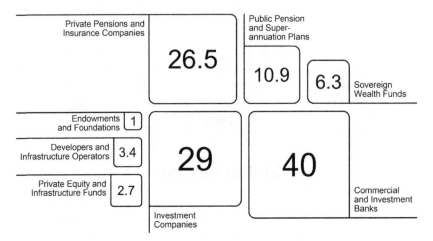

Figure 2.1. Total assets under management (in trillion USD)

As of 2017, SWFs are among the largest institutional investors, with nearly twice as much investment as global hedge funds and private equity funds combined. The fifteen largest SWFs had a combined AUM of $6.3 trillion that year—large if compared, for example, to the US GDP of approximately $18.6 trillion (SWF Institute 2017). However, their asset size represents only a fraction of total international financial assets. By comparing the volume of SWF assets with the volume of AUM by other institutional investors—worth approximately $113.5 trillion—the picture changes (see figure 2.1).

But SWFs are not a homogenous group of actors. They differ in mandates and corporate governance structures, which relate to their distinct investment.[1] Some funds, such as the Chinese Investment Corporation or the Qatar Investment Authority, follow an active investment strategy (i.e., holding controlling stakes in companies) aimed at promoting national development agendas. Others, such as the Government Investment Corporation (Singapore) or the Norway Global Fund, pursue a portfolio strategy (i.e., holding minority stakes) with the purpose of risk diversification and long-term savings (see table 2.1).

SWFs share similarities with other institutional investors, such as pension funds. For example, the bulk of both pension funds and SWF assets is concentrated in a small number of funds. The largest 300 pension funds together comprise $ 10.4 trillion (Watson Wyatt 2006, 4). Out of this, each of the twenty largest pension funds has an average size of $ 171.4 billion (calculated with data from Watson Wyatt 2006, 14). From these top twenty, the Government Pension Fund of Japan constitutes the biggest pension fund, with a volume of $ 935.6 billion. The majority of SWF assets are similarly concentrated in a small number of funds. The largest fifteen SWFs hold around 85 percent of all AUM. The largest SWF, the Norwegian PFG (Pension Fund Global), possesses assets worth approximately $ 1 trillion. PFG alone is estimated to own an average of 1.25 percent of the holdings of every listed company in the world (*Financial Times*, 8 August 2013).

This chapter introduces SWF variation both across and within countries. First, it draws on established studies that differentiate types of SWFs through a set of organizational features (Hammer et al. 2008; Al-Hassan et al. 2013). Second, it outlines standard explanations for each of these SWF types. Third, it advances a critique of these standard explanations, which serves as a basis for "Bringing Politics In" in the next chapter.

Waves of SWF Creation

The first SWF wave related to commodity revenue—in particular, petrodollar flows. Oil exporting countries began recycling resource revenue surpluses into the international financial system, to be eventually reintermediated via Western financial institutions (see Schena et al. 2018). The first traces of SWFs can be found in the early 1950s, which marked a clear transformation in the power relationship between private international oil companies and governments, in favor of the latter (Penrose 1968). This period was characterized by emancipating developing states, which demanded more power over domestic economic matters. Particularly in oil producing countries, notably in the Gulf, governments pressed toward higher oil taxes on multinational petrol enterprises (see Tétreault 1995; Tugwell 1975; Petras et al. 1977). The higher income from raised oil taxation resulted in dramatically enlarged state revenue, which was the basis for SWF creation in some countries.

In the early 1950s, Saudi Arabia became the first Middle Eastern country to raise its corporate oil tax, in the same 50–50 fashion that Venezuela had implemented a decade earlier (Petras et al. 1977, 13). This nearly doubled the Saudi governmental revenue from $56.7 million in 1950 to $110 million the following year (Young 1983, 21). Confronted with this massive increase, King Abdul Aziz Al Saud, supported by his Finance Minister Shaykh Abd Allah Sulayman, officially asked the US government for financial advice in December 1950 (Young 1983, 27). The United States responded by sending a mission of financial experts, under the direction of Arthur N. Young, to Saudi Arabia. Young's team created the Saudi Arabian Monetary Agency, tasked with the same obligations as a Western national bank, such as providing monetary stability and financial and economic research. However, it also had fiscal functions such as centralizing the enormous government revenues from oil export (Mallakh and Mallakh 1982).

Following in the footsteps of Saudi Arabia, Kuwait imposed an oil tax. Together with substantial growth in its output rate state oil revenues increased tenfold in the early 1950s (Al-Atiqi 2005; Baker 1986). The political crisis in Iran, where Prime Minister Mohammad Mossadeq had nationalized the oil industry, was responsible for this sharp increase in output. The nationalist Mossadeq insisted that agreements with the Anglo-Iranian Oil Company (later British Petroleum) were not in the national interest of Iran (Tetreault 1995). As a result of nationalization, an embargo against Iranian oil led to an increase in exploitation activities in neighboring Kuwait (Tetreault 1995). This helped Kuwait become the largest single Middle Eastern oil producer by the 1950s.

The high oil revenues of that time were the basis of the Kuwaiti welfare state and the foundation of power for the ruling family. According to Mary Ann Tetreault (1995, 3), in order to sustain the welfare state that provided the citizens of Kuwait one of the highest living standards in the world, the Shaikh agreed to establish the Kuwait Investment Office in London, with the official purpose of "investing the surplus oil revenue in order to provide a fund for the future and reduce its reliance on its single finite resource" (Kuwait Investment Office 2008). The core concept was that a portion of oil income should be put in the Kuwait Investment Office, in order to ensure sufficient revenue to maintain the welfare state at times when oil prices were low.

The second wave of SWFs was strongly associated with emerging economies carrying persistent trade surpluses—especially in Asia. These countries finance their SWFs largely through surplus capital, generated from export activities. East Asia, for example, has witnessed a rapid growth of sovereign wealth, particularly with the creation of the first Chinese SWF in 2007 (Schena et al. 2018). That year, China established one of the largest SWFs by transferring $200 billion from its foreign exchange reserve overhang into the Chinese Investment Corporation (Martin 2008).

Parallel to this, a third wave of SWFs evolved what have become known as sovereign development funds. These funds are capitalized by using state commercial assets and are well-represented by the likes of Temasek in Singapore, Khazanah in Malaysia, Mumtalakat in Bahrain, and

Samruk-Kazyna in Kazakhstan. Their objective was initially to improve the management of state assets and subsequently, if required, to restructure them in pursuit of privatization and monetization.

The currently accelerating wave of SWFs is focused on broader economic objectives, as countries seek innovative ways to leverage foreign capital to finance economic transformation (e.g., Rietvield and Toledano 2017). SWFs designed to catalyze foreign direct investments into strategic sectors of the host country's domestic economy include Italy's CDP Equity and the Ireland Strategic Investment Fund (Schena and Ali 2016; Schena et al. 2018). As investors these SWFs can seed risk capital to strategic sectors or projects, particularly when domestic capital markets are underdeveloped, shallow, or repressed (e.g., Senegal's FONSIS) (Schena et al. 2018). For example, Morocco created Ithmar Capital as a strategic investment fund in 2011 with the purpose of mobilizing national and international investment into the tourism sector (*PrivateEquityWire* 2016). Beyond these, a number of other development-focused funds have recently been announced, including funds in Turkey, Egypt and Guyana.

This brief historical trajectory illustrates that SWFs emerge in specific historical contexts, which in turn shape their purposes. Reflecting on different purposes, we can distinguish among a variety of funds (see table 2.1).

2.1 Sovereign Fund Types

Although no universally accepted definition exists in the burgeoning SWF literature, SWFs share a set of broad similarities (Clark et al. 2013).[2] Common to all SWFs is their (a) ownership (SWFs are owned by the government, either directly or indirectly via the appointment of a board), (b) liabilities (SWFs have no direct liabilities), and (c) beneficiaries (SWFs are managed according to the objectives of the government, and this mandate drives their investment; Clark et al. 2013). This definition allows for the inclusion of both SWFs that invest primarily internationally and those that invest both domestically and internationally.

Typologies range from simple distinctions between oil/commodity funds and nonoil funds/noncommodity funds (Rozanov 2005; Kimmitt 2008) to large typologies embracing up to five cells (IMF 2008). Although recent attempts have been made to categorize SWFs in terms of historical-geographical maps, notably Clark et al. (2013), the most established way to differentiate is based on their objectives (see IMF 2008; Gilson and Milhaupt 2008). Using function as the main defining criteria, scholars such as Gilson and Milhaupt (2008) as well as institutions, most notably the IMF

TABLE 2.1. Variation and characteristics of sovereign wealth funds

Country	SWF Name	Date of creation	Size in $ billion	Main funding source	Primary mandate
Algeria	Revenue Regulation Fund	2000	8	commodity	stab
Angola	Fundo Soberano de Angola	2012	5	commodity	stab
Australia	Australian Future Fund	2006	99	fiscal	sav
Azerbaijan	State Oil Fund	1999	33	commodity	stab
Bahrain	Mumtalakat Holding Company	2006	11	fiscal	dev
Botswana	Pula Fund	1994	6	commodity	stab
Brunei	Brunei Investment Agency	1983	40	commodity	sav
Canada	Alberta Heritage Fund	1976	13	commodity	sav
Chile	Pension Reserve Fund	2006	9	commodity	sav
Chile	Economic and Social Stabilization Fund	2006	14	commodity	stab
China	China Investment Corporation	2007	813	fiscal	dev
China	National Social Security Fund	2000	295	fiscal	sav
China	SAFE Investment Company	1952	514	fex	stab
Colombia	Colombia Savings and Stabilisation Fund	2011	4	commodity	stab
East Timor	Timor-Leste Petroleum Fund	2005	17	commodity	stab
Hong Kong	HKMA Investment Portfolio	1935	456	fex	stab
Iran	National Development Fund of Iran	2011	91	commodity	dev
Ireland	Ireland Strategic Investment Fund	2001	9	fiscal	dev
Kazakhstan	Samruk-Kazyna JSC	2008	61	fiscal	dev
Kazakhstan	Kazakhstan National Fund	2000	65	commodity	dev
Kuwait	Kuwait Investment Authority	1953	524	commodity	sav
Libya	Libyan Investment Authority	2006	66	commodity	sav
Malaysia	Khasanah Nasional	1993	35	fiscal	dev
Mexico	Oil Revenues Stabilisation Fund of Mexico	2000	6	commodity	stab
New Zealand	New Zealand Superannuation Fund	2003	23	fiscal	sav
Nigeria	Nigerian Sovereign Investment Authority	2012	1	commodity	sav
Norway	Government Pension Fund Global	1990	922	commodity	sav
Oman	State General Reserve Fund	1980	18	commodity	stab
Palestine	Palestine Investment Fund	2003	1	fiscal	dev
Panama	Fondo de Ahorro de Panama	2012	1	fiscal	stab
Peru	Fiscal Stabilisation Fund	1999	8	commodity	stab
Qatar	Qatar Investment Authority	2005	320	commodity	sav
Qatar	Qatar Diar				dev
Russia	National Welfare Fund	2008	72	commodity	sav

TABLE 2.1.—Continued

Country	SWF Name	Date of creation	Size in $ billion	Main funding source	Primary mandate
Russia	Russian Direct Investment Fund	2011	13	commodity	dev
Saudi Arabia	Public Investment Fund	2008	183	commodity	dev
Saudi Arabia	SAMA Foreign Holdings	1952	514	commodity	stab
Senegal	FONSIS	2012	1	fiscal	dev
Singapore	MAS	1971	273	fex	stab
Singapore	Temasek	1974	197	fiscal	dev
Singapore	GIC	1981	359	financial	sav
South Korea	Korea Investment Corporation	2005	108	fex	sav
Trinidad	Heritage Stabilisation Fund	2000	6	commodity	stab
UAE-Abu Dhabi	Mubadala	2002	125	commodity	dev
UAE-Abu Dhabi	Abu Dhabi Investment Coundil	2007	110	commodity	dev
UAE-Abu Dhabi	Abu Dhabi Investment Authority	1976	828	commodity	sav
UAE-Dubai	Investment Corporation of Dubai	2006	210	fiscal	dev
UAE-Ras Al Khaimah	RAK Investment Authority	2005	1	financial	dev
UAE-Federal	Emirates Investment Authority	2007	34	commodity	dev
US-Alaska	Alaska Permanent Fund	1976	55	commodity	sav
US-Texas	Texas Permanent School Fund	1854	38	commodity	sav
US-Texas	Permanent University Fund	1876	17	commodity	sav
US-Wyoming	Permanent Wyoming Mineral Trust Fund	1974	7	commodity	stab
US-North Dakota	North Dakota Legacy Fund	2011	4	commodity	sav
US-Idaho	Idaho Endowment Fund Investment Board	1969	2	commodity	sav
US-Utah	Utah-SITFO	1896	2	commodity	sav
US-Louisiana	Louisiana Education Quality Trust Fund	1986	1	commodity	sav

Source: Information compiled from SWF websites and SWF databases (e.g., SWFInstitute, ESADEgeo, SovereigNet).

Notes: sav=savings, stab=stabilization, dev=development, fex=foreign exchange reserves

(2008) and OECD (2011), have created heuristic typologies. For example, the IMF (2008) distinguishes among Stabilization SWFs, Reserve Investment Corporations, Savings SWFs, Contingent Pension Reserve Funds, and Development SWFs. Gilson and Milhaupt's typology instead includes three cells: Stabilization SWFs, Savings SWFs, and Development SWFs (Gilson and Milhaupt 2008). Most authors and commentators, such as Lyons (2007) and Gilson and Milhaupt (2008), highlight that SWFs as a group can be located on a "continuum" of other sovereign investment vehicles. The two extremes of this continuum are central banks and state-owned enterprises.

The threefold typology used in this book is based on the view that SWFs can be systematically differentiated by their organizational characteristics—relating to their official mandate, ownership, and legal status. Ownership and legal status refer to whether the SWF is organized as a separate legal entity under specialist law or under an existing entity (e.g., central bank), and whether the SWF owns the assets that it manages or whether it manages the assets on behalf of the central government or the ministry of finance. This is directly connected to the investment mandate/objective (stabilization, development, or savings), which influences asset allocation in terms of geography (domestic or abroad), asset class (bonds, equity, direct investments, or real estate), and investment horizon (short- or long-term oriented).

Sovereign Wealth Funds with Savings Mandates

SWFs with savings mandates, such as the Australian Future Fund and the Kuwait Investment Authority, differ from other state finance institutions in the savings domain—notably state-run Central Provident Funds (CPFs) or state-owned savings banks.[3] The most prominent differences between these institutions and CPFs relate to their liability structures. While public pension funds have explicit liabilities (e.g., workers' pensions), SWFs do not. In contrast to SWFs, state-owned savings banks and CPFs manage private wealth (e.g., deposits from the population). Yet there is a direct link between the creation of SWFs and public pension funds, particularly in countries with limited domestic investment opportunities. Public pension funds under trustee legislation accumulate private wealth and try to gain exposure to risk-free and secure assets, notably government bonds.[4] However, countries with budget surpluses do not need to issue bonds in order to finance public expenditure. One way to address this is through SWF creation, as an institutional means of investing proceeds from the issuance of government bonds in international assets with higher risk-return profiles.

In organizational terms, SWFs with savings mandates differ from other SWF types, as they are commonly created as private corporations under company law, in combination with constitutional law or by decree (see Hammer et al. 2008), and do not usually own the assets they manage. They are established as separate legal fund management entities, under a mandate from the ministry of finance or the central government, and with full authority to act (Al-Hassan et al. 2013, 9). They manage assets on behalf of the central government or the ministry of finance, which are the formal owners of the assets. Their organizational features are directly related to their primary function of maintaining long-term purchasing power of national wealth. Unlike SWFs with development or stabilization mandates, the principal objective of SWFs with savings mandates is return maximization. This type of SWF is also known as "reserve investment corporations" or "future generations funds," "contingent pension reserve funds" or "generic sovereign wealth funds'" (Blundell-Wignall, Hu, and Yermo 2008; IMF 2008; Griffith-Jones and Ocampo 2010).

Sovereign Wealth Funds with Development Mandates

SWFs with development/diversification mandates, such as Mumtalakat (Bahrain) and the Public Investment Fund (Saudi Arabia) differ from other state finance institutions in the industrial domain, notably development banks, statutory boards, and state holding companies.[5] Although the line of differentiation is thin, it becomes most prominent in terms of their legal status. While state holdings, statutory boards, and development banks are often established as public law entities and invest primarily in domestic assets, SWFs with development mandates are not purely public entities under state ownership. Instead, SWFs with development mandates are often established under private company law with constitutional status. In terms of mandate and investment structure, SWFs with development mandates are similar to development banks and state holdings. Like these, SWFs with development mandates may have direct holdings in companies and may raise capital by issuing bonds. A number of similarities in these structural characteristics make it difficult to sharply differentiate between SWFs with development mandates on the one hand and state holdings and state development banks on the other.

Unlike SWFs with stabilization or savings mandates, SWFs with development mandates usually own the assets they manage and follow the "investment company model," where assets are actively managed and the SWF takes majority stakes in companies (e.g., see Al-Hassan et al., 2013; Halland et al. 2016; Gratcheva and Anasashvili 2017). They usually "take the form of state-owned corporations also with distinct legal persona" (Al-Hassan et al. 2013, 9). Commentators, most notably Fernandez (2008), describe these types of SWFs as government vehicles that manage government direct investments in companies. Direct investments are generally referred to as investments that are sufficiently large as to affect a firm's management decisions. For conceptual reasons, this book applies a narrow view by categorizing an SWF ownership stake of at least 51 percent as majority/direct investment. SWFs of small open economies with between 51 and 100 percent ownership of companies include Temasek, Mumtalakat, Qatar Holding, and the Investment Corporation of Dubai.[6] Unlike other SWFs, those with development mandates issue bonds. Schena and Chaturvedi stated that "[f]unds with a development or transformational mandate often have a different operating model, which requires sizeable amounts of both short and long-term operating capital to support their investment programs and the liquidity or capital needs of portfolio companies," highlighting the rationale behind the bond issuance (Schena and Chaturvedi 2011, 2). Another reason behind the issuance of bonds by SWFs with development mandates is the desire to develop and deepen domestic capital markets (Schena and Chaturvedi 2011).

SWFs with a development mandate are typically created under company law, in combination with constitutional law or by decree, as a formally private company which is owned by the state—often with a structure differentiating between the owner, board, and operational management (Hammer et al. 2008; Al-Hassan et al. 2013). Although SWFs with development mandates own the assets they manage, they themselves are usually formally owned by the ministry of finance or the government. This makes them directly accountable to the ministry (or, in some cases, to the government or the parliament).

The ministry of finance is commonly the major shareholder and thus is responsible for board appointments. Hammer et al.'s statement that "[t]he Minister of Finance ensures that the Board is competent to oversee the activities of the SWF, but the government operates at arm's length and does not get involved in the business and investment decisions of the SWF" suggests strong links between the SWF and the Ministry of Finance (Hammer et al. 2008, 10). The appointment of senior officials often ensures a close connection between SWFs and the political elite.

The principal objective of SWFs with development mandates relates to the governments' aim of securing economic growth, socioeconomic development, and economic transformation (IMF 2008; Schena and Chaturvedi 2011). Al-Hassan et al.'s statement that "[d]evelopment funds are established to allocate resources to priority socio-economic projects" highlights the important role of economic transformation objectives (Al-Hassan et al. 2013, 5). As a result, these types of SWFs are also referred to in the literature to as "development SWFs," "development funds," "industrial SWFs," "productivist SWFs," and "state investment holdings" (Griffith-Jones and Ocampo 2010; IMF 2008; Clark et al. 2013; Kumar 1992). Common overall is the broad aim of supporting economic diversification and transformation, or diversification in other asset classes, through direct investment or strategic partnerships.

Sovereign Wealth Funds with Stabilization Mandates

Sovereign wealth funds with stabilization mandates, such as the Hong Kong Monetary Authority and the Monetary Authority of Singapore, have organizational features that make them distinct from other SWF types.[7] They are established under general fiscal law or central bank law. Instead of creating a separate legal entity, it is common for the principal owner (e.g., either the central government or the ministry of finance) to utilize the central bank as an agent. These funds are typically owned and controlled by the ministry of finance and operationally managed by the central bank (Hammer et al. 2008; Al-Hassan et al. 2013). When the central bank acts as an agent, the principal remains accountable to the legislature (Hammer et al. 2008, 9). The fund is often a unit within the central bank, and is integrated into the broader framework of fiscal/monetary policy and budgetary processes. The functions of SWFs with stabilization mandates can include smoothing of budget revenues and currency fluctuations, or hedging against capital supply shocks in an international environment of high capital mobility (Al-Hassan et al. 2013; Velasco and Parrado 2012). They absorb excessive liquidity (i.e., money supply) in periods of high external income (Lee 1997, 1).

Though many SWFs can be classified as SWFs with stabilization, savings, or development mandates, this book asserts that these are "ideal" types of SWFs.[8] As such, it is important to emphasize that meaningful variation can be found within these SWF types. For instance, SWFs with stabilization mandates can be differentiated between those that focus primarily on monetary stabilization and those that focus on budget smoothing and fiscal stabilization. Furthermore, SWFs with stabilization mandates can involve investment portfolios that are not primarily used for stabilization purposes but for return objectives, as is usually the case when the funds are larger than what is needed for stabilization purposes. In this case, the SWF outsources portions of the funds to third-party investment managers. Alternatively, it can also create a subunit with a different investment mandate. In turn, SWFs with savings mandates can allocate a part of their portfolio in domestic assets for stabilization purposes. Similar to SWFs with savings mandates, SWFs with development mandates can invest minority stakes in long-term assets for return purposes. Additionally, some SWFs have multiple objectives, such as stabilization, savings, and development (e.g., Nigeria's SWF; Orji and Ojekwe-Onyejeli 2017) or stabilization and savings (e.g., Norway, Azerbaijan, or Botswana; Al-Hassan et al. 2013). In cases where an SWF has multiple mandates, meaningful organizational variation within the SWF can also be found in the existence of subunits with specific mandates.

2.2 Standard Explanations of Sovereign Wealth Fund Types

Standard explanations of SWF types typically refer to arguments of economic efficiency, emphasizing that the creation of SWFs follows functional imperatives. Although many economists, such as Truman (2008) and Kimmitt (2008), acknowledge the important role of politics, they believe that economic indicators are the predominant explanatory variables of SWF variation. Efficiency-based approaches suggest that the decision-making process of resource allocation—in terms of whether and what kind of SWF is established—is driven by "objective" identifiable challenges, such as the need for additional pension liabilities, stabilized fiscal revenues, or for development purposes.

The common assumption is that countries with similar macroeconomic characteristics make similar SWF choices. Most analyses have been written by economists (Aizenman and Lee 2005; Aizenman and Glick 2007, 2009; Truman 2008; Udaibir at al. 2009; Blundell, Hu, and Yermo 2008; Frankel 2011). These studies draw on well-established economic models, such as on foreign exchange reserve management (Flood and Marion 2001) or resource endowment (Lee 2007); they use well-established concepts, such as that of Dutch Disease (*Economist*, 26 November 1977; Lee 1997), and well-established hypotheses, such as the permanent income hypothesis (IMF 2008) or the precautionary savings hypothesis (see Carroll and Jeanne 2009).

TABLE 2.2. Different sovereign wealth fund types in small open economies

Funding Sources	Stabilization	Savings	Development
		Mandate	
Commodity	Revenue Equalization Fund (Kiribati), Trust Fund (Tonga) Trust Fund (Tuvalu) Stabilisation Fund (Papua New Guinea) Compact Trust Fund (Marshall Islands) Compact Trust Fund (Micronesia) Compact Trust Fund (Palau)	Qatar Investment Authority, Brunei Investment Agency, Government National Oil Account (Sao Tome and Principe), Abu Dhabi Investment Authority, Heritage Fund (Trinidad), Kuwait Investment Authority Timor-Leste Petroleum Fund Phosphate Royalties Trust Fund (Narau)	Investment Corporation of Dubai, Qatar Holding Qatari Diar Mubadala (Abu Dhabi) ADIC (Abu Dhabi)
Foreign Exchange Reserves	Hong Kong Monetary Authority Ex. Fund Monetary Authority of Singapore Currency Fund		
Fiscal/ others		Government Investment Corporation (Singapore)	Temasek (Singapore), Mumtalakat (Bahrain) IPIC (Abu Dhabi)

Sources: Information compiled from SWF websites and SWF databases (e.g., ESADEgeo, 2014, p. 102; SWF Institute, 2014).

Referring to national economic factors, these models expect that countries' SWF choices are steered by identifiable challenges, such as the need to cover additional pension liabilities or to stabilize fiscal revenues. These models propose the investigation of key economic indicators, such as reserve levels, macroeconomic openness, fuel export levels, ongoing current-account surpluses, the type of resource endowment, and the level of economic development. Accordingly, SWF variation is assumed to follow certain underlying economic logics or laws, which must be uncovered by the researcher in order to explain SWF variation. Stabilization SWFs, for examples, are primarily found in resource-rich economies, which use them as a mechanism to avoid Dutch Disease.

In order to avoid Dutch Disease, commodity exporting countries can use their receipts to create a stabilization fund (Flood and Marion 2001; Lee 1997; Aizenman and Glick 2009). "Dutch Disease," a term coined by the *Economist* (1977), described the economic situation in Holland at the end of the 1970s, where large quantities of gas had been discovered in 1959. The exploitation of these deposits, in particular in the years of high oil prices, led to massive inflows of petro dollars that caused an appreciation of the Dutch guilder. This undermined the competitiveness of Dutch manufacturers, since a strong guilder made Dutch manufacturing expensive compared to other countries (*Economist* 1977). Thus the question of "how to spend . . . oil money" but prevent deindustrialization at the same time became crucial (*Economist* 1977, 86). Stabilization funds typically have an investment mandate that is oriented towards highly fluid and safe assets, such as currency derivatives or bonds. These have a short-term international investment horizon in order to guarantee liquidity for fiscal or monetary purposes (Hammer et al. 2008).

If stabilization funds outgrow their original purpose, countries often set up a separate fund with a long-term investment mandate. Funds above the sum needed for stabilization can be used for intergenerational wealth transfer. SWFs with savings mandates share wealth across generations by "transforming nonrenewable assets into diversified financial assets" (Al-Hassan et al. 2013, 5). For example, countries with greater surpluses/ reserves than are needed for stabilization purposes and with an ageing population are expected to create SWFs with savings mandates, which are "set up to meet identified outflows in the future with respect to pension-related contingent-type liabilities" (Al-Hassan et al. 2013, 6).

Efficiency-based explanations would expect availability of surpluses and funding sources to be a strong predictor for SWF type. However, an initial analysis of fifty-six SWFs suggests that their types do not necessarily follow macroeconomic country characteristics in terms of funding sources.[9] This suggests that even in instances in which SWF variation is clearly associated with a set of macroeconomic factors, other variables may need to be integrated in order to avoid spuriousness.

While efficiency-based approaches have clarified the important link between macro variables and SWFs, constructivist approaches have made important contributions in expanding the scope of SWF analyses by integrating the role of ideas. Constructivist analyses emphasize the role of exogenous expert networks as well as perceptions about the potential consequences of creating SWFs. However, constructivist accounts are not without problems.Constructivist frameworks consider the spread of SWFs across countries as a result of the diffusion of financial fads or fashions via emulation (Chwieroth 2014). Constructivist studies were inspired by the observation that SWFs emerged at particular times in countries with geographical and cultural proximity (Chwieroth 2014) and specific geo-strategic characteristics (Cohen 2009). As such, even the starkest SWF variations, among oil-exporting economies, should be explained in terms of ideas, culture, and strategy. According to constructivist explanations, countries create SWFs when other countries in their peer group have also created SWFs in order to address similar challenges, such as windfall commodity revenues.

Perceptions guide the decisions of whether to establish an SWF (Chwieroth 2014). These can be informed by the perceived opportunities and constraints of having an SWF in the context of strategic alliances. Helleiner and Lundblad (2008) provide an explanation of why some nations decide not to establish an SWF. Their examples are Saudi Arabia[10] and Japan. Rather than diversifying their large reserves via SWFs into other asset classes with higher premiums, these countries' preference for holding surpluses in low-yield US treasury bonds seems like a puzzle. However, it is explained on the grounds of preserving their relationship with the United States. Under certain circumstances, international political factors (e.g., international alliances and security considerations) outweigh the economic benefits of SWFs. Hence, the nonproliferation of SWFs in some surplus countries can be the result of precautionary considerations. Perceptions about potential geostrategic consequences can influence a country's decision of whether to establish an SWF as a mechanism for sovereign wealth management.

Likewise, the perceived efficacy considerations of SWFs in other countries also play an important role in a country's SWF choice. Particular types of SWFs are symbols that "signal conformity with a peer group's standards of behaviour" (Chwieroth 2010, 3). In this process, the creation of an SWF is constructed as an adequate response for a country with certain characteristics and exposed to a specific challenge. Constructivist explanations highlight that the creation of SWFs reflects a process of contingent emulation among countries in similar peer groupings (Chwieroth 2014). It occurs when countries emulate the policies of other countries "without reflection on the evidence of the efficacy of that policy" (Chwieroth 2010, 3). Most SWFs are nontransparent and this makes it very difficult to assess the efficacy of SWFs for other countries (Chwieroth 2014).[11]

Unlike "learning," emulation takes place when countries adopt a similar policy or "best practice" (e.g., by creating an SWF with a savings mandate) without deliberating on the evidence of the effectiveness of that practice

(Chwieroth 2010, 3). From this perspective, SWFs are "fads" or "socially constructed appropriate institutional forms of policy" across countries that possess similar structural features (e.g., similar export profiles) (Chwieroth 2010, 3). The observable expectation of a constructivist explanation is that countries in similar peer groups confronted with similar economic policy challenges follow their peers in the creation of comparable SWF types. Central to this process are bounded actors that act in an environment of uncertainty.

The expectations of constructivist accounts are that countries that are close and similar in certain ways (e.g., in structural characteristics, especially in their export profiles) will adopt similar SWFs when confronted with similar but separate challenges. If macro aspects and geographic proximity are the central factors for explaining SWF differences, then it would be expected that economies that are similar—in terms of international economic exposure, level of development, size of their domestic market, and resource endowment and culture—would make similar choices regarding SWFs. However, a cursory look at countries within certain peer groupings and the timing of SWF creation suggests a more ambiguous picture (see table 2.2). Even small open economies within similar peer groupings, confronted with similar but separate challenges create different types of SWFs, indicating that factors other than "emulation" influence the creation of SWF types.

Conclusion

This chapter has outlined the different types of SWFs according to their organizational characteristics. Efficiency-based explanations treat the creation of various SWF types as rational responses of policymakers to policy problems—independently of any other country's policy responses. Constructivist accounts treat the creation of different SWF types as the outcome of contingent emulation of "best practices" among peers facing similar challenges. Efficiency-based approaches and constructivist work have made major contributions to the understanding of the drivers and variability of SWF creation, though their focus on macro-level variables is overly narrow. The creation of different SWF types across small open economies presents a puzzle for both constructivist- and efficiency-based explanations.

The next chapter develops a third perspective—within established analytical frames—to analyze unexplained SWF variation across countries. Efficiency- as well as constructivist-based approaches would benefit from the insights of a domestic-politics perspective in two crucial ways. Efficiency-based approaches would gain accuracy in clarifying SWF outcomes unexplained by economic factors. Similarly, constructivist-based approaches would benefit from a domestic politics account because it provides a structure that allows linking ideas to policy outcomes. A domestic politics perspective helps to assess why ideas—the "fad" of creating an SWF—have dissimilar impacts on economies within similar peer groups facing similar challenges.

THREE

Bringing Domestic Politics In

A Policy Network Analysis of Sovereign Wealth Funds

After much macro-level analyses on SWF variation, attention is now turning to "inside-out approaches" that study the effects of domestic politics. Empirically rich, domestic-politics-informed case studies of well- and long-established SWFs have begun to emerge (e.g., Seznec 2008; Raphaeli and Gersten 2008; Diwan 2009; Abdelal 2009; Kéchichian 2010; Bahgat 2010; Bazoobandi 2013). "Inside-out" approaches emphasize the need to link decisions about SWF choices to domestic politics (see Helleiner 2009). Scholars such as Clark et al. (2013) conceptualize SWFs as the result of policy decisions. Choices must be made about the allocation of windfall oil revenues in spending and saving. In turn, choices themselves are the results of policymaking (e.g., see Griffith-Jones and Ocampo 2010). Domestic politics is an important intermediating variable that links national macro-level features and international factors to the creation of SWFs (Monk 2010).

Inside-out approaches provide important insights into the drivers of SWF decisions. These studies present detailed empirical data on the history of the respective SWFs. A number of country case studies, such as on Singapore (Yeung 2011) and the United States (Rose 2011), illustrate how individual SWFs have evolved over time in line with their countries' developmental trajectories. Yet, little noticed by existing inside-out research are the important implications of SWFs for socioeconomic actors. Establishing an SWF can create winners and losers—at least in the early stages.

SWFs typically manage a country's excess savings and surpluses through investment and diversification into international assets. By withdrawing liquidity from the domestic market and channeling surpluses abroad, SWFs can be intrusive for domestic financial actors. For example, the creation of a large mandatory state-run central provident fund (CPF) that is linked to an SWF implies distributional consequences for domestic private organizations (e.g., private pension funds, private insurers, private banks, private asset managers, and private fund managers). This is because state finance institutions can compete in the accumulation and allocation of savings with the private sector.

In line with existing inside-out approaches, this book treats the creation of SWFs as an economic policy outcome. But unlike existing studies, *Capital Choices* accounts for the organizational effects of non-state actors. The role of non-state actors in policymaking can vary across and within countries. Out of the entire range of actors interested in a policy issue, only a few are directly involved in the policymaking process, while others can merely advocate positions and ideas in hopes of influencing outcomes (Montpetit 2005; Howlett 2002).

This chapter presents an overview of existing inside-out approaches on SWFs. It offers a critique of domestic politics and highlights the gap: sectoral SWF variation. It responds to the critique by providing a framework on sectoral SWF variation (i.e., a policy network analysis of SWFs).

3.1 Existing Inside-Out Approaches

Inside-out approaches share a common understanding of SWF variation as a policy outcome. Existing inside-out work on SWF variation can be separated into analyses of differing investment behavior or on the creation of divergent SWFs. While the former explains institutional behavior, the latter investigates the creation of different institutions.[1]

Studies on the variation of SWF behavior have made important contributions about how domestic politics affect SWF governance and investment strategies. While there are a few, notably Angela Cummine (2016), who examine the ways SWF behavior can constitute a source of conflict in the domestic political system, the majority of studies focus on the impacts of domestic politics on SWF behavior. To understand SWF behavior, academics, notably Helleiner (2009), suggest the use of comparative political analysis. Scholars such as Shih (2009), Eaton and Zhang (2010), and Wang and Li (2016) follow Helleiner's suggestion by comparing the effects of domestic structure on SWF governance and behavior across different countries. Fascinated by differing investment moves by SWFs, Shih (2009) seeks to determine why some follow longer-term goals whereas others have more short-term targets. By conceptualizing SWFs as tools for domestic political survival, Shih (2009) examines how political unity affects SWF behavior. Shih (2009) finds that SWFs of highly unified autocratic states are able to pursue long-term profit maximization strategies, whereas in fragmented regimes, such as China, SWF investment behavior is much less predictable. In a similar vein, Pekkanen and Tsai (2011) investigate why some SWFs seem to have more coherent strategies than others. Inspired by constructivist work, Pekkanen and Tsai (2011) are interested in the sources of SWF ambiguity—the lack of a coherent SWF strategy. Their analysis goes beyond regime characteristics to include the role of popular perceptions about SWFs. According to Pekkanen and Tsai (2011), SWF ambiguity reflects a diversity of domestic expectations and is the unexpected product of accommodating varied domestic stakeholder expectations.

A recent study on "Understanding the Politics of Bailout Policies in Non-Western Countries" examines the use of SWFs during periods of financial pressure (Braunstein 2017). Unlike their Western counterparts, non-Western countries tend to mobilize their SWFs for financial bailouts. To investigate why even very similar non-Western countries adopt different SWF responses, the author uses select case studies on the responses to financial crisis in Hong Kong and Singapore between the 1960s and 1990s. The author found that the differing uses of SWFs reflected the regulatory environments and institutional settings of the respective countries, and vary across state-business relations.

Another research stream studies the effects of politics on the creation of SWFs. Most of these analyses are single historical case studies, such as on SWFs in South Korea (Kim 2012), Kazakhstan (Kemme 2012), Australia (Eccleston 2012), Malaysia (Jikon 2012), Vietnam (Duc Tho et al. 2012), China (Wu et al. 2012), the United States (Rose 2011), and Singapore (Elson 2008). These studies aim to explain the trajectory of SWFs by embedding their emergence in their respective countries' geopolitical and domestic economic contexts. In an edited volume, Xu and Bhagat et al. (2010) emphasize the variety of contrasting interests within the state apparatus. Factions in different state bodies compete for resources (Liew and He 2010; Fortescue 2010). These self-interested elites, which are associated with state bodies and their competition for influence, shape the form and function of SWFs. Other scholars, notably Clark et al. (2013), go beyond individual country studies by relating SWF variation to their historical contexts. Clark et al. (2013) treat the creation of SWFs as institutional innovations, occurring when states with varying capacities respond to the contradictions between global financial markets and sovereignty. The form and function of SWFs reflect these underlying conflicts, and any shift in these conflicts results in a corresponding change of SWFs. Authored by economic geography scholars, Clark's book focuses on historical country contexts in which particular SWF variations emerge.

To capture the characteristics of political systems in terms of democratic and nondemocratic regimes, authors such as Reinsberg (2009) have started to use well-established frameworks from comparative politics, such as veto players. This term refers to influential societal actors, in particular the central bank and regulating agencies, whose formal or informal approval is required for policy change. Veto players are more likely to resist policy change, such as the creation of an SWF, if the prospective outcome departs from their optimal position (Reinsberg 2009). For example, central banks have an institutional self-interest in holding the monopoly for reserve management. This causes opposition to SWFs, as they could compromise parts of this monopoly (Reinsberg 2009). SWFs are also less likely to be created in democracies (Reinsberg 2009). If veto player postulates hold, it should be difficult to observe the creation of SWFs in democratic countries, which are characterized by electoral competition and the existence of many veto players with an interest in maintaining the status quo. But many democracies have created SWFs, which necessitates a further development of veto player argument.

Other authors, notably Li and Wang 2011, have suggested that if democracies have SWFs then veto players play an important role in the institutionalization of SWFs. They identify a set of veto players, such as ministries, involved in domestic decision making and examine their influence on the institutional design of SWF variation. Li and Wang (2011) draw on an existing dataset (Truman 2008) to test their argument that the number of veto players influences the degree of SWF institutionalization. They measure and compare the veto points of official actors, such as legislative, executive, and judiciary, to explain variability in the institutionalization levels of SWF variation. Their conclusion is that the more veto players there are in the political system, the more institutionalized SWFs will be. They make also explicit the role of policy decisions and SWF variation, by focusing on veto players and interest clashes between competing policymaking institutions (Wang and Li 2011).

3.2 Comments on Existing Inside-Out Approaches

These studies illustrate how competition for influence and resources among state agencies influences SWF variation. They recognize the role of individual actors in economic policy choices and SWF variation. Without explicitly referring to a theoretical frame, studies such as those of Fortescue, map out a number of different actors responsible for SWF variation. Many of the existing political economy-informed accounts, such as Liew and He (2010) and Fortescue (2010), offer valuable insights into individual SWF histories, but have difficulty explaining cross-country variation. They lack theoretical guidance and provide no analytical frame where hypotheses could be systematically tested or developed. Furthermore, most of these studies suffer from a confirmatory bias, because they only choose cases, such as Russia (Fortescue 2010) and China (Liew and He 2010), where bureaucracy and state actors play the central role in economic decision making.

These studies have difficulty accounting for the role of non-state actors and their effects on SWF creation. Existing inside-out approaches overemphasize the insulation of the state from civil society, and thereby fail to account for or remain vague about the role of non-state actors (e.g., see Pekkanen and Tsai 2011). Consequently, inside-out studies have difficulties explaining SWF variation that is affected by non-state actors. Their principal units of analysis are competing policymaking organizations, most notably the Ministry of Finance and the Central Bank. These organizations are the key shapers of SWF variation and can be treated as unitary actors. The explanatory factor refers to the concentration of power across these actors (e.g., see Shih 2009; Easton and Ming 2010; Wang and Li 2016). These studies assume actors to be self-interested, aiming to maximize their power through the control of SWF resources via policymaking organizations. It is implied that political bodies influence the form and function of SWFs independently of societal interests.[2]

Little noticed, the establishment of SWFs has important implications for socioeconomic actors and creates winners and losers—at least in the early stages. Different SWFs are characterized by organizational features which particular distributional implications. The creation of state finance institutions with savings mandates has implications for the allocation and accumulation of domestic wealth, and thus has direct distributional consequences for socioeconomic actors. For example, it is common to observe SWFs with savings mandates spreading their risks through portfolio investments across a large spectrum of assets with an international focus. They usually have an explicit mandate to invest in international assets, notably international equity. SWFs with savings mandates often privilege international finance houses, to the disadvantage of domestic private financial institutions. Similarly, through their operations, state-run central provident funds withdraw capital from the domestic economic system and transfer current wealth/consumption into future wealth/consumption. For private domestic finance actors (e.g., private commercial banks and pension funds), CPFs can be competitors in the quest for savings. In stark contrast, international finance actors can benefit from SWFs and CPFs with savings and international investment mandates in a number of ways, such as through investment outsourcing, wealth management, or co-investment. Likewise, SWFs with strategic and industrial mandates can assume a competitive role vis-à-vis domestic private socioeconomic actors, such as in bidding for contracts, and can thus harm private businesses operating in similar sectors (e.g., real estate, retail banking, fund management, commerce, and logistics). Due to their size, their special legal status, and state backing, these types of SWFs enjoy a number of advantages vis-à-vis private sector corporations in market power, political access, and credit access. There are close connections between SWFs, subsidiaries, and the banking system, as some of the SWF have banks as their subsidiaries, which may then supply preferential credit.

A Policy Network Analysis on SWF Variation

Based on these observations, this book integrates socioeconomic actors, such as finance, commerce, and labor, into an analysis of SWF creation, without neglecting the important independent role of the state. The role of non-state actors in policymaking can vary across and within countries.

A policy network (PN) analysis approach accounts for business and non-business actors as well as for state autonomy. Policy networks are a shorthand to capture the organizational features of actors (both private and state) in the policymaking processes, and shift the focus to the importance of organizational context in policymaking. A PN analysis provides a valuable framework for categorizing complex formal and informal decision-making structures. These are reflected in the type of state autonomy, degree of business mobilization, and level of state concentration/fragmentation. Differences between these structural characteristics give rise to different types of PNs. In turn, PNs inform the types and power of various actors in policymaking processes and policy outcomes. As such, PNs are independent of the dependent variable, which is the creation and mandate of SWFs.

A PN analysis offers a way to map the organizations involved in poli-cymaking, and the relationship of this map to policy outcomes. This facilitates the exploration of the domestic politics behind different policy outcomes within countries and across countries. Policy network theories maintain that policy outcomes, and thus institutional choices, emerge from the structure of state-society relations. The structures of these relations shape the interactions among actors, thereby influencing consultation, negotiation, and bargaining in formal and informal institutional arrange-ments. This makes it an excellent framework for investigating policy pro-cesses characterized by the involvement of peak organizations leading to policy choices that defy formal political institutional logic or reflect the underlying economic power of interest groups.

Policy networks are not only descriptive maps; they also hold explana-tory power. Over the past thirty years, a wide range of scholars from vari-ous disciplines, including political science (Atkinson and Coleman 1989) and sociology (Laumann and Knoke 1987), have drawn on different meth-ods and theoretical frameworks to contribute to PN analysis. These range from typological to inter-organizational approaches and reflect differing methodological traditions (Thatcher 1998). Börzel (1998) differentiates between qualitative and quantitative approaches. The former are process-oriented and focus on the structure and content of interactions between actors using qualitative methods, whereas the latter analyze the relations between actors with quantitative methods. A number of well-established studies in this tradition find that the forms of state-society relations affect different policy choices in terms of financial institutions (Hall 1986; Kat-zenstein 1985; Zysman 1983). Given that different financial institutions represent the outcomes of policy decisions, and that policy decisions are influenced by state-society relations, this book can construct a direct link-age between state-society relations and the creation of different SWF types.

A policy network analysis supports such an approach by accounting for business actors as well as state autonomy. PN analysis shifts focus to the importance of the organizational and political contexts of policymak-ing. PN analyses are well-established analytical frames within comparative political economy emphasizing the structural aspects of state-society rela-tions in different national settings, and helping to explain industrial and financial policy.[3] A PN analysis offers a combination of factors, like the concentration of state power, bureaucratic arrangements, the relationship between officials and the private sector, and the organizational properties of the private sector. These factors provide information about the central-ization and power of the state and the mobilization of business in a policy domain (see table 3.1).

For example, the notion of clientele pluralist PNs describes a state-society relationship where decision-making structures are highly concentrated, state officials have low levels of autonomy, and there are high levels of business mobilization. The essence of clientele pluralism is the permission of asymmetry in the representation of private interests (Atkinson and Coleman 1989). This facilitates interaction between the public and private sectors and shapes the content of the interactions (Atkinson and Coleman 1989). Unlike in other PNs (e.g., state-directed PN, pressure pluralist PN, corporatist PN), policymakers in a clientele pluralist PN are strongly influenced by a particular segment of society, which follows their sector-specific economic preferences (Atkinson and Coleman 1989; Dunn and Perl 1994). Typically, pluralist PN lead to reactive policies—structured around the immediate needs of particular firms, which are often short-term oriented ad hoc solutions that are uncoordinated with previous decisions—aimed at creating an attractive investment climate (Atkinson and Coleman 1989).

At the other extreme are state-directed PNs, which are characterized by officials with high levels of autonomy, a low level of business mobilization, and high levels of concentration in state decision-making structures. These particular characteristics shape the organizational logic of policymaking (see Atkinson and Coleman 1989; Dunn and Perl 1994). Business is divided and often "considered untrustworthy by officials," and "the political administrative style is one of managerial directive followed by a polite briefing" (Atkinson and Coleman, quoted by Dunn and Perl 1994, 313). This allows the adoption of a long-term view of economic policymaking, involving policies requiring close coordination and cooperation. In so-called "anticipatory" policies, the "emphasis [is] on intrusive policy instruments, [strongly driven by the state] integrated with one another and aimed at structural transformation"; these are organized around comprehensive structural transformation (Atkinson and Coleman 1989, 60). Highly mobilized and autonomous, "the state embarks upon economic

TABLE 3.1. Atkinson and Coleman's factors of policy networks

	State Structure			
Mobilization of business interests	*High autonomy, high concentration*	*High autonomy, low concentration*	*Low autonomy, high concentration*	*Low autonomy, low concentration*
Low	State-directed	Pressure pluralism	Pressure pluralism	Parentela pluralism
High	Concertation	Corporatism	Clientele pluralism	Industry dominant pressure pluralism

Source: Atkinson and Coleman (1989, p. 54).

projects that have serious repercussions for the investment decisions of business" (Atkinson and Coleman 1989, 59).

SWFs are instances of such anticipatory policies. They manage a country's excess savings and surpluses through investment and diversification into international assets. They can also be crucial for a country to implement and coordinate its savings policy in a context of high capital mobility and openness. By withdrawing liquidity from the domestic market and channeling surpluses abroad, SWFs are also important for addressing inflation pressures. As such, SWFs are institutional policies that are highly integrated and coordinated with other policy areas, such as monetary policy. As companies with state backing, SWFs enjoy preferential access to resources and thereby can affect other domestic private financial actors. Due to their central role in the accumulation and allocation process of domestic savings, the creation of SWFs can be intrusive for domestic financial actors.

PNs can differ from one another and are bound by the policy domain. A policy domain refers to a field of policy activity, and is commonly given a label such as "health" or "environment" (Laumann and Knoke 1987). Thus far, PN analysis has been applied in a large number of single and comparative studies on definable separate policy domains and sectors, including the industrial domain (Atkinson and Coleman 1989; Wright 1990; Dunn and Perl 1994), the finance and savings domain (McConnell 1993; Josselin 1995; Coleman 1994), the health sector (Rhodes and Wistow 1988; Proven and Milward 2001; Kay 2006), the education sector (Raab 1992; Homeshaw 1995), the energy sector (MacInnes 1991; Toke 2000), the environment (Howlett and Rayner 1995; Jost and Jacob 2004), and agriculture (Daugbjerg 1998a, 1998b; Montpetit 2002; Botteril 2005).

Central to all PN studies is their support for a disaggregated view of policymaking and their emphasis on the existence of different subsystems across countries and across domains. They highlight organizational differences between interest groups and the state across policy domains (see Boerzel 1998). A number of comparative studies, such as Wilks and Wright (1987) and Hall (1986), have illustrated that meaningful variation in single countries can occur with regard to the role of state and society in the policymaking processes and the nature and extent of state intervention. In countries with a strong state tradition such as France and Japan, Hall (1986) and Boyd (1987) illustrate that the supposedly centralized and autonomous states are frequently internally divided and policies are often closely coordinated with the business sector in certain areas. In contrast, in countries with a weak state tradition, such as Canada and Britain, policies in particular areas, notably monetary policy, are led by highly autonomous and strong central banks (Atkinson and Coleman 1989). PNs offer a structural analysis of civil society and state actors in the policymaking process, by which different structures create different policy outcomes.

By focusing on a combination of structural factors, a PN approach accounts for a number of the elements that interact with the policymaking process. Through its disaggregated approach, a PN analysis allows for the investigation of both within-country and cross-country variations in domestic structures and their effects on policy choices concerning state finance institutions.

Conclusion

In line with inside-out approaches, this book treats the creation of an SWF as an economic policy outcome. In turn policymaking is a collective enterprise involving state and non-state socioeconomic actors. Inside-out approaches overemphasize the insulation of the state from civil society, and thereby fail to account for the role of non-state actors or remain vague in terms of what they define as civil society and non-state actors. As such, most of these accounts have difficulties in explaining SWF variation affected by non-state actors. The role of non-state actors in policymaking can vary across and within countries. By using cross-country and cross-sectoral comparison this book offers a complementary perspective—within established analytical frames—for analyzing unexplained SWF variation within and across countries.

FOUR

Capital Choices in Industrial Policy

Asian City-State Economies and the Emergence of Temasek

In fall 2008, when the world economy appeared on the brink of meltdown, industrial policy experienced a revival in nearly every country. Stiglitz et al. (2013) define industrial policy as "government policies directed at affecting the economic structure of the economy." The state can play an important role in the correction of market failures and make up for lost demand (Wade 2012; Rodrik 2004; Weiss 2015; Mazzucato 2013). For example, the state can compensate for market imperfections by addressing liquidity and acting as a long-term financier for investment projects in developing economies (OECD 2015). Industrial policy has typically been associated with BRIC countries. For example, China has increased state intervention significantly over the last decade (Kurlantzick 2016). While state-owned enterprises in China controlled 60 percent of all assets in 2003, this number increased to 66 percent in 2012 (Lee 2012). Some commentators, notably Bremmer (2009), consider this evidence for the resurgence of state capitalism. Even leaders of liberal market economies such as former US president Barack Obama and former UK prime minister David Cameron expressed the importance of industrial strategies as engines of economic growth.

The recent resurgence of industrial policy is closely connected to the spread of SWFs with industrial and strategic investment mandates. In the period between 2011 and 2017, twenty SWFs were created with development and diversification mandates (Schena et al. 2018). This was the fastest growing segment of SWFs in recent years. Governments around the globe increasingly challenge the efficacy of investing surplus wealth in foreign markets. Consequently, states redirect funds back to domestic use for combined financial and economic return. This is in line with economists such as Mazzucato, who posit that governments should be "actively creating new markets, instead of just fixing them," and provide a variety of examples of how the state has played an "entrepreneurial" role, such as through equity funds (including venture capital) and "industrial development corporations." SWFs increasingly serve as anchor investors for international investors in domestic projects. The World Bank in particular has acknowledged this in its recent initiative to consider SWFs as tools for domestic development (Halland et al. 2016). In a similar fashion, the United Nations Industrial Development Organization (UNIDO) recommends the deployment of sovereign wealth for national economic development (UNIDO 2016).

Many strategic funds are being proposed and launched in countries that have not enjoyed sizeable surpluses, notably Senegal. It is even more surprising that some countries with large surpluses, notably Switzerland, have not yet created such funds—despite domestic calls to do so. Overlooked in the debate, the creation of an SWF with development mandates has implications for the allocation of capital, and, as such, has consequences for socioeconomic actors. This is particularly the case when state finance institutions are created without an explicit mandate to cater to private companies in their respective sector. Hence, choices made about creation of SWFs with development mandates have varying consequences for socioeconomic actors in the respective policy domains. Capital flow and allocation can be biased towards priority projects and lead to potential crowding out effects on domestic private organizations in the respective policy domain. Based on these observations, the key argument advanced in this chapter is that the existence of a strong and politically well-organized private sector in the industrial domain tends to suppress the development or constrain the use of SWFs in relevant activities, such as real estate and manufacturing. This argument is based on the finding that SWFs with a development mandate make majority and direct investments in companies, and compete at both the international and domestic level.

The chapter begins by examining Hong Kong's and Singapore's common background with regard to their historical and macroeconomic context. This is followed by a comparative investigation of state-society structures and their effects on SWF choices. Recently released archival material together with interviews offer new insights into the policymaking processes and policy debates about different capital choices in Hong Kong and Singapore. The subsections consider actors', such as the chambers' of commerce and industry, their financial policy preferences, and the policy choices made.

4.1 Hong Kong and Singapore: Similar Backgrounds and Different Institutional Responses

In the years following World War II, Singapore's and Hong Kong's long-established entrepôts were confronted with an increasingly hostile trade environment. Sparked by the Korean War (1950–53), the United Nations imposed an embargo on China—Hong Kong's largest trading partner in 1951. This caused China to try to bypass Hong Kong as a trade intermediary (see Chen and Li 1991; Szczepanik 1958, 45), dropping from first place among Hong Kong's trading partners in 1950 to seventy-third place by the late 1970s (Wang 1991, 450). Singapore's entrepôt trade declined similarly, as neighboring countries increasingly tried to bypass Singapore to trade directly with Western countries (Nyaw 1991). Following its expulsion from the states of Malaya in 1965, Singapore embarked on an ambitious program of export-oriented industrialization. This strategy has relied on attracting multinational corporations and expanding Singapore's state enterprise sector. In 1967, shortly after the loss of the common market with Malaya, the British government announced its intention to withdraw its entire military from Singapore by 1975 (Rodan 1989). This was problematic because British forces spent around $450 million annually, which was equivalent to 12 percent of Singapore's annual GDP (Rodan 1989, 87). It was estimated that the withdrawal would lead to a loss of 100,000 jobs in Singapore.[1]

Responding to the decline in entrepôt trade, Hong Kong and Singapore began establishing themselves as industrial centers. By the mid-1960s, both city-states were following a similar industrial trajectory focused on labor-intensive industrialization. Hong Kong's and Singapore's prosperity largely relied on trade- and export-oriented industrialization because their domestic markets were not large enough to serve as an initial base for industrialization (Chen et al. 1991; Yeung 1991; Nyaw 1991). Thanks to their strategic locations as well as their abundance of labor, both were able to follow an industrialization strategy of export promotion of labor-intensive manufactured goods. In both Hong Kong and Singapore, labor-intensive industries accounted for more than 50 percent of total gross manufacturing output (Nyaw 1991, 192–94). Hong Kong focused on the production and export of textiles, plastics, toys, watches, electronic products, basic metal, machinery, and equipment, whereas Singapore's focus was on textiles, electrical machinery, petroleum products, transport equipment, foodstuffs, printing, and publishing (Chen and Li 1991; Nyaw 1991).

However, by the 1970s, rising domestic labor costs in an increasingly competitive international environment and protectionist sentiments in Western markets put diversification and upgrading pressures on the labor-intensive industries in Singapore and Hong Kong. According to Peter Bocock—then an official in the World Bank Department for Information and Public Affairs—"[i]t was clear that the rate of growth of Singapore's traditional sources of income would be insufficient to cope with the island's economic and social needs" (1970, 27). According to the United Nations Development Programme (UNDP), Singapore's overall development goal for the 1970s was "to transform Singapore within ten years, at an economic development rate of 15 percent per annum (and a possible doubling of per capita income by 1975) into a regional centre for brain services and brain service industries" (UNDP 1972, 5). This pressured Hong Kong and Singapore industrialists towards diversification. Additional pressures towards higher value-added sectors came from rising wages. As a result, Hong Kong's labor-intensive industries found it increasingly difficult to compete internationally (Hong Kong Hansard, 9 October 1970, 112). Singapore had achieved full employment by the late 1970s (Chiu et al. 1997). Thereafter, its prime goal was to upgrade and restructure its industrial base (Winsemius 1982a, 152). A leading expert of Singapore's economic policy highlighted that the country's policymakers were concerned about its ability to compete long-term (anonymous, personal communication, 18 April 2014).

Although Hong Kong and Singapore greatly benefited from the international trade liberalization of the 1950s, 1960s, and 1970s, it also afforded other newly industrializing economies with large labor surpluses such as Taiwan, South Korea, Thailand, and Malaysia, the opportunity to export to Western markets (see report of the Advisory Committee on Diversification 1979a). These countries began to industrialize in the labor-intensive manufacturing sectors targeted by trade liberalization, similar to Hong Kong and Singapore (reports of the Hong Kong Commerce and Industry Department from April/June 1964, October/December 1964, January/March 1965, October/December 1967; Lim and Pang 1986, 13). Emerging economies with low wages offered more competitive prices than Singapore for a variety of products, such as electrical machinery appliances and textiles (see Nyaw 1991). From the 1970s onwards, Singapore's labor supply was shrinking, increasing pressure on wages, which in turn put pressure on labor-intensive manufacturing (Chen et al. 1991).[2] Singapore's and Hong Kong's major export markets (i.e., OECD countries) began to introduce non-tariff trade barriers that covered a wide range of labor-intensive industries. Until the late 1960s, a significant portion of Singapore's industry share of GDP was related to labor-intensive manufacturing including food, beverages, wood products, cork products, printing, metal products, rubber, plastic, and textiles (Nyaw 1991, 201). At this time, around 70 percent of Hong Kong's total exports (in value terms) shipped to the United States, the United Kingdom, West Germany, Japan, Australia, and Canada (Lee 1976, 16). In addition to traditional forms of protectionism such as quotas, new forms emerged, notably free-trade areas (e.g., United States and Canada; Australia and New Zealand). These areas, such as "Fortress Europe," were characterized by free trade flows within and high tariffs outside the areas (Chen et al. 1991). Hence, between the 1950s and 1980s Hong Kong and Singapore were confronted with similar external pressures to which they had to respond.

Finance Institutional Responses

While Singapore created a development bank in the late 1960s, accompanied by an expansion in government-linked companies, and followed by an SWF (Temasek) in the 1970s, policymakers in Hong Kong repeatedly decided against the creation of state finance institutions that could have supported Hong Kong's industrial upgrading and diversification. This decision was made in the context of the lack of an existing heavy industry base. Singapore and Korea each had four oil refineries by the 1970s; Taiwan had three. But given China's hostility towards Hong Kong in the period before 1977, no actors wanted to build a refinery in the colony (David O'Rear, personal communication, 23 October 2013). Likewise, just as discussions about reuniting Hong Kong and China were emerging in the late 1970s, the Hong Kong government decided to not do anything unusual, such as swerving towards an entirely new and untested economic model. According to David O'Rear—former chief economist of the Hong Kong General Chamber of Commerce (HKGCC)—when Deng Xiaoping was asking Hong Kong industrialists to invest in China, it would have been insulting for the government to suddenly change course, seeking to compete with China, and keeping those investors in Hong Kong instead. Indeed, it might have been seen as a hostile act. As a result, Hong Kong deindustrialized, recreating itself as the premier business and financial center in the Asian half of the world (David O'Rear, personal communication, 23 October 2013).

Despite calls for government intervention in the industrial domain between the 1960s and '80s, no large state-enterprise sector emerged in Hong Kong. Unlike in Singapore, the public sector in Hong Kong remained very small, with basic public utility companies, such as electricity and transport providers, in private hands but under government regulation (Riedel 1974).[3] Most of these public-utility companies, such as Hong Kong Electric Co., China Light & Power Co., Hong Kong Telephone Co., China Motor Bus Co., Hong Kong Tramways, Star Ferry Co., and Yaumati Ferry, were controlled by Hong Kong's large private conglomerates and listed on its stock exchange (Ngo 1996; *Far Eastern Economic Review*, 20 December 1956).

Instead of focusing on state industrial financing facilities, Hong Kong's policymakers emphasized the upgrading of educational and private finance institutions, especially private commercial banks. In making industrial competition and upgrading an issue of education and other services, rather than of inadequate industrial financing facilities, focus was removed from state finance institutions. This was in line with the preferences of Hong Kong's finance and commerce community. Private commercial banks in Hong Kong, notably Hang Seng Bank and Hong Kong Bank, had begun establishing industrial financing schemes (Goodstadt 2005).[4] Bank loans and advances to manufacturing were a central and growing area of banking business in the years after 1965.[5] For example, between 1965 and 1971, the manufacturing sector accounted for about 20 percent of total bank loans and advances.

Little noticed by most academic accounts of Hong Kong's industrialization was the potential that existed for the state to develop into a much more active and powerful economic player.[6] The British government in London supported the idea of "economic planning" in their colonial territories as a means of achieving growth and development (Goodstadt 2005, 2007,). As a result, Hong Kong even prepared a ten-year development plan (*Far Eastern Economic Review*, 19 May 1948). In the early postwar period, Hong Kong's government was actively buying up large stocks of cotton yarn with the purpose of keeping local mills in operation at a time when it was difficult to obtain supply (Goodstadt 2005, 2007). Goodstadt (2005, 2007) highlights a contest between the British government in London and the administration in Hong Kong with respect to the level of state intervention and creation of state finance institutions. Hong Kong's manufacturers demanded the creation of state finance institutions, notably a state development bank and industrial-development corporations. This could have created the possibility for a Development Bank of Singapore or for a Temasek-like institution to emerge in Hong Kong.

In contrast, the government of Singapore set up the Minister for Finance Incorporated (MFI) with a government act (Minister for Finance Incorporation Act 1959). According to the MFI Act, "[a]ll property, movable and immovable, which immediately before [independence] was vested in the Chief Secretary, Colony of Singapore, under the provisions of the Chief Secretary" was transferred to the MFI. This made the Ministry of Finance the direct holder of corporate assets. The MFI served as the corporate body representing the Ministry of Finance's ownership stakes in local companies (*Straits Times*, 25 June 1999; *Straits Times*, 16 February 1977, 12). In 1961, Singapore's government created the Economic Development Board (EDB), a statutory board that made loans but also took equity positions.[7] After the British withdrawal, Singapore's government transferred installations and assets left by the British into national assets, which were directly held by the MFI (Ajith Prasad, personal communication, 21 March 2014).

The period after 1965 witnessed a rapid increase in the number of statutory boards and state enterprises directly owned by the MFI.[8] By the early 1970s, Singapore's state sector had expanded rapidly, and was involved in almost all industries (Deyo 1981). Public policy expert Peter Chen's statement that "[d]uring the period 1960–1974, the private-consumption expenditure increased 263 percent, whereas the Government consumption expenditure increased 532 percent at constant prices" illustrates the rapid growth of the state enterprise sector (Chen 1976, 80–81). Singapore's government companies operated across a wide range of unrelated sectors, notably the transport sector (e.g., Singapore Airlines, Singapore General Aviation Service), leisure industries (e.g., Jurong Bird Park, Singapore Zoo), the food industry (e.g., National Grain Elevator, Sugar Industries of Singapore), engineering (e.g., National Engineering Services), heavy industry (e.g., United Industrial Corporation, National Iron), and chemicals (e.g., Chemical Industries Far East) (*Business Times*, 3 September 1979). In 1968, the EDB's rapid expansion led to the hiving off of its industrial financing function to the newly created Development Bank of Singapore (DBS), and its industrial estates development and maintenance function to the newly created Jurong Town Corporation (EDB Annual Report 1968). As a result, in the early 1970s Singapore's government became the "most important entrepreneur in the Singapore economy" (Chen 1976, 81).

In 1973 this led to a restructuring of Singapore's state enterprise sector into Temasek. Temasek differs fundamentally from state enterprises and from Singapore's other SWF, the Government Investment Corporation (GIC). Temasek was set up with a coordination, development/diversification mandate, while the GIC had a pure saving mandate, focusing on return maximization through investing in international financial assets. These differing mandates were reflected in divergent investment structures with regard to asset classes (i.e., to what extent the SWF makes minority and majority investments), time horizon of investments (i.e., to what extent the SWF makes long or short-term investments), and allocation of investments (i.e., to what extent the SWF invests in domestic or foreign assets). While Temasek holds majority/controlling stakes in firms, using its voting power to influence enterprise policy, the GIC acts as a passive investor primarily making minority investments. The GIC invests predominantly in international long-term assets, such as equity and government bonds, whereas Temasek's focus is on both domestic and international assets.[9] While Temasek owns the assets it manages, the GIC does not.

Temasek also differs from state-owned enterprises, as it was created under the Singapore Companies Act in 1974 as a private exempt company, meaning a private company that is wholly owned by the government (Singapore Company's Act Chapter 50/4). In addition to this exempt status, Temasek enjoys the constitutional status of a Fifth Schedule company, releasing it from filing reports with the Registrar of Companies. In 1983 the Statutory Bodies and Government Companies Act further limited access to data, allowing more flexibility for the government (*Straits Times*, 16 February 1977, 12). As an unlimited entity under special law, Temasek was exempted from the public budget and allowed to expand into different economic sectors.

4.2 Diffusion and Efficiency Accounts of Institutions in Hong Kong and Singapore

Differing capital choices in Hong Kong and Singapore's industrial policy offer weak support for a diffusion-based explanation. Such an account implies that given certain country characteristics, the choice of creating an SWF with a development mandate reflects a process of emulation vis-à-vis peers with similar characteristics and organizations (see Chwieroth 2014). Accordingly, we would assume that Singapore created Temasek in 1974 after other countries in its peer group created SWFs with development mandates, when faced with a similar problem of diversification. However, not one of Singapore's peers had created a similar institution at the time. It was highlighted by Suppiah Dhanabalan—a former chairman of Temasek—that the SWF shared similarities with the Swedish Industrial Investment Holding Company AB (Suppiah Dhanabalan, cited by the *Straits Times*, 25 June 1999, 74–76). Yet, according to J. Y. Pillay, former permanent secretary of the Ministry of Finance and Temasek's first chairman, there was no visit to Sweden or any particular attempt to follow the Swedish AB model at that time (J. Y. Pillay, personal communication, 26 March 2014; Singapore Infopedia 2015). Examples could be found but not in peer countries, and evidence suggests that no emulation took place.

Hong Kong shared many similarities with Singapore. As such, from the early 1970s onward, Hong Kong had a peer that was confronted by a set of separate but similar pressures and created an SWF. In newspapers and Legislative Council (LegCo) debates, Hong Kong's manufacturers proposed modeling state finance organizations after those of other newly industrializing economies in East Asia (Hong Kong Hansard, 29 October 1981, 120). They highlighted the experiences of South Korea, Taiwan, and Singapore to recommend more active state involvement (Hong Kong Hansard, 14 January 1987, 729–30). International organizations like the World Bank had recommended the creation of a state-run industrial bank in Hong Kong even earlier, beginning in the late 1950s (*Far Eastern Economic Review*, 20 May 1968; *Far Eastern Economic Review*, 30 May 1968). Even Hong Kong's administration officials had been studying other examples of development corporations, such as the Development Corporation of Malaya and the Development Finance Corporation of Ceylon (Industrial Bank Committee Proceedings, 1959–66). However, although Hong Kong's policymakers surveyed other countries, they decided against the creation of state finance institutions in the industrial domain (see Industrial Bank Committee 1960).

Differing capital choices in Hong Kong's and Singapore's industrial policy offers some—albeit mixed—support for an efficiency-based argument. Such accounts emphasize the role of national interest in the diversification and upgrading of a country's industrial base as one of the major drivers behind the creation of SWFs with development mandates (see Lee 2007; IMF 2008). National economic factors (e.g., factor endowment such as land, labor, or capital) are important predictors of a country's SWF choice. Precisely because of their lack of land and natural resources, small open economies like Singapore are expected to use labor and capital factors for development. In the late 1960s and the early 1970s, the entrance of new competitors with abundant labor, such as Malaysia and Thailand, put diversification pressures on Singapore's labor-intensive industries. Consequently, an efficiency argument would suggest that it is not surprising to observe the emergence of state financing institutions and Temasek in the 1970s. Confronted with powerful international competition pressures and domestic constraints (e.g., full employment and wage pressures), Singapore needed to diversify its industrial base and upgrade into higher value-added sectors. The creation of Temasek is in line with what efficiency-based accounts would predict.

Yet an efficiency argument has difficulties in explaining Hong Kong's industrial capital choices. Pressure for upgrading and diversification were especially high between the late 1960s and late 1970s. For example, the *Report of the Advisory Committee on Diversification* emphasized that "[s]ome of the cost advantages that Hong Kong enjoyed at the beginning of the period have undoubtedly diminished over time" and that this was "partly because of the success of other economies in expanding their lower-cost output capacity" (Advisory Committee on Diversification 1979a, 37). It repeatedly highlighted that Hong Kong's neighboring countries were abundantly endowed with resources (e.g., land and labor), which made it easier for them to compete with Hong Kong in labor-intensive industries (Hong Kong Hansard, 29 October 1981, 119–21). Given that China did not effectively initiate its opening until the early 1980s, Hong Kong's industrialists did not have the option of outsourcing labor-intensive production into labor-abundant mainland China in the 1970s. From the late 1960s on, observers emphasized that Hong Kong's industrial input needed more capitalization in order to address increasing labor costs (*South China Morning Post*, 25 February 1968). An efficiency argument would expect the creation of state finance institutions with development mandates. These would have supported the structural change from labor-intensive capital-intensive manufacturing, by helping upgrade Hong Kong's production to higher value-added industries.

4.3 Policy Networks and Capital Choices in Hong Kong's and Singapore's Industrial Policies

Cross-national comparison of the capital choices in industrial policy of Hong Kong and Singapore suggests the effect of state-society structures. As previously mentioned, Hong Kong and Singapore shared a number of similarities from the 1950s through the '90s, especially in terms of their outward-oriented industrial strategies. Standard explanations would expect their industrial strategies to have been marked by restricted choices as a consequence of limited domestic markets and extreme openness to international competition pressures. In both city-states, discussions commenced about how to respond to such pressures, with similar economic actors involved but organized differently.

Take, for example, Singapore's state directed policy network (PN)—

characterized by a highly autonomous and concentrated state. This PN facilitated the systemic exclusion of weakly organized domestic manufacturers and the cementing of a strong alliance with multinational firms. While many different socioeconomic actors—notably domestic finance and manufacturers—held a substantive interest in this issue, only a small group of state actors were directly involved in the policymaking process. This in turn lead to the emergence of an SWF with a development mandate in Singapore.

In contrast, Hong Kong's private-interest dominant structures were characterized by a highly concentrated state with low autonomy from well-organized domestic trade and finance groups. Although industrialists had a substantial interest in issues regarding the creation of a state development bank and development fund, only finance and commerce organizations were directly involved in important policymaking processes. Hong Kong's clientele pluralist PN led to decisions against Singapore-type capital choices in Hong Kong.

Business Mobilization and State Structure

Decision-making in Hong Kong's industrial domain was concentrated within the government's Finance Branch, which had strong linkages to highly mobilized domestic finance and commerce actors. The domestic finance and commerce sector was represented by the HKGCC. The HKGCC held a clear monopoly in the representation of business between the 1960s and 1980s, and was the most powerful business association in Hong Kong (Helmut Sohmen, personal communication, 19 September 2013; Ho Sai Chu, personal communication, 25 November 2013). Most of the HKGCC chairmen and vice-chairmen came from the commerce or trade sector. The government department that formally contained industrial policymaking was the Department of Commerce and Industry, established in 1950. From its launch the main function of the Department of Commerce and Industry's was collecting trade statistics (Ngo 1996, 129). The structure of this department was heavily biased towards trade and commerce (Ngo 1996).

The HKGCC had a strong structure, deep formal and informal linkages with the state, and an extensive internal research capacity (David O'Rear, personal communication, 23 October 2013). Unlike the HKGCC, the Hong Kong Chinese Chamber of Commerce was characterized by high levels of internal fragmentation, power struggles among factions with different ideologies, and low research capacity. This complicated the ability of the Hong Kong Chinese Chamber of Commerce to take a unified position vis-à-vis policymakers. Small Chinese traders, which could not become members of the HKGCC, typically joined the Hong Kong Chinese Chamber of Commerce. Since 1997, the Chinese Chamber has greatly improved its formal and informal linkages, both within Hong Kong and with the various governments in the mainland (David O'Rear, personal communication, 13 June 2018).

Hong Kong's manufacturers, conversely, were weakly mobilized. No single association could claim monopoly representation of industrial actors. However, industry's small size compared to trade produced little coherent demand for either stronger lobbying voices or significant pro-industry policy adjustments. Manufacturing was never more than 25 percent of GDP, and two-way trade never less than 85 percent (David O'Rear, personal communication, 13 June 2018). According to a former Hong Kong governor, between the 1960s and '80s, the Chinese Manufacturers' Association (CMA) and the Federation of Hong Kong Industries (FHKI) competed for members (anonymous, personal communication, 1 November 2013; *Far Eastern Economic Review*, 6 June 1963, 563–65). The CMA is Hong Kong's oldest and largest association for industrial interests.[10]

Culture and long-standing traditions influenced the CMA's organizational structure. Many of the key actors on powerful internal CMA committees were "still steeped in traditional Chinese mentality" and were "showing little awareness of the British style of governmental practice" (P. C. Lund, personal communication, 15 November 2013). As a result, the CMA invested very little in engaging with governmental policies. According to a former CMA employee, the "CMA's confidence in shaping industrial policy and in fully engaging with the government was below its potential to do so" (P. C. Lund, personal communication, 15 November 2013). Instead of shaping government policies, the CMA followed a practice of adjustment, changing their own industrial practices to match the British style of government practice.

Cultural differences led to a split between Cantonese and Shanghainese manufacturers. The CMA was predominantly Cantonese, and most of its members were local family enterprises (P. C. Lund, personal communication, 15 November 2013). Members of the CMA strongly resented large Shanghainese industrialists, chiefly on the grounds of tradition and language. Most Shanghainese entrepreneurs in Hong Kong had received a Western education at elite universities, such as the Massachusetts Institute of Technology, the University of Chicago, the London School of Economics, and the Imperial College, and spoke English (Wong 1988). Furthermore, Shanghainese entrepreneurs tried to adopt a Western appearance by registering their companies under English names and by appointing well-known British merchants to their boards of directors (Wong 1988). As a result, instead of joining the CMA, most of the Shanghainese manufacturers joined other associations, such as the HKGCC, which also created an industrial unit (Ngo 1996).[11] A former Hong Kong governor noted that the Hong Kong government of the day was very skeptical of the CMA (anonymous, personal communication, 1 November 2013), a view supported by Ngo (1996), who claims the government considered the CMA as a "mahjong club."[12]

Business representation in Singapore's industrial domain was typified by multiple chambers and associations with overlapping jurisdictions, all competing for members. Singapore has had three ethnic chambers of commerce and industry: the Singapore Chinese Chamber of Commerce and Industry (SCCCI), the Singapore Malay Chamber of Commerce and Industry (SMCCI), and the Singapore Indian Chamber of Commerce and Industry (SICCI). These organizations competed for members with the Singapore Manufacturing Association (SMA).

Singapore's ethnic chambers were voluntary organizations, and as such had little capacity to bind their members to agreements, which could then be negotiated with the state. Business representation in the industrial domain was also characterized by relatively low levels of organizational density.[13] For example, the SICCI had a membership of only 450 firms, mainly operating in textiles, trade, and importing and exporting tailored garments (*Business Times*, 6 January 1978, 6). It kept a low profile in terms of policymaking, not attempting to influence government policy (*Business Times*, 6 January 1978, 6). Unsurprisingly, this passivity was criticized by its members. For example, one major complaint was that the SICCI did not conduct market surveys for its members (*Business Times*, 6 January 1978, 6). Likewise, the SMCCI was described as a "not very active association" which was internally divided along ethnic groups (*Business Times*, 13 January 1978). This ethnic division was also reflected in a divided stance in the policymaking process. Although this ethnic bias within the SMCCI has decreased since the 1970s, in a sense that the SMCCI has placed more emphasis on representing a trade than an ethnic community, the SMCCI has remained very weak, particularly because of its small membership base (*Business Times*, 13 January 1978, 6). In 1978 the SMCCI had around 200 members, most of them active in general trade (*Business Times*, 13 January 1978, 6).

Among Singapore's ethnic chambers, the SCCCI has been the largest and most important. During the 1970s it had a wide network of about

6,730 members operating in finance, trade, commerce, and manufacturing (*Business Times*, 20 January 1978, 6; Visscher 2007, 186). Dialect, in terms of geographical origin, was used as an organizing principle within the Chamber (Hsieh 1976). As a result, the internal organization consisted of different groupings originating from various regions of China, including Hokkien, Teochew, Fuzhou, Canton, Hakka, and Hainan (Hsieh 1976). An observer's statement that "[t]he SCCCI is the only trade organization in Singapore still internally sectionalized along historical communal and dialect-group lines" highlights the organizational distinctiveness of the Chamber (*Business Times*, 20 January 1978, 6). Reflecting this, the SCCCI had a traditional election system where members of the Chamber's committee were elected by each of the different community groups (Hsieh 1976). However, this organizational specificity led to a number of internal conflicts during the 1960s and 1970s (see Visscher 2007). The SCCCI's influence in policymaking was significantly weakened due to the internal fragmentation and tensions among dialect groups (*Business Times*, 20 January 1978, 6). This discouraged many Chinese entrepreneurs from becoming members. Export-oriented Chinese manufacturers in particular began to join the SMA instead of the SCCCI (*Business Times*, 20 January 1978).[14]

The influence of the fragmented business representation system was further weakened in the late 1970s through the creation of the partially state-run Singapore Federation of Chambers of Commerce and Industry (SFCCI). The SFCCI was a coordinating body for the four chambers under the guidance of government representatives and the SMA. Its members were the SMCCI, the SICCI, the SCCCI, the Singapore International Chamber of Commerce, and the SMA (*Business Times*, 28 March 1978, 12). The formation of the SFCCI was announced by Minister of Finance Hon Sui Sen during a 1976 speech.[15] Because the government saw the ethnically-based chambers as old-fashioned, it advocated that the SFCCI should be dominated by the SMA, which was mostly comprised of MNCs (Visscher 2007).[16] While the stated objective of the SFCCI was to "provide a permanent forum for discussion among the five bodies, and to have a national body" (*Business Times*, 5 May 1978, 7) according to some scholars, notably Visscher (2007, 194) it was more of a façade of a united front on a national level.

State society structures in Singapore's industrial domain stand in stark contrast to those of Hong Kong. The literature on Hong Kong's industrial policy highlights the asymmetry in its industrial domain through the dominant role of finance and commerce in policymaking (Harris and Harris 1988; Rear 1971; Chan 1998; Chiu 1994; Ngo 1996). Unofficial members

of the Legislative Council (LegCo) and Executive Council (ExCo) represented the interests of a narrow segment of society: commerce, finance,
and a small share of industrial interests from the Shanghai business community (Rear 1971). Although these unofficial members of the ExCo and
LegCo could not determine policies, they nevertheless wielded tremen-
dous influence because the government rarely refused their requests (Rear
1971). The governor was not legally bound to act according to the advice
of the ExCo, but it was long-standing convention to respect its majority
views, and mandated that it be consulted on all major policy issues.[17]

The LegCo's role was defined by law. According to Leo Goodstadt,
former chief of Hong Kong's Central Policy Unit no money could be spent
by the government without its approval, and no law could be passed except
by the LegCo (Leo Goodstadt, personal communication, 12 February
2015). Hong Kong's state apparatus was also characterized by high levels of
autonomy from the Colonial Office in London and from weakly mobilized
domestic industrial actors. When Hong Kong's policymakers received
policy directives from London with regard to its industrial domain, they
typically ignored them. Goodstadt's statement that "[London] permitted
the colony a degree of freedom [. . .] without precedent in British imperial history" affirms this (Goodstadt 2005, 49). Goodstadt stated that Hong
Kong's policymakers "were very prepared to clash with London when the
colonial administration was asked to follow a course of action which might
be convenient or economically advantageous to the United Kingdom, but
which was unacceptable to Hong Kong" (Goodstadt 2005, 50).

While Hong Kong's government had low autonomy from one part of
society (i.e. finance and merchant groups), Singapore's enjoyed high levels of autonomy across society. This influenced policymaking in its industrial domain regarding the kinds of financial institutions set up, together
with high concentration of decision-making power within the Ministry of
Finance[18] and low levels of mobilization among domestic producer groups.
Singapore had a unitary government and a government dominated by one
party.[19] Its ruling elite was homogeneous in terms of educational, social,
and ideological background (Ho Khai Leong 2000).[20] According to George
Bogaars—a former senior civil servant in Singapore—when the People's
Action Party came into office in 1959, Prime Minister Lee Kuan Yew
created the Political Study Centre, where every senior civil servant was
required to take courses (Bogaars 1981). The "objective of the Prime Minister, Mr Lee Kuan Yew, was to make the senior reaches of the civil service
more politically sensitive with the formation of the Political Study Centre," which indicates a politicization of senior civil servants (Bogaars, 1981).

From the late 1950s on, high-level bureaucrats were key components of Singapore's state-society structures. To ensure loyalty, civil servants were carefully selected via the Directorship and Consultancy Appointments Council and the Public Service Commission. The Public Service Commission was a powerful agency that managed the recruitment of talent for government support (Ho Khai Leong 2000). The Directorship and Consultancy Appointments Council, which consisted of leading ministers and senior civil servants, appointed officials to the boards of government-linked companies. In turn, the Directorship and Consultancy Appointments Council was responsible to a Coordinating Board, which reported to the prime minister (see Vennewald 1994; Barr 2014).

Executive power was concentrated in the hands of the Cabinet ministers (Tan Jake Hooi 1972).[21] After the ministers were the permanent secretaries, who were responsible for large areas of government business.[22] According to Tan Jake Hooi—one of Singapore's chief planning officers—policy was typically initiated by top political leaders and bureaucrats, and not by the parliament (Tan Jake Hooi 1972). In stark contrast to Hong Kong, "[o]nly about one-tenth of the members in [Singapore's] parliament [were] businessmen" (Lee Sheng-Yi 1976, 50), and most were associated with the People's Action Party. An important implication of high levels of hierarchical power concentration was that even when tensions emerged about policy choices, they would be solved rapidly.[23] Arrangements were in place that encouraged formation of close linkages between political executives and senior civil servants (Schein 1996).

In Hong Kong and Singapore we can find similar actors with similar policy preferences which were organized differently. Debates reveal that similar policies were discussed in both economies and the actors were aware of alternative capital choices.

4.3.1 Reviews on State Finance Institutions in Hong Kong (Late 1950s–80s):

Between the late 1950s and the late 1970s, decisions about the kind of finance institutions to be set up in Hong Kong's industrial domain grew out of a number of policy reviews, including by the Industrial Bank Committee (1959–60), the Working Committee on Productivity (1963–64), the Trade and Industry Advisory Board (1968), and the Advisory Committee on Diversification (1979a; 1979b). Central to these was the question of how Hong Kong should address increasing external pressures, notably international competition and protectionism in labor-intensive industries. All reviews were influenced by Hong Kong's clientele pluralist PN. Thanks to their prominent positions in legislative and executive bodies, banking actors and merchants had developed close links to Hong Kong's key policymakers in the industrial domain (see Rear 1971; Chiu 1994; Brewer and MacPherson 1997; Chan 1998). Hong Kong's clientele pluralist PN operated by appointing finance and commerce actors to these committees. At the same time, high power concentration within the state apparatus, combined with low levels of autonomy from highly mobilized finance and commerce actors, allowed for bypassing domestic industrial organizations in policymaking processes.

While a small section of the Hong Kong Commerce and Industry Department (i.e., the Industry Section), together with Hong Kong's industrialists, supported the creation of a state finance institution that would channel capital on a preferential basis to domestic industry, the government's Finance Branch, together with finance and commerce actors, supported the expansion of private finance institutions in the industrial domain (Ngo 1996). The Finance Branch, led by the financial secretary, together with commerce actors (e.g., the HKGCC) and banks, were highly critical of the creation of state finance institutions in Hong Kong's industrial domain (Hong Kong Hansard, 9 October 1970; O'Rear 2013; Sohmen 2013). Banks especially feared competition with a state institution that provided cheap credit. Because the industrial credit market was highly profitable, private commercial banks were keen to keep the state out of it (*Hong Kong Standard*, 24 January 1968). According to Hong Kong's former chief secretary, Anson Chan, the official position was that it is not the government's role to pick winners and that therefore it should let market forces decide (Anson Chan, personal communication, 2 December 2013).

Apart from financing industrial exports, Hong Kong's merchants had little interest in supporting Hong Kong's industrial production (Ngo, 1996). They feared that an industrial policy could compromise Hong Kong's existing trade policy (Ngo 1996). A more unofficial position among key policymakers was not to interfere with the preferences of domestic finance interests (correspondence between the CEO of the Chartered Bank and the financial secretary, quoted from the Proceedings of the Industrial Bank Committee, 1959–66, letter from the 22 October 1959 from A. O. Small, 7).

Industrial Bank Committee (1959–60)

The first review of industrial capital choices focused on the creation of a state-run industrial bank, and was undertaken by the Industrial Bank Committee. Discussions on the creation of state finance institutions with development mandates started in the late 1950s. In 1958, it became public that Hong Kong's government had allocated a significant part of its foreign reserves to foreign assets, including equities. A statement in the *Far Eastern Economic Review* that "the Hong Kong Government has over [HK]$400,000,000 tucked away in sterling investments, and [HK]$20,000,000 invested in Federation of Malaya Stock," was followed by the question of whether it would be "desirable to lend [HK]$50,000,000 from these reserves to a Development Corporation?" (*Far Eastern Economic Review*, 25 December 1958, 850). It was suggested that HK$ 50 million could help diversify Hong Kong's economy by creating new industries of advanced types, such as by attracting the British Motor Corporation to start a plant in Hong Kong (*Far Eastern Economic Review*, 25 December 1958). Attention was drawn to the role of development corporations in other countries, notably the Development Finance Corporation of Ceylon (*Far Eastern Economic Review*, 25 December 1958, 848–51).

Hong Kong's manufacturers complained about the high interest rates charged by private commercial banks and the conditions under which they provided industrial credit (see Report of the Industrial Development 1960). According to the manufacturers, this made it very difficult to finance industrial upgrading and diversification, which was seen as necessary in addressing increasing levels of international competition and protectionism. Specifically, the CMA emphasized the need to create a state industrial bank to support the diversification efforts and long-term financing needs of domestic industrialists (letter from the CMA, 27 July 1959, quoted from Industrial Bank Committee Report 1960). The CMA "requested the government to set up a special agency responsible for industrial lending, and the CMA's chairman and vice-chairman were entrusted to pass the demand to the authorities" (Chiu 1994, 77). The CMA also suggested using Hong Kong's fiscal surpluses or currency reserves as a financing source for the creation of an 'industrial development fund'" (Hong Kong Hansard, 28 March 1979, 652; Hong Kong Hansard, 29 October 1981, 119–21; Hong Kong Hansard, 14 January 1987, 719).

Inclusion of Commercial Banks and Exclusion of Industrialists

The decision against creating a state industrial bank with the objective of channeling capital into the domestic industrial domain at competitive rates grew out of a review in 1959–60 by the Industrial Bank Committee. On behalf of Hong Kong's governor, the financial secretary appointed the Committee with the aim of investigating the creation of an industrial bank (Report of the Industrial Bank Committee 1960). According to a former Hong Kong chief secretary and governor, the financial secretary was "very closely involved" in choosing the membership of the Industrial Bank Committee (anonymous, personal communication, 1 November 2013). The financial secretary's comment that "[he] ensured that there was strong banking representation on it" indicates the intended overrepresentation of the banking sector in the review (correspondence between the CEO of the Chartered Bank and the financial secretary, quoted in Industrial Bank Committee Proceedings, 1959–66, letter from the 22 October 1959 from A. O. Small, 7).

Only private commercial bankers and officials with a banking background were appointed to the Industrial Bank Committee. It consisted of six members, including J. J. Cowperthwaite, who chaired the committee in his position as financial secretary, as well as five unofficial members: Y. H. Kan (chief of the Bank of East Asia), Q. W. Lee (director of the Hang Seng Bank), Dhun Ruttonjee (legislative councilor with a degree in law), A. O. Small, and G. O. W. Stewart (Manager of the Hong Kong Bank; see Industrial Bank Committee 1960, 17). None had an industrial background or a direct affiliation with the industrial sector. This large-scale inclusion of banking actors informed the operation of the Committee. Neither industrialists nor representatives of the Industry Section of the Department of Commerce and Industry were appointed. Thus, industry representatives were not involved in the policy processes leading to the decision against a state-run industrial bank. Industrialist associations, notably the CMA, were merely allowed to submit a position paper. Interestingly, there was only one official meeting between the Industrial Bank Committee and representatives of the industrial sector, during which the latter was represented by the CMA and written memoranda were presented by other stakeholders, including the HKGCC, the Working Party of the FHKI, and the director of Commerce and Industry Department (see Report of the Industrial Bank Committee 1960).

The exclusion of industrialists from the Committee was justified by mistrust among Hong Kong's key policymakers. The government took a highly critical attitude toward the CMA. Its view of the CMA as inefficient and unreliable in policy processes was revealed in a confidential letter of 12 July 1960 from the Secretariat for Chinese Affairs to the financial secretary. The secretary for Chinese Affairs noted: "It seems to me that the publication of the exchange of correspondence with the [CMA] could certainly do no harm, in view of their present tactics, in that it does not show them up in a particularly good light as an efficient body" (Industrial Bank Committee Proceedings 1959–66, 67). This was carefully indicated by the Report of the Industrial Bank Committee of 1960, which questioned the data forwarded by the industrial associations, notably the CMA. The Industrial Bank Committee Report (1960) continued that "[a]n appeal to individual industrialists or intending industrialists to come forward to the Committee would not, we feel, have been an appropriate course of action, as the Committee was not in a position to investigate and judge the status of individual industrial enterprises or projects" (Industrial Bank Committee Report 1960, 4). As a result, it noted that "[t]he Committee was therefore forced to rely very largely on its members' own knowledge of the position and on their private enquiries" (Industrial Bank Committee Report 1960, 14).

This highly influential report instructed policymakers not to create a state industrial development bank, and reflected the preferences of Hong Kong's banking community. By drawing on this report, Hong Kong's government decided not to create a state finance institution in the industrial domain. The report noted that developed countries created industrial banks in order to respond to the "[commercial] banker's reluctance to borrow short and lend long" and that developing countries had created such institutions in order to respond to the "lack of capital resources" (Industrial Bank Committee Report 1960, 2). Although the report outlines some of industry's financing problems, it claimed that there was no lack of capital resources in Hong Kong and that commercial banks did not hesitate to finance good projects. The report thus concluded that there was no need for the creation of state finance institutions with development mandates in the form of an industrial bank or a development finance corporation (Industrial Bank Committee Report 1960).

Discussions on the Industrial Bank Committee and Choices Made

Discussions on state finance institutions between the 1960s and 1980s reflected the clientele pluralist PN. Industrialists highlighted the need to develop and upgrade traditional industries through active government support (Hong Kong Hansard, 14 January 1987). Their proposals and demands were made separately and were not coordinated. For example, the CMA complained that existing loan schemes in Hong Kong were insufficient for small-scale enterprises, which represented the majority of Hong Kong firms in relative and absolute terms (see Lee 1976). By drawing attention to Japanese commercial banks' industrial loan schemes and Britain's Finance Corporation for Industry, the CMA called for another review of finance institutions in the industrial domain (*Far Eastern Economic Review*, 12 March 1965, 469–71). The CMA's chairman stressed that the process of moving to more sophisticated manufacturing requires long-term low-interest rate loans (*South China Morning Post*, 25 February 1968, 10). The CMA also argued that a state-run development bank or fund could channel more financial resources into upgrading existing industries and establishing new industries, such as oil refineries (Hong Kong Hansard, 31 July 1974, 1100; Urban Council Annual Conventional Debate 1975). Individual manufacturers not associated with the CMA highlighted the problem of undercapitalization (*Star*, 20 January 1968). Even professionals not directly affiliated with manufacturing supported the industrialists' demand for cheap loans and assistance. For example, LegCo member Maria Chu highlighted Hong Kong's loss of competitive advantage and the need to support domestic industry (Hong Kong Hansard, 29 October 1981). Chu illustrated this point by emphasizing that garment production in the early 1980s was around one-third more expensive in Hong Kong than in Taiwan or South Korea (Hong Kong Hansard, 29 October 1981).

Low levels of mobilization among industrial actors were reflected in their uncoordinated and fragmented stance during discussions of state finance institutions. Later, the *Far Eastern Economic Review* repeatedly noted that Hong Kong could have created a development fund with part of the surplus money that was used by the Exchange Fund for Hong Kong's currency stabilization policies and bank bailouts of the 1960s (see *Far Eastern Economic Review*, 11 March 1960; 9 April 1964; 12 November 1964; 12 March 1965; 10 October 1966; 30 November 1967; 4 April 1968). Interestingly, the government argued that insufficient funds were available for the creation of a development bank (*Hong Kong Standard*, 5 January 1968). Although the *Far Eastern Economic Review*'s reports were in the interest of Hong Kong's industrial community, and particularly the CMA, there was little coordinated interaction between the CMA and the FHKI or with individual industrialists and professionals with similar preferences (see Hong Kong Hansard, 29 October 1981, 119–21; Press release, Federation of Hong Kong Industries, on 10 March 1981, in Industry Financial Assistance 1979–83).

Individual industrial actors, professionals, and industrial associations such as the FHKI and the CMA separately supported the creation of state finance institutions. Because of their voluntary nature, as well as the lack of in-house capacity for information gathering, industrial associations, notably the CMA, struggled to collect relevant data about the specific financing needs from their members. For example, a former CMA employee mentioned that a number of organizational factors led to the CMA's difficulties in representing its constituency's preferences in a systematic way (Lund 2013). Industrialists criticized the CMA's inability to collect information about the financing situation of Hong Kong's manufacturers.[24] According to the CMA, the information about the financial situation of Hong Kong's manufacturers required by the Industrial Bank Committee was difficult to obtain. The CMA director's statement that "it is an extremely difficult requirement put forward by the Industrial Bank Committee for the [CMA] or others concerned to gather 'concrete examples' of the matter" draws attention to the CMA's difficulties in obtaining information (*Hong Kong Standard*, 5 August 1960).

Hong Kong's private finance and commerce actors were highly skeptical of the creation of state finance institutions in the industrial domain. According to them, state finance institutions would distort the flow of capital and lead to inefficient allocation decisions (see Ngo 1996). Instead, bankers suggested relying on existing private industrial financing schemes (*Hong Kong Standard*, 24 January 1968). The finance/commerce sector's view was shared by the government's Finance Branch. The financial secretary's statement that it is "still the better course to rely on the nineteenth century's 'hidden hand' than to thrust clumsy bureaucratic fingers" indicates the "deep-seated dislike and distrust" of economic planning and controls among high-level government officials (Hong Kong Hansard 1962, 133).

Hong Kong's government was able to ignore the industrialists' requests for the creation of an industrial bank. According to Goodstadt (Leo Goodstadt, personal communication 12 February 2015), the government refused to set this up because the manufacturers' associations could provide no evidence of a shortage of loan financing for industry. As a consequence, industrial producer groups criticized the composition of the Industrial Bank Committee, which reflected Hong Kong's PN. Industrial associations such as the CMA regarded the report as vague as well as biased, and demanded that the government reconsider its decision (*South China Morning Post*, 5 August 1960; Hong Kong Standard, 5 August 1960). A high-level CMA representative expressed "great dissatisfaction" over the Industrial Bank Committee decision, and specifically with the way the Industrial Bank Committee collected information (*Hong Kong Standard*, 5 August 1960). The Industrial Bank Committee's decision was reported as "unfair and mysterious" since it was not published publicly (*Star*, 20 January 1968). Soon after the controversial Industrial Bank Committee Report (1960), a number of other reviews were initiated between the early 1960s and late 1970s.

Further Industrial Reviews (1960s–80s)

The Working Committee on Productivity was appointed in 1963 to conduct another review addressing the issue of increasing international competition. Hong Kong's governor appointed this committee with a clearly specified mandate. This referred to advising on (a) methods of gaining greater productivity, with specific reference to Japan, (b) the desirability of a Productivity Council, and (c) the desirability of a Productivity Centre (Hong Kong Working Committee on Productivity 1964). This time, the government carefully excluded topics related to industrial financing facilities from the official mandate. Instead, its focus was on policies addressing competition in labor-intensive industries that did not directly harm or interfere with the preferences of finance and commerce actors. Competition pressures were readdressed as an issue of education, training, and research, as well as information services and coordination among these issues in official bodies, most notably the Productivity Centre and the Productivity Council. This time, the industrial sector was well represented on the committee, notably via the CMA, the FHKI, and the director of the Department of Commerce and Industry (Hong Kong Working Committee on Productivity 1964). The committee recommended setting up a Productivity Council and a Productivity Centre, which would provide various services to improve productivity in Hong Kong. Subsequent demands by the FHKI to introduce more comprehensive support schemes such as R&D development were opposed by the Finance Branch on financial grounds (see Ngo 1996, 193). Through their central position in the debate and in the policymaking process, finance interests managed to keep broader support for state finance institutions in the industrial domain weak.

Following the Working Committee on Productivity's review (1963–64), the issue of finance institutions in Hong Kong's industrial domain was under discussion again in 1968. In consultation with the Trade Industry Advisory Board, the Department of Commerce and Industry undertook an informal review. During the 1960s, the Trade Industry Advisory Board was a key body for advising the secretary for Commerce and Industry on industrial policy (Trade and Industry Department 2014). The members of the Trade Industry Advisory Board included one Shanghainese industrialist, one representative from the semigovernmental FHKI, a representative from the HKGCC, three bankers, and two merchants (Civil and Miscellaneous Lists, Hong Kong Government, 1 April 1968). Within the Trade Industry Advisory Board, the Hong Kong Bank, the Hang Seng Bank, and the Chartered Bank were strongly against the creation of any form of state finance institution in the industrial domain (Ngo 1996). This, together with the financial secretary's objection, led again to the decision not to create a state finance institution in Hong Kong's industrial domain (Ngo 1996; *Far Eastern Economic Review*, 17 April 1969).

The global oil shock of 1973–74, which translated into the 1974–75 recession, provoked another review of Hong Kong's diversification. The Advisory Committee on Diversification was appointed in October 1977 with the purpose of reinvestigating a variety of industrial policy issues, notably existing industrial financing facilities (Advisory Committee on Diversification 1979a, 1979b). The official mission of the committee was to advise on "whether the process of diversification of the economy, with particular reference to the manufacturing sector, [could] be facilitated by the modification of existing policies or the introduction of new policies" (Advisory Committee on Diversification 1979b, 2). In an attempt to address increasing protectionist sentiments, specifically in the textile and clothing sectors, the governor highlighted the need to investigate the desirability of diversification into new industrial activities. It was also noted that the origins of the committee stemmed from earlier calls, dating back to the 1960s, to reevaluate the government's role in the economy (report of the Advisory Committee on Diversification 1979a). These included the evaluation of existing financial institutions in Hong Kong's industrial domain (see Advisory Committee on Diversification 1979b, iii). The structure of the Advisory Committee on Diversification reflected Hong Kong's clientele pluralist PN.

The demand for creating Singapore-like state finance institutions continued in Hong Kong throughout the 1970s. Along with calls for creating a state development bank and fund, there were calls for establishing a state-run industrial estate (business park) authority. Originally proposed by the Hong Kong Industry Department, domestic industrialists also supported the idea of creating such an authority (Tsim 1989, 110; Hong Kong Hansard, 2 February 1977). A state-run industrial estate authority was perceived as a means of fostering production of precision machines and quality products, thereby making Hong Kong the "Switzerland of the Orient" (Hong Kong Hansard, 24 March 1976, 677; 28 April 1976).

An initial step towards creating such an authority had already been made in 1974 with the establishment of a working group composed entirely of government officials (Hong Kong Hansard, 2 February 1977). This was possible only because of support from Hong Kong's governor, on the condition that this authority would be converted into an independent corporation (Hong Kong Hansard, 6 October 1976; 2 February 1977). The Hong

Kong Industrial Estates Corporation was established in 1977 by statute as a nonprofit autonomous body funded by government loans, with the aim of operating industrial estates for high-tech firms and providing ready-made factory buildings (Sung and Lawrence, 1991). Nevertheless, an observer highlighted that it "was a tough job to get government to agree to set aside land for such [an authority]," particularly because of the financial secretary's opposition (Tsim 1989, 110; Hong Kong Hansard, 11 February, 1976).

However, the Hong Kong Industrial Estates Corporation remained largely insignificant as a state finance institution in the industrial domain. The criteria for industrial companies to qualify for support under this authority were very strict (Tsim, 1989, 110). As a result, the Hong Kong Industrial Estates Corporation posed little competition to Hong Kong's banks in industrial and estate financing. And, interestingly, the chairman of the Hong Kong Industrial Estates Corporation was one of Hong Kong's major local bankers (Hong Kong Hansard, 30 March 1977). In the early 1990s, the organization operated only two estates, the Tai Po Industrial Estate with seventy-one hectares and the Yuen Long Industrial Estate with sixty-seven hectares (Sung and Lawrence 1991, 202). These were small compared to Singapore's Jurong Town Corporation, which by 1973 had developed more than 3,700 hectares of industrial estates comprising 506 factories and employing more than 50,000 people (Yoshihara 1975, 22).

Concrete ideas about the specific form of a state development fund were proposed quite late in the 1980s, when pressure towards diversification started to ease. This was the context in which China started its effective opening, and many of Hong Kong's manufacturers started to reallocate labor-intensive industries to mainland China. According to Ho Sai Chu, the honorary chairman of the Chinese Chamber of Commerce, Hong Kong's industry moved production to mainland China to take advantage of cheap labor and land (Ho Sai Chu, personal communication, 25 November 2013). Proponents of a development fund had, by then, clearer ideas about designing and sourcing a fund with a development mandate. Interestingly, they came not from the industrial sector but from actors with a professional background. They suggested the use of part of Hong Kong's reserves and the appointment of a development fund committee consisting of government and private sector representatives (Hong Kong Hansard, 14 January 1987). The most explicit call for the creation of a state-run development fund was made in 1986 by LegCo member Chung Pui Lam (Hong Kong Hansard, 6 November 1986, 393). Interestingly, he had a professional background as a lawyer and was a representative of Sham Shui Po district, one of Hong Kong's earliest industrial centers, with many small and medium enterprises. Chung Pui Lam proposed "setting up an industrial development fund" in order to help "medium and small-sized factories by providing low interest, long-term loans" (Hong Kong Hansard, 6 November 1986, 393). The major objective of such a fund was to "help to promote industrial diversification and the development of [. . .] small and medium-sized factories" (Hong Kong Hansard, 14 January 1987, 719). It would provide preferential loans to selected industries, support industrial mergers and takeovers, and facilitate technology transfer (Hong Kong Hansard, 14 January 1987). Chung's statement that the "fund could also flexibly be engaged in other types of capital investment" suggests a potentially wide investment spectrum for the development fund (Hong Kong Hansard, 14 January 1987, 719). However, these ideas were not taken up, due to heavy resistance by commerce and banks, who argued that diversification pressures disappeared with the effective opening of China.

The 1977 review, initiated by the governor, was not welcomed by the government's Finance Branch. The financial secretary, who was against the creation of state finance institutions, insisted that a review could be undertaken only under the condition that he was the chairman of the committee (Hong Kong Management Association 1978). The financial secretary was thus able to control the scope and agenda of the Advisory Committee on Diversification (Ngo 1996). It included thirteen unofficial members and three official members. The three official members were the financial secretary, the director of Trade Industry and Customs, and the secretary for Economic Services. The unofficial members consisted of three individuals from domestic banks, two from merchant houses, one journalist, one representative of the Finance Branch, and one from the Department of Industry (report of the Advisory Committee on Diversification 1979a, 5). To preempt criticism from manufacturing, unofficial members were also drawn from the industrial sector (three came from the FKHI and one from the CMA). These included advocates of state finance institutions, who highlighted their support for creating a development bank, fund, or corporation (Hong Kong Hansard, 28 March 1978; 25 April 1979). However, the committee members were again divided into specialist subcommittees.

Industrialists were carefully allocated to subcommittees, notably the Subcommittee on Industrial Development, which were not mandated to discuss policy issues regarding the kind of finance institutions set up in Hong Kong's industrial domain (Advisory Committee on Diversification 1979a). Industrialists in the Subcommittee on Industrial Development emphasized the need for state intervention in terms of support facilities. For example, they highlighted that Hong Kong should follow other countries' examples, such as that of Singapore (Advisory Committee on Diversification 1979a, 272). However, Ngo's statement that "[b]y marginalizing the CMA in the advisory bodies, or by appointing its leaders to the less important committees, the government thus created a subordinate position for the CMA vis-à-vis [other associations]" indicates that socioeconomic actors can be excluded from important committees by including them on less relevant bodies (Ngo 1996, 151). Proponents of state finance institutions were not included on the Working Group on Financial Facilities, the subcommittee responsible for discussing the kinds of finance institutions set up in Hong Kong's industrial domain.

The Working Group on Financial Facilities consisted of one chairman, M. G. R. Sandberg, who also served as the chairman of the Hong Kong Bank, and five official members, including the secretary of monetary affairs, the commissioner of banking, the commissioner of securities, and the secretary for economic services (Advisory Committee on Diversification 1979b, v. 5). The Working Group on Financial Facilities highlighted that domestic industry had no difficulty acquiring loans from private commercial banks (Advisory Committee on Diversification 1979a). Drawing on the Working Group's suggestion, the report of the Advisory Committee on Diversification (1979a) concluded that there was no need for the creation of a state finance institution with a development mandate. The Subcommittee on Industrial Development, which authored the report's chapter on "Industrial Development," contradicted the view of the chapter authored by the Working Group on Financial Facilities. These tensions among different subcommittees about financial institutions reflected the structure of state-society relations in Hong Kong's industrial policy domain.

Beneficiaries of Capital Choices in Hong Kong between the 1960s and 1980s

The role of private commercial banks in financing Hong Kong's diversification has been controversial. While there are those, notably Goodstadt (2005), who highlight that there was no shortage of credit for industrial undertakings, others, such as Chiu (1994), emphasize the shortage of industrial financing. Interestingly, a study published in 1962 noted that the prime rate of leading British banks in Hong Kong was competitive with commercial banks in the United Kingdom (EIU 1962). For example, in 1961, the prime rate was 6 to 7 percent in Hong Kong, compared to 8 percent in the United Kingdom (EIU 1962, 17). However, it is misleading to compare Hong Kong commercial banks' lending rates with those in developed countries. Industrial enterprises in developed countries were to a large extent not funded by private commercial banks but by state-related development banks or industrial banks with preferential interest rates that were much lower than those of commercial banks (e.g., in the United Kingdom the Industrial and Commercial Finance Corporation and the Finance Corporation, in Canada the Canadian Industrial Development Bank, in Japan the Japanese Central Bank for Commercial and Industrial Co-operation; see Industrial Development Committee Report 1960). Furthermore, there is no public evidence on whether the British banks in Hong Kong applied this prime rate to industrial creditors. If they did, it was only to well-established large firms. Most of Hong Kong's firms were small-scale enterprises that usually did not get credit from large British banks (Leo Goodstadt, personal communication, 15 November 2013). Even some high-level bank officials in Hong Kong, notably W. C. L. Brown, chief manager of the Chartered Bank, indicated the inappropriateness of existing industrial financing. In a speech to a FHKI luncheon meeting on 17 February 1981, he drew attention to the difficulties in creating industrial financing at attractive terms. Brown's comment that "[t]he availability of relatively long-term funds at acceptable costs is none too promising in the very near future, in view of the prevailing high and unstable interest rates" suggests unfavorable industrial financing conditions in Hong Kong.

Hong Kong's manufacturers did not benefit from this choice for three reasons. First, Hong Kong's commercial banks had a preference for short-term "self-liquidating loans," in stark contrast to the needs of industrial long-term finance (*Far Eastern Economic Review*, 24 February 1966, 367–70). For example, an industrialist highlighted that Hong Kong's commercial banks had an "escape clause" in all loans that allowed them to recall the loan at any time (*China Mail*, 20 December 1967). This meant that industrialists could use these loans only for working capital but not for large-scale investments in fixed assets (*China Mail*, 20 December 1967). Second, to obtain a loan from the banks, manufacturers had to provide security via complex mortgage agreements. Manufacturers had to mortgage their land in order to build the factories, mortgage their factories to buy machinery, mortgage machinery to buy raw materials, and mortgage materials to pay wages (*China Mail*, 2 June 1965). It is estimated that, in the 1960s, around 95 percent of Hong Kong's factories operated on a very risky financing basis (*China Mail*, 2 June 1965).

Third, large private banks in Hong Kong provided credit with favorable terms only to already well-established large firms with good reputations (EIU 1962a, 1962b; Riedel 1974). The former president of the Hong Kong Economic Association Y. C. Jao emphasized this lending practice on numerous occasions. Y. C. Jao's statement that the Hong Kong Bank had "a very hard-headed, prudent and shrewd lending policy towards Hong Kong's manufacturing industries" indicates high levels of selectivity among Hong Kong's large banks (Jao 1983, 553). However, most of Hong Kong's firms in absolute and relative terms were small and medium enterprises. For example, more than 90 percent of the firms in Hong Kong employed fewer than fifty workers, and only 1.2 percent of Hong Kong's firms employed more than 200 employees (Nyaw 1991, 199). Consequently, most enterprises in Hong Kong had to rely on smaller banks or on financial intermediaries. Financial intermediaries received loans from large commercial banks and relent the money at higher rates to industry (Wong 1988). These rates commonly ranged between 16 and 20 percent and had a maturity of 12 to 18 months maximum (*Far Eastern Economic Review*, 11 February 1960, 315; Topley 1964, 208). Between 1970 and 1980, the growth in industrial investment exceeded the growth rate in bank loans to manufacturing (Brown 1981, 8–9, quoted in Industry Financial Assistance 1979–983). This suggests that other capital sources, notably informal private channels, were behind the growth in industrial investment. However, informal private channels charged even higher interest rates of between 20 and 30 percent (Industrial Bank Committee Report 1960, 4). Experts, notably Monks (2010, 46), claim that some industries, such as Hong Kong's toy industry, were actually charged interest rates of 40 percent or more. This made it very difficult, especially for small and medium enterprises, to address competition in labor-intensive sectors by upgrading and diversifying into higher value-added sectors. While capital choices in Hong Kong benefited, especially the domestic private finance sector, choices in Singapore were perceived as highly intrusive by the private sector.

4.3.2 Singapore Review

The creation of Temasek in 1974 arose out of an informal review of how Singapore should reorganize its state enterprise sector and respond to pressures in an internationalizing environment. As of the early 1970s, most of Singapore's state-owned enterprises—which grew dramatically between the mid-1960s and early 1970s—were under the direct ownership of the MFI. Policymakers sought ways to upgrade Singapore's industrial base from labor-intensive light manufacturing into higher value-added and more capital-intensive sectors. Confronted with a complex international environment—characterized by increasing competition and protectionism—it became increasingly difficult for the Ministry of Finance to manage its numerous companies via the MFI.

Evaluation about which kind of institution to set up took place during the first oil crises in 1973–74.[25]Although there was no particular event that triggered the creation of Temasek in 1974, it was brought about in an overall context of full employment and the concern of policymakers about the future governance of state enterprises in an international environment characterized by increasing competition and protectionism. According to J. Y. Pillay—Temasek's founding chairman—the context of a thriving state sector necessitated restructuring existing governance arrangements, which referred to the MFI (Pillay 2014). The MFI Act of 1959 Section (4) required the presence of the finance minister for all documents that required the seal of the MFI. Pillay's statement that "[it was very difficult] for the Minister for Finance Incorporated to own so many [enterprises] direct" draws attention to governance aspects behind the creation of Temasek (Pillay 2014). This is supported by Ajith Prasad, former director of the Budget Division in the Ministry of Finance, who highlights that the logic behind the creation of Temasek was "better governance" of a rapidly expanding government sector in a highly international environment (Ajith Prasad, personal communication, 21 March 2014). Likewise, Suppiah Dhanabalan—a former Cabinet minister and a former chairman of Temasek—emphasizes the important intermediary role of Temasek in the early years. Dhanabalan's statement that "[i]t was more to find a home for monitoring activities that were necessary, to collate all the information of various government investments and to keep the Minister for Finance and the Cabinet informed about the performance of the companies" underlines the central coordination function of Temasek from its creation (Suppiah Dhanabalan, cited by the Straits Times, 25 June 1999, 74–76).

Singapore's state-directed PN influenced the creation of Temasek in 1974. It enabled the smooth transfer of industrial capital accumulated between the 1960s and early 1970s into a new organizational format. From the beginning, Temasek was an institutional means of increasing coordination among Singapore's state-owned enterprises. In 1974 Temasek was vested with the shares of the MFI in exchange for twenty-one million shares, which were equivalent to the entire capital issued by Temasek (*Straits Times*, 16 February 1977 12).[26] Temasek's gross assets by board control were estimated at more than S$3.5 billion, making it the largest conglomerate in Singapore and Southeast Asia in 1978 (*Business Times*, 3 September 1979, 1). It controlled the largest ship repair and building complex, the national shipping line, the third-largest bank, the national airline, held significant stakes in listed companies, and additional stakes in other companies through the Development Bank of Singapore. This was commented upon at that time by the *Business Times* as "a daunting assortment of companies which give the impression of an all pervasive government presence in business" (*Business Times*, 8 August 1978, 40).

Temasek has remained the largest corporate entity in Singapore and the region (*Straits Times*, 16 February 1977, 12; *Far Eastern Economic Review*, 25 April 1980, 23 May 1991; *Business Times*, 31 July 2002).[27] Initially, it was created to hold S$ 345 million equity invested in thirty-six government-linked companies, and it has since grown significantly (*Straits Times*, 25 June 1999, 74). It has acquired control over monopoly firms, sectoral leaders, and other state holdings in Singapore, notably Sheng-Li, later known as Singapore Technologies, as well as MND Holding.[28] In 1977 Temasek employed around 24,000 people via its companies, and its gross assets were estimated at about S$ 3.5 billion (*Straits Times*, 16 February 1977, 12). Most of Temasek's companies have been active in pillar industries, such as manufacturing, technology, telecommunications, financial services, utilities, logistics, and real estate.[29] Although Temasek initiated its international equity investments in the late 1970s, its basic structure and governing rules have remained the same. Temasek formally owns the assets it manages, and has always been fully accountable to the Ministry of Finance. It was created under the Companies Act as a private exempt company, which is any private company that is wholly owned by the Singapore government (Singapore Companies Act, Chapter 50/4). This status has allowed more flexibility, because Temasek was not subject to the same legal limitations as other private companies (*Straits Times*, 16 February 1977, 12; Krause 1987, 114). Furthermore, Temasek enjoys a number of operational advantages that Statutory Boards MFI could not provide (*Straits Times*, 16 February 1977, 12). For example, as an entity under special law, Temasek was exempted from the public budget, and was allowed to expand into new economic sectors and compete freely with the private sector.

To fully understand the decisions leading to the creation of Temasek, J. Y. Pillay highlights that it is necessary to understand previous decisions leading to the emergence of a large state enterprise sector in Singapore between the 1960s and 1970s (Pillay 2014). Pillay's statement that "[Temasek] could have been set up at any stage" suggests a closer investigation of this period. Between 1965 and 1973, state enterprises emerged in a number of different unrelated sectors, such as food manufacturing, logistics, steel, engineering, and tourism. As such, it is important to understand the historical trajectory whereby the once powerful Singapore business elite were removed over time from Singapore's policymaking structure.

Inclusion of State Actors and International Experts

A small group of international experts from the UN was systematically integrated into policy processes in Singapore's industrial domain. Experts such as UN economist Albert Winsemius and I. F. Tang were repeatedly invited by key actors of Singapore's PN to consult with Singapore's policymakers on industrial institutional policy.[30] Winsemius described himself as an economic advisor to the Singapore government, with free access to Singapore's key economic policymakers, notably the finance and Deputy Prime Minister Goh Keng Swee (Winsemius 1982b, 213–14). The arguments used by the government to create the Economic Development Board (EDB) in the State of Singapore Development Plan (1961) reflected the arguments of an earlier report by Winsemius. He recommended a set of incentives to attract foreign MNCs and creating the EDB as an institution to provide loans and to make equity investments. As such, Winsemius's key arguments were directly transferred into Singapore's Development Plan (Low 2005). The first managing director of the EDB was E. J. Mayer, also an international expert who had previously worked as a director of the Industrial Planning Development Board in Israel (Schein 1996). Apart from international experts, only a small group of senior civil servants were involved in the first five-year plan and the creation of the EDB.[31]

Following Singapore's expulsion from Malaysia in 1965, Tang and Winsemius developed a new proposal suggesting a shift from import substitution to an export orientation (Winsemius 1982c). They identified hostilities with neighboring Malaysia and Indonesia as the major causes behind the economic slowdown. To address these problems, Winsemius emphasized the need to deal with high domestic wages and conquer world markets with the help of MNCs and a modified EDB to reach out to potential investors through a network of representative offices in Japan, the United States, the United Kingdom, and Europe (Winsemius 1982c). Again, the government's identification of problems, and accordingly its wage policy (i.e., following a low wage policy), as well as its institutional policy responses, were reflected in Winsemius's and Tang's suggestions. The government swiftly implemented Tang's and Winsemius's proposals (Ngiam 2006). With the expansion of the EDB, the industrial loan function was outsourced to the newly created DBS and the EDB's equity function was outsourced to Jurong Town Corporation, also newly created.

The decision to create Temasek in 1974 grew out of an informal review about reorganizing Singapore's large state enterprise sector. This occurred among a small circle of people in the Ministry of Finance. At that time the minister of finance and his permanent secretary were looking for a better way to govern Singapore's fledging government-linked enterprise sector (Pillay 2014). By then Singapore had full employment and its economy was growing very fast (Pillay 2014). The execution of this review was delegated by the Ministry of Finance to the permanent secretary of finance—at that time, J. Y. Pillay. Minister of Finance Hon Sui Sen and Permanent Secretary of Finance J. Y. Pillay decided to form Temasek to create a buffer and coordination tool between the Ministry of Finance and its enterprises (Pillay 2014).[32]

Lim Siong Guan, former head of Singapore's Civil Service, noted the government's strategy of systematically placing civil servants on the boards of Temasek's companies following its creation (Lim Siong Guan 2006, 182). This was to guarantee that the Temasek control structure was in line with the ultimate shareholder: the Ministry of Finance. Dhanabalan's testimony that "[t]he Government's main interest was to make sure the right people were in charge [. . .] after that the management was to chart its own course" indicates a clear rationale behind the selection of key people on the board of Temasek (Suppiah Dhanabalan, cited by the *Straits Times*, 25 June 1999, 74–76). This was crucial for the government because the Ministry of Finance had no direct influence over the appointment of Temasek subsidiaries. At the beginning of Temasek's operations, six high-level civil servants were appointed to build the core element of Temasek governance (*Straits Times*, 16 February 1977, referring to 1974). Due to the specific selection of these people, which included one company secretary (Cheong Boon Liang) and five directors (J. Y. Pillay, permanent secretary from the Ministry of Finance; F. J. D'Costa, director of the Revenue Division of the Ministry of Finance; Moh Siew Meng, from the Ministry of Finance; Elisabeth Sam, from the Monetary Authority of Singapore; and Chua Kim Yeow, Account General), the government exerted control over the controlled companies or subholdings (*Straits Times*, 16 February 1977). Directors were appointed who also held multiple chief executive positions in companies controlled by Temasek. For example, Temasek's founding chairman, J. Y. Pillay, was also chairman of Singapore Airlines, deputy chairman of the Monetary Authority, director of the DBS, and a board member of Sembawang Shipyards (*Straits Times*, 16 February 1977; *Straits Times*, 18 July 1977).

Exclusion of Domestic Finance/Commerce and Manufacturers

Thanks to the structure of its state-society relations, Singapore could easily bypass domestic private business and finance actors in industrial policymaking. No representative of Singapore's private business sector was part of the review that led to the creation of Temasek in 1974. The PN allowed for the adoption of a long-term view on industrial policy and financial institutions. The emergence of Singapore's large state sector between the 1960s and 1970s was accompanied by the systematic exclusion of its business elite from policymaking and consultations. This allowed for easy exclusion of business in the 1970s and smooth creation of Temasek.

The exclusion of domestic business from policymaking structures started in the mid-1950s under British rule. It began with the establishment of the Rendel Commission, entrusted with reviewing Singapore's constitution (Liu and Wong 2004). This Commission drafted a new constitution abolishing the institutional representation of business in Singapore's legislation process. Singapore's domestic business elite (the Chinese Chamber of Commerce, Singapore Chamber of Commerce, and the Indian Chamber of Commerce) consequently lost their prerogatives of appointing representatives to Singapore's legislative council (Tan 2011). The chambers, specifically the Chinese Chamber, protested heavily against these measures (Visscher 2007). However, despite the loss of their seats in the legislative council, the domestic business elite remained influential in Singapore throughout the late 1950s (Goh 1958, 1). Up to the mid-1960s, local private entrepreneurs were powerful forces in Singapore's economic policy domains. Low's statement that "there was a dynamic, influential Chinese business community in commodities, trading, real estate and banking which had emerged during the colonial period and were among the largest Chinese enterprises in Southeast Asia" highlights the existence of politically powerful domestic entrepreneurs (Low 2001, 417).

The exclusion of domestic industry and finance from decision-making processes was justified on the grounds of expertise and trust. This point was repeatedly made by Lee Sheng-Yi, a leading academic on the financial development of Singapore. Lee Sheng-Yi's statement that "[a]lthough some businessmen [were] appointed as ambassadors, they [were] not so trusted as an inner political group to hold key position in policy matter" highlights the uneasy relationship between the state and the domestic business sector (Lee Sheng-Yi 1976, 50). Actors forming the core of Singapore's PN, notably policymakers and high-level civil servants, shared the same political ideology, interests, and objectives. They were highly suspicious of the domestic private business elite (Low 2001); the "government saw local capital largely synonymous with unproductive rentier activities," which further indicates the government's distaste for businesses related to trading and serving the domestic economy (Low 2001, 417). Singapore's policy advisors from the UN also had little trust in Singapore's domestic business associations, notably the Singapore Chinese Chamber of Commerce and Industry (SCCCI) (Winsemius 1982d).[33] Instead, Singapore's government identified MNCs as reliable economic partners for its industrial development.[34] According to a number of academics, notably Deyo (1981), and international organizations, such as the UNDP (1972), as well as other observers, specifically correspondents from the *Far Eastern Economic Review* (28 October 1977), Singapore's government privileged MNCs over domestic firms in the industrialization process. In turn, MNCs were not particularly interested in competing or cooperating with domestic private enterprises, but in dealing with the Singaporean state directly, and as such did not object to the creation of SWFs with development mandates.[35]

Beneficiaries of Temasek

Skepticism about capital choices was common among domestic manufacturers and businesses in Singapore's industrial domain. Under the leadership of the SCCCI, private domestic businesses were opposed to Temasek and its subsidiaries (Winsemius 1982d; Low 2001; *Far Eastern Economic Review*, 18 October 1977, 36–37; *Far Eastern Economic Review*, 28 October 1977). To them, the government's choice to create Temasek directly conflicted with their business. As a result, they demanded the retreat of the state from business, and made subtle suggestions to privatize Temasek. There were explicit calls for the privileging of Singapore private enterprises over state enterprises controlled by Temasek and over foreign enterprises in public projects, as well as the reduction of regulatory restraints for small and medium enterprises (SMEs) (*Straits Times*, 3 August and 20 October 1985). Furthermore, domestic manufacturers called for the creation of a development bank to cater "exclusively" to small and medium private enterprises (*Sunday Times*, 8 May 1988, 17). The manufacturing sector highlighted that the EDB should set up a guarantee fund for SME loans, and the government should require that banks apportion a certain percentage of their loans to SMEs (*Business Times*, 4 May 1988). According to the SCCCI, domestic commercial banks were unwilling to provide such loans because of the lack of collateral.[36]

Similarly, Singapore's private commercial banks were uncomfortable with the creation of Temasek. Their critique was directed at Temasek's banking subsidiaries—notably the DBS—and their loan policy. Singapore's private banks complained about unfair competition in retail and industrial banking with state-related banks—the DBS in particular. Between 1974 and 1986 the average annual compound rates of growth for the DBS (20.6

percent) and the government owned Post Office Savings Bank (POSB) (36.1 percent) were significantly higher than the average growth of private commercial banks (15.7 percent) (Schulze 1990, 54). As of 1983, the DBS and POSB alone accounted for about 20 percent of the total financial assets in Singapore (Schulze, 1990, 52). Schulze highlights that "[g]rowing government market shares [provides] evidence that public sector competition had a restraining effect on private [banks]" (1990, 54). The domestic private finance sector felt that the DBS and POSB enjoyed a number of advantages regarding tax and reserve requirements. Occasional evidence suggests that this may have allowed the DBS and POSB to provide industrial and retail banking and retail at better rates. For example, Singapore's private banks considered the POSB loan to Singapore Airlines unfair competition. A local banker's statement read that the loan "was on such a low margin that it could not be matched by profit-conscious banks," drawing attention to the concerns of domestic financial actors (*Straits Times*, 17 November 1979, 18). However, the extent to which the DBS and POSB affected private banks in terms of industrial banking in Singapore remains unknown.

From the early 1970s on, discussions began about the kinds of institutions set up in Singapore's industrial domain. Interestingly, domestic private business actors did not perceive other countries as their key competitors. For them, competitors were MNCs and government-linked enterprises under the umbrella of Temasek, and companies of the MND Holding and Sheng-Li Holding (*Straits Times*, 1 April 1977, 11).

As mentioned, between the early and late 1980s most of the companies of the MND Holding and Sheng-Li Holding were transferred into the portfolio of Temasek. According to domestic private entrepreneurs, the government entered sectors via its SWF and its subsidiaries that hitherto were reserved for private business (*Business Times*, 8 August 1978, 40). For example, the SCCCI formulated a memorandum asking the government to delineate the roles of the state and private sector in industrial and commercial domains. Indeed, "[t]here was widespread fear then that government would compete, and compete unfairly, with private organizations, diverting much of the business to companies with official backing," which highlights the critical stance of the domestic private business sector vis-à-vis the kinds of institutions that were set up (*Straits Times*, 16 February 1977, 12). In addition, domestic enterprises illustrated their case by showing that they were already in fierce competition with MNCs, such as Lever Brothers in domestic soap products and ice cream, Japanese MNC Bata in the domestic shoe industry, Japanese Yaohan in domestic shopping centers, and Japanese construction companies backed by Japanese banks (*Asian Wall Street Journal*, 6 September 1977).

Domestic businesses and manufacturers identified a lack of reasonable financing as one of their key obstacles to upgrading. Responding to this the government introduced the Small Industry Finance Scheme in 1976 (later renamed the Local Enterprise Finance Scheme), initially financed through the DBS—a subsidiary of Temasek (see Yeung 1999, 267). However, the DBS charged high fees and set very strict lending conditions, which made borrowing from it unattractive for domestic firms (see Li Choy 1985). According to a DBS analyst, the minimum interest rate under the Small Industry Finance Scheme was 9.5 percent per year and the minimum rate for hire and purchase loans was 10.5 percent (Ho Kum Koon 1977). Observers also indicated that the DBS had a particular preference for government companies (*Straits Times*, 17 November 1979). Unable to get cheaper finance, the domestic private business sector directed its critique to government policies in general, and Temasek's firms in particular (see *Far Eastern Economic Review*, 18 and 28 October 1977). For example, the SCCCI highlighted that companies owned by Temasek were not only duplicating and competing with private business but also competing on unfair terms (*Business Times*, 8 August 1978, 40).

The Early Years of Temasek (1974–85)

Between the late 1970s and the mid-1980s Temasek became active in industrial upgrading and diversification, particularly in the electronics sector, by providing finance, coordination, and direction, producing intermediary products for MNCs, and investing in technology sectors.[37] Competition between the 1970s and 1980s was not necessarily driven by efficiency motives (e.g., improving industry standards, diversification, or upgrading) but by profit and opportunism. Temasek began competing in multiple unrelated sectors with private entrepreneurs via its directly owned subsidiaries. Although Temasek's companies were primarily involved in strategic capital-intensive sectors in which private capital was hesitant to invest, they also actively competed with domestic entrepreneurs in nonstrategic sectors, such as food, manufacturing, and retail.

A number of government-linked companies—controlled by Temasek—emerged in sectors that were in direct competition with domestic private entrepreneurs. These included logistics, manufacturing, food processing, hospitality, printing, heavy industry, real estate, insurance, and finance

(*Straits Times*, 13 March 1985, 19). Given the strong reputation of Singapore's government, Temasek's companies had a particular advantage in credit rating (Hwang Peng Yuan 2003, 214). High-level officials, such as Ajith Prasad—former director of the Budget Division in the Ministry of Finance—noted that the rapid expansion of companies controlled by Temasek was also partly opportunistic (Prasad 2014). Prasad's statement that "[SWF subsidiaries] invested whenever there was an opportunity so you had a situation where Sembawang which was originally a shipyard, diversified and acquired many other industries including the DeliFrance chain of eateries" draws attention to the potential for opportunistic investment behavior by SWFs (Prasad 2014). Another example is SAFE Super Store, owned by SingTechnologies—later a subsidiary of Temasek—which became a major competitor for domestic commerce. SAFE Super Store originated as a welfare facility for the armed forces by selling TV sets and fridges at reasonable prices, but soon opened to the wider public (Hwang Peng Yuan 2003, 214). Other examples including the roast duck business and food manufacturing, controlled by Singapore Technologies and Singapore's International Trading Company INTRACO (Hwang Peng Yuan 2003).

The Crowding Out Debate of the 1980s

The so-called crowding out debate took place in the 1980s, and concerned the impact of MNCs and companies owned by Temasek on the local business and finance sector.[38] Apart from practitioners, the debate also included academics, such as Koh (1987a, 1987b) and Yuan et al. (1990), concerning the effects of Singapore's state institutions on the private sector. It gave socioeconomic actors who were not part of Singapore' state-directed PN an opportunity to leverage their criticism vis-à-vis the kinds of financial institutions set up in Singapore's industrial domain. They specifically used the international public press, such as *The Economist*, the *Financial Times*, and the *Far Eastern Economic Review*, as platforms to convey their positions on institutional policy to a wider audience. The question raised publicly was whether MNCs and Singapore's SWF were crowding out the private domestic sector.

To domestic private business, the major problems were the expansion of government-linked companies under the auspices of Temasek and the large influx of MNCs. Companies under Temasek and its subsidiaries were "perceived to have unfair advantages in terms of access to funds, tenders and opportunities" (Ramirez and Tan 2003, 513). For example, firms owned by Temasek or integrated into Temasek, such as the Construction Development Corporation and MND Resource Development Corporation, bid for government tenders. This was seen as unfair competition by domestic private entrepreneurs (Prasad 2014). The local business sector repeatedly expressed concern about the increasing role of government in the areas it occupied (see Deyo 1986; Low 2000). The crowding out of the local private duck roasting businesses via Temasek and its subsidiaries was another prominent case in the debate (Yuan et al. 1990).

Singapore's 1985 Recession and the Economic Committee

A global downturn in demand for electronics and petrochemical products triggered Singapore's first recession in 1985, putting pressure on Singapore's policymakers to review existing policy and institutions in the industrial domain. As a result of previous policy decisions to focus on electronics and petrochemicals, Singapore's SWF was specifically exposed to the 1985 worldwide downturn in electronics and a dramatic slump in oil prices (Report of the Economic Committee 1986).

To investigate and respond to the causes of Singapore's 1985 recession, the government formed a high-level Economic Committee. It was created under the chairmanship of Minister of State Lee Hsien Loong with the official purpose of investigating "the longer term problems and prospects of the Singapore economy, identify new growth areas, and define new strategies for promoting growth" (Report of the Economic Committee 1986, 1). It delineated the future strategy of Singapore as an exporter of offshore services and a base for the regional operational headquarters of MNCs (Report of the Economic Committee 1986).

The Economic Committee was divided into eight specialist subcommittees.[39] The subcommittee concerning Temasek included international bankers and senior civil servants from Temasek and its subsidiaries.[40] The committee was initially appointed with senior representatives of Temasek, notably its deputy chairman and general manager, and executives from Temasek's subsidiaries, such as the chairman of Fraser & Neave, MRT, Singapore Press Holding, and the senior vice president of DBS (*Straits Times*, 3 February 1986, 1). Shortly after the initial appointment round, two international bankers joined the Public Sector Divestment Committee (PSDC). One was the senior vice president of Union Bank of Switzerland in Singapore, and the other was a former deputy managing director of the MAS and managing director of Banque International Asia (*Straits Times*, 17 April 1986, 9). The PSDC was appointed by the minister of finance in January 1986. Its official task was the formulation of "a programme for the divestment of government-linked companies [. . .] and make recommendations on the implementation of the programme" (PSDC report, letter from the PSDC to the Ministry of Finance 1987, 1). The official objectives of the PSDC related to the deepening of Singapore's stock market through the divestment and listing of nonstrategic government-linked companies (Public Sector Divestment Committee 1987, 1). The existence of a well-developed stock market was considered a prerequisite for convincing MNCs to set up their operational headquarters in Singapore (*Straits Times*, 6 September 1986, 21).[41]

The specific organizational arrangement of the review of Temasek's divestment process excluded domestic private entrepreneurs, and the PSDC was supported by the staff of Temasek. Interestingly, the Temasek headquarters at the same time served as the official secretariat of the PSDC, which had thirty-seven internal meetings and fifteen discussions with officials from other ministries and Temasek as well as its subsidiaries.[42] The following organizations were included on the committee: the Ministry of Communication and Information, the Ministry of Defence, the Ministry of Labour, the Ministry of National Development, Temasek, Sheng-Li Holding, the Central Provident Fund, the Civil Aviation Authority, the Commercial and Industrial Security Corporation, the Economic Development Board, Jurong Town Corporation, the MAS, the Public Utilities Board, SBC, Telecom Authority, INTRACO, the National University of Singapore, and Singapore's Stock Exchange (Public Sector Divestment Committee 1987).

The effect was that only a small number of people associated with Singapore's state-directed PN were in full control of the divestment process; they could stop and reverse this process at any time. The PSDC report influenced the particular divestment procedure and as such hampered the potential full-scale privatization. The divestment process itself was quite complex. First, Temasek's subsidiary companies submitted proposals to Temasek (*Straits Times*, 6 April 1985, 1).[43] Temasek submitted its proposals to the PSDC, which then prepared a report that was submitted to the Economic Committee (Public Sector Divestment Committee 1987). Then, the Economic Committee, headed by the minister of state trade and industry, decided which recommendations to endorse before forwarding suggestions to the Cabinet (*Straits Times*, 19 December 1985, 1–12). Finally, after the Cabinet approved the divestment, Temasek placed the respective company shares of the subsidiary with DBS Securities—the stockbroking arm of DBS—which itself is owned by Temasek. DBS Securities then sold these shares to other companies, linked to other state enterprises (*Straits Times*, 3 September 1986, 17).

The Growth of Temasek Following Singapore's Recession (1985-90s)

Partial divestment was followed by Temasek's subsequent expansion and regionalization. Drawing on the Interim Report of the Committee to Promote Enterprise Overseas (Teo Chee Hean 1993), Henry Yeung—a leading economic geographer—estimates that at the end of 1990s around 60 percent of Singapore's GDP could be traced to the public sector, in which Temasek played an important role (Yeung, 2004, 46). From the late 1980s on, Temasek experienced a considerable expansion into international, regional, and domestic equity. For example, between 1990 and 1991, Temasek sold equity for S$ 118.4 million and purchased equity for S$ 305.9 million on the stock market (*Straits Times*, 14 June 1991). Consequently "Temasek bought three times what it sold in the stock market" (*Straits Times*, 14 June 1991). It used the income generated from its divestments (e.g,. the sale of shares in Singapore Airlines) to buy equity in strategic sectors on both a domestic and global basis (*Business Times*, 18 March 1988, 1). Up until 1989, the government yielded S$2.5 billion from its divestment program. Temasek began reinvesting in global companies, which thus far had no presence in Singapore, as well as investment funds (*Business Times*, 19 March 1991).

Between the mid-1980s and the late 1980s, Singapore's state-directed PN enabled the smooth transfer of companies from the Ministry of National Development and the Ministry of Defence into the portfolio of Temasek. For example, in 1984 MND Holdings began transferring some of its assets from government-linked companies related to land and housing development to the Ministry of Finance, which in turn transferred it to Temasek. The original plan was to consolidate MND Holdings under Temasek (Prasad 2014).[44] However, in the late 1980s it became clear that Temasek had started to invest on a global basis, including in the United States. Temasek also needed to acquire stakes in banks; however, US legislation at that time forbade industrial holding companies with a direct interest in industries to take controlling stakes in banks. Therefore, it was necessary to separate bank-related activities from industrial-related investment activities. It was thus decided to retain MND Holdings as a vehicle for the Singapore government's investment in banks.[45]

In the late 1980s, Sheng-Li Holding transferred its assets to Temasek.[46] Although Sheng-Li Holding operated under the Ministry of Defense, it had been directly owned by the Ministry of Finance (*Straits Times*, 20 April 1989). In the late 1980s, Sheng-Li Holding employed more than 11,000 people and was restructured and transferred into the portfolio of Temasek. Lee Hsien Loong, by then the trade and industry minister of Singapore, emphasized that by diversifying Sheng-Li Holding's operations into industrial products and services, it would not "rely on the military markets alone" (Lee Hsien Loong, cited by the *Straits Times*, 20 April 1989, 27). Sheng-Li Holding was reorganized in 1989 into five subsidiaries, including Singapore Shipbuilding & Engineering, Allied Ordinance of Singapore, Singapore Aircraft Industries, Singapore Food Industries, and Singapore Technologies Industrial Corporation, which sought investments in the high-technology, electronics, services, and communication sectors. After restructuring in 1989, all Sheng-Li companies adopted the name of Singapore Technologies (*Straits Times*, 20 April 1989, 27).

Between the 1990s and 2000s, Temasek became the majority owner in former statutory boards that were corporatized: Sing Tel in 1992, Singapore Power in 1995, the Post Office Savings Bank in 1998, and the Port of Singapore International in 1997—the second biggest global port operator. The Singapore Broadcasting Corporation was corporatized in 1994 as Telegroup Corporatisation, and it became part of the Media Corporation Group, which was also owned by Temasek. The Public Works Department was corporatized as CPG Corporation in 1999—under Temasek—and one year later it became a part of Australia Downer EDI Group. Likewise, the Commercial and Industrial Security Corporation, previously a statutory board, has been owned by Temasek since 2005. As of the 2000s Temasek emerged as a role model for other countries, such as Turkey and Kazakhstan, in their state owned enterprise reforms. Policy makers of these countries trying to emulate Temasek without being aware of the underlying domestic policies that shaped the SWF

Conclusion

Variation in capital choices is neither solely the result of macroeconomic characteristics combined with efficiency considerations nor the outcome of cross-national diffusion. This chapter illustrates that even city-states with similar export profiles make very different decisions in terms of their industrial-finance institutions. Singapore established a wide range of highly coordinated state finance institutions with industrial and development mandates, whereas Hong Kong Hong repeatedly opted against the creation of state finance institutions with development mandates, choosing instead decentralized and uncoordinated private financing arrangements. The result was the creation of a state-run development bank, a large state-owned enterprise sector, and a sovereign wealth fund in Singapore and the advancement of private sector finance schemes in Hong Kong. This divergence in finance institutions can be explained by how differently state-society structures have played out in Hong Kong and Singapore.

In both city-state economies, similar socioeconomic actors existed, but were structured differently. Hong Kong's clientele pluralist policy network (PN) hindered the pursuit of industrial policy and finance institutions with a long-term horizon characterized by high levels of coordination and state involvement. A highly mobilized domestic banking sector, together with a centralized state with low levels of autonomy influenced discussions and policymaking processes concerning the kinds of finance institution that were set up. State-society structures permitted policymakers to bypass domestic industrialists, which demanded the creation of a state-run industrial development bank and a more activist industrial policy, underpinned by state finance institutions with a development mandate. Instead, they affected finance institutional arrangements structured around the immediate needs of Hong Kong's finance and commerce sector.

By contrast, Singapore's state-directed PN enabled the pursuit of industrial policy and finance institutions with a long-term horizon characterized by high levels of coordination and state involvement. The hierarchical structure of the Ministry of Finance allowed a small group of state actors to bypass domestic finance and industrial interests on decision-making processes. High levels of autonomy enabled state actors to create and reorganize the state enterprise sector—leading to the emergence of Temasek—without interference from domestic private interest groups. For them, the government's choice to create Temasek came in direct conflict with their business, and they made subtle suggestions to privatize Temasek.

Based on the findings, this chapter argues that the existence of a strong and politically well-organized private financial sector tends to suppress the creation of SWFs with an industrial financing function. In contrast, the presence of a state-directed PN, which is characterized by a weakly organized private sector and centralized autonomous state decision making structures leads to the creation of an SWF with a development function.

FIVE

Capital Choices in Savings and Financial Policy

Asian City-States and the Emergence of the Government Investment Corporation

Global savings in 2019 bear little resemblance to those of earlier decades.[1] A significant portion now originates from non-OECD countries. While in the 1980s about 25 percent of world savings[2] could be attributed to non-OECD economies, by 2015 this had doubled to around 50 percent of world savings (see fig. 5.1).[3] This is equal to a 10,000 percent absolute increase. The shift in world savings also reflects an underlying shift in global reserve holdings.[4] By 2019 states have amassed over $7 trillion in reserves. Previous debtor nations have become creditor nations. A major part of this increase can be attributed to China. According to the World Bank, China will continue to dominate global savings over the coming years. By 2030, China's absolute savings will the largest among all economies worldwide, estimated at around $9 trillion (Global Saving in 2030).

The shift in global savings is strongly linked to the rise of SWFs. The 2000s export boom led to persistent current account surpluses and accumulation of net foreign assets, especially in Asia. Net exporting countries began holding more reserves than needed for prudential purposes. In the process of diversifying these reserves into globalized asset portfolios with long-run higher returns, governments began transferring sovereign assets into newly created SWFs (Aizenman and Glick, 2007). Yet a number of net exporters with sizable savings and foreign exchange reserves, notably Hong

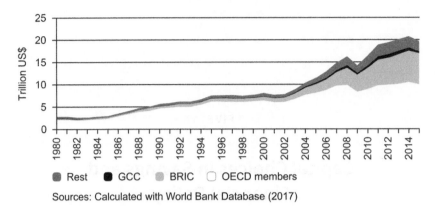

Rest ● **GCC** ● **BRIC** ○ **OECD members**

Sources: Calculated with World Bank Database (2017)

Figure 5.1. Global gross domestic savings in trillion USD

Kong, have resisted calls to create such funds. Overlooked in the debate is the frequent linkage between creation of SWFs with saving mandates—particularly economies without resource wealth—to other state finance institutions, such as Central Banks or Central Provident Funds. The allocation and investment decisions of SWFs, together with these related finance vehicles, can impact other firms in the respective policy domain.

Capital choices have differing implications on capital allocation, and, as such, have distinctive consequences for various socioeconomic actors. The creation of large SWFs with savings mandates impacts domestic socioeconomic actors, especially if they are created without specified directives catering to private actors in the respective policy domain (e.g., private pension funds, private insurers, or private banks). An SWF with a savings mandate accumulates significant amounts of domestic wealth and channels it into international financial assets including equity, debt, and international real estate. This is either done directly or via international financial intermediaries. This can lead to competition for capital with the private domestic finance sector.

This chapter begins by examining Hong Kong and Singapore's common historical and macroeconomic background. This helps in assessing efficiency and constructivist aspects explained by standard explanations of SWFs. This is followed by an investigation of state-society structures and their effects on SWF choices. The subsections consider actors' preferences and the policy choices they make.

5.1 Hong Kong and Singapore: Similar Backgrounds
but Different Finance Institutions

Hong Kong's and Singapore's public and private savings' levels were among the highest in the world, particularly in the 1970s and '80s. Despite their extreme financial openness, this chapter finds that their domestic state-society structures permitted a wide range of different capital choices. While Singapore experienced the expansion of its mandatory state-run Central Provident Fund (CPF) and creation of the Government Investment Corporation (GIC), Hong Kong witnessed the emergence of private pension schemes and a finance sector dominated by private actors. Interestingly, debates about the creation of a CPF and a GIC-like SWF also took place in Hong Kong, but its state-society structures allowed the exclusion of labor and social welfare organizations. It were these organizations which demanded the creation of an SWF with a savings mandate. In contrast, Singapore's state alliance with domestic labor and international finance facilitated creation of an SWF, at the cost of the domestic private finance sector.

Singapore and Hong Kong were both once British colonies with similar economic trajectories. In the nineteenth and early twentieth century Hong Kong emerged as the main entrepôt for China as Singapore did for Southeast Asia. In the 1950s and 1960s, an increasingly hostile regional environment (e.g., the Korean War and the Malaysian/Indonesian Confrontation) affected both states' entrepôt and trade activity. In order to produce surplus wealth, they needed to follow an export-oriented strategy given their small domestic market size. Between the 1960s and 1970s, both embarked on a labor-intensive, export-oriented development strategy (Lim and Pang 1986; Nyaw 1991). Hong Kong and Singapore became leading manufacturers of textiles, plastics, toys, watches, electronic products, basic metal, machinery, and equipment (Chen and Li 1991; Nyaw 1991). Thanks to high levels of economic growth, combined with their conservative fiscal policies, Hong Kong and Singapore accumulated large surpluses (see table 5.1). Likewise, a high propensity to save among the populations led to high savings levels in Hong Kong and Singapore, reflected in high savings ratios (see table 5.2). For example, in the 1980s, savings ratios in Hong Kong and Singapore surpassed even those of OECD economies, such as Germany, Austria, and the United States (World Bank 2015).

Between the 1970s and 1980s, Singapore and Hong Kong began establishing themselves as regional financial centers. This was a period of

TABLE 5.1. Surpluses in Singapore and Hong Kong between 1960 and 1980

	Singapore in million Sing$	Hong Kong in million HK$
1960	88	14
1965	136	77
1970	100	449
1975	551	488
1980	1,214	2,500

Sources: Youngson (1982), p.60),; Low (2005), p.170).

Note: The Singapore figures refer to current account surpluses, whereas the Hong Kong figures refer to budget surpluses.

TABLE 5.2. Public and private savings in Hong Kong and Singapore (1980–87)

	Saving Ratio as a Percentage of GDP	
Year	Singapore	Hong Kong
1980	38.8	31.4
1981	41.7	30.4
1982	42.3	28.2
1983	45.0	25.1
1984	45.3	28.9
1985	40.6	27.3
1986	38.9	28.5
1987	40.5	31.6

Source: James (1991), p. 308.

challenges and opportunities. As small open economies with high import needs, policymakers in both city-state economies were faced with the question of how to sustain the purchasing power of their ageing population in the context of high inflation pressures (Hong Kong Greenpaper 1977; Singapore Hansard, 17 June 1976). Inflation rates in Hong Kong and Singapore during the early 1970s and 1980s reached double-digit levels (*Economist*, 19 July 1975, 15; Li 1999; Jao 2001; Moreno 2012, 185; MAS Economic Explorer 2014). In Hong Kong, a significant portion of savings flowed into highly speculative domestic stock and real estate markets, leading to a number of banking crises (see Goodstadt 2005). In contrast, since the late 1970s Singapore's large savings have been managed conservatively by the Monetary Authority of Singapore (MAS), which invested the proceeds from the issuance of government securities primarily in highly liquid assets such as conventional foreign reserves (e.g., cash deposits of other currencies).

Over the same period, international markets and asset classes became highly lucrative. The period between the late 1970s and early 1980s has been described as the "turning point in global finance" (Helleiner 2004). It witnessed capital account liberalization and stock market development, making international public and private equity investments more attractive (Eichengreen 2004; *Straits Times*, 6 October 2007). It also experienced a solid development of the Euro Dollar Market, which grew from $75 billion in 1970 to $1 trillion by 1984 (Strange 1988, 107). High interest rates combined with technological advances were among the main drivers of the international financial securitization (Walter 1991). The 1980s US interest rate shock had a particularly significant effect on small open economies, which were highly exposed to the US economy (Glick and Moreno 1994). The dramatic rise of interest rates (up to 20 percent), commonly referred to as "interest rate shock," together with the appreciation of the US dollar, had varied consequences for debtor nations and creditor nations. For surplus countries such as Singapore and Hong Kong, this opened up the scope for diversified long-term investments, and in the early 1980s it became very lucrative to buy US treasury bonds.

Finance Institutional Responses

While Singapore's policymakers responded to the changing international financial environment with the creation of an SWF (the Government Investment Corporation, GIC), Hong Kong's policymakers opted against the creation of such state finance institutions. Little-noticed by the wider academic community, there was a real possibility for the creation of a large state-run CPF in Hong Kong, and linked to that, a GIC-type SWF (see fig. 5.2). A report from the Legislative Council—Hong Kong's parliament—reveals that such a state-run CPF covering Hong Kong's labor could have reached, over a period of ten years, a size similar to Singapore's CPF (Hong Kong Hansard, 13 March 1987). Over ten years this might have led to a CPF with a volume of between HK$ 80–90 billion net (Hong Kong Hansard, 5 November 1986, 327).[5] If interest rates were included in this calculation, this figure would significantly increased. Given an annual addition of HK$ 8,500 million and a minimum annual interest rate of 10 percent (during the 1980s, the average prime interest rate was even higher), the CPF would have grown in a period of ten years to around HK$ 140 billion.[6] Compared with the total estimated government revenue in 1986 of about HK$40 billion, this would have amounted to a very large sum (Hong Kong Hansard, 5 November 1986, 327).

The creation of such a CPF in Hong Kong might have led to the creation of an SWF. CPFs are usually governed by trustee legislation and need to allocate their capital into highly secure asset classes. This typically requires an inactive management.[7] Such a CPF usually translates its members' contributions into secure bonds issued by the government or a monetary authority. The proceeds from the issuance of such bonds are usually used to finance budget deficits (Hong Kong Hansard, 13 May 1987). Like Singapore, Hong Kong enjoyed structural surpluses and, therefore, did not need to issue bonds for this purpose. Consequently, one alternative option would have been the creation of an SWF (see Mok 1986). This idea was brought up on several occasions in Hong Kong's LegCo (Hong Kong Hansard, 13 March 1987). It was highlighted that if a large CPF were created, its funds would need to be invested professionally by a state investment agency into international assets, and the return on the investments would be used to pay the interest on CPF members' accounts ("Implications of Establishing a CPF in HK," Hong Kong Hansard, 13 May 1987, 1591).

But instead of creating such state finance vehicles, Hong Kong's policymakers were determined to rely on private financial institutions. They promoted deposits in private commercial banks and private provident fund schemes. As a result, each month approximately fifty new private pension schemes were approved (Hong Kong Hansard, 13 May 1987, 1537). Reflecting this, the number of approved private provident fund schemes also increased dramatically from 540 in 1970 to 4,105 in 1986 (Li 1988, 71, taken from *Hong Kong Economic Journal*, 27 August 1988). In the 1980s these covered around 300,000 workers (Hong Kong Hansard, 13 May 1987, 1537). Together with Hong Kong's domestic commercial banks, these institutions allocated significant funds into the burgeoning property sector and Hong Kong's speculative stock market (Jao 2001). From the 1970s onward, Hong Kong's stock market started to become an important source for financing property (Wong 1991, 217). This had important implications. Because of the banking sector's high exposure to the property sector and later to the stock market, this translated into a number of banking crises between the 1960s and the 1980s (Jao 2001, 23–48).

Singapore's policymakers relied on state rather than private finance institutions. In stark contrast to Hong Kong, the number of private provident funds in Singapore had increased to only about 100 by 1977 and most of them were weakly funded (Lee 1974, 203; *Business Times*, 23 June 1979, 9). Simultaneously, mandatory contribution rates to Singapore's CPF from employee wages as well as from employers' incomes, increased progressively from 5 percent in 1955 to 38.5 percent in 1980, 42 percent in 1981,

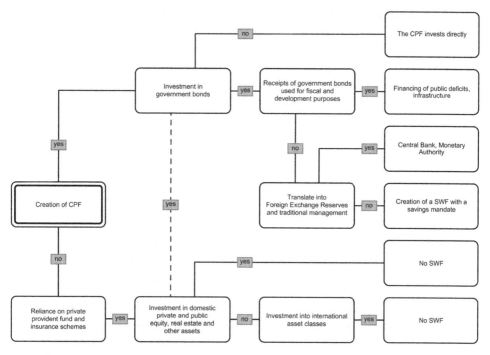

Figure 5.2. Decision-making model on the link between CPFs and SWFs

45 percent in 1982, and to its highest level of 50 percent in 1985 (S. Y. Lee 1984, 258; Skully 1984; Skully and Viksnins 1987). The CPF's membership size increased from 180,000 in 1955 to 504,828 in 1968 to 1,518,755 in 1980, and its members' outstanding balance grew from S$9.1 million in 1955 to S$539.7 million in 1968, approximately S$10 billion in 1980, and approximately S$27 billion in 1985. By law, the CPF was required to deposit its members' contributions to the MAS, which in return issued Singapore Government Securities. This made the CPF the major holder of Singapore Government Securities (Lee Tsao 1987).

Singapore's SWF, the GIC, was established in 1981 with the objective of maintaining long-term purchasing power of Singapore's savings. However, the GIC does not own the assets it manages. Its mandate requires the GIC to invest exclusively in international assets. Through its investments, the GIC has been channeling liquidity out of Singapore since 1981.[8] It launched its international investment operations with about S$10 billion, which reached approximately S$110 billion—equivalent to $82 billion—by 1997 (K.Y. Lee 2006; *Straits Times*, 14 April 1999).

5.2 Diffusion and Efficiency Accounts of Different Institutions in Hong Kong and Singapore

The cases of SWF variation in Hong Kong and Singapore offer mixed support for an efficiency-based explanation. The observed policy outcome in Hong Kong's savings domain is contrary to what an efficiency argument would have predicted. In light of an ageing population, and given that no old-age security and welfare system had been put in place, pressures were rising in Hong Kong to create state finance institutions with savings mandates in order to secure the future purchasing power of the population.[9] Between the 1960s and the 1980s, a highly volatile real estate and stock market made investments in other domestic assets highly risky (Hong Kong Hansard, 13 May 1987). Given the lack of alternative domestic asset classes, and in the context of an attractive international investment environment, an efficiency argument would have expected the creation of a state finance institution channeling savings into international assets.[10] Interestingly, at this time Hong Kong already had the capacity and "know-how" to manage savings abroad via state finance institutions (Hong Kong Hansard, 3 February 1993). For example, the Hong Kong government already had a small state-run CPF (the Subsidized Schools Provident Fund), which mainly invested in highly secure international assets (Hong Kong Hansard, 13 March 1987).[11]

While the case of Hong Kong offers little support for an efficiency argument, the creation of the GIC in Singapore provides evidence on the impacts of efficiency. Given significant amounts of savings and limited domestic investment opportunities, an efficiency argument would have predicted the creation of an SWF with a savings mandate in Singapore. Like Hong Kong, Singapore enjoyed structural surpluses, and as such it did not need to issue government securities for fiscal purposes. By the early 1980s, Singapore's government continued issuing large amounts of government securities, specifically for the Central Provident Fund—Singapore's mandatory state pension fund. By law, the CPF Board is required to invest in securities issued and guaranteed by the Singapore government (S. Y. Lee 1984). Given Singapore's domestic investment constraints in the 1970s and 1980s, one way of allocating high levels of domestic savings without the creation of bubbles and without fueling inflation was to set up an SWF channeling savings abroad into long-term financial assets. Given its small domestic markets and large savings levels in an international environment of high-return opportunities, the GIC's was highly rational from a macronational perspective.

However, the cases of Hong Kong and Singapore offer little support for diffusion-based explanations. A diffusion argument would argue that countries create an SWF with a savings mandate when members of its peer group have created a similar SWF when faced with comparable problems of wealth accumulation and long-term investment. However, at the time of the GIC's creation, none of Singapore's peers had established an SWF with a savings mandate. This is particularly emphasized by GIC's former managing director J. Y. Pillay: "The formation of GIC was actually quite a novel idea, groundbreaking because no other government that we knew of had set up such a specific agency to manage the surplus assets on a diversified portfolio basis." This suggests that Singapore did not follow any other country in its decision to create an SWF (J. Y. Pillay, quoted by MAS Commemoration 2011, 95). In terms of small open economies without hydrocarbon resources, Singapore was the first to create such an SWF. During the 1980s, only countries outside Singapore's peer group had created SWFs with savings mandates.

Although small economies of the Middle East had already established SWFs with savings mandates, they cannot be considered peers of Singapore, because of their very different export profile structure. Singapore's policymakers considered examples in the Middle East, but pursued an entirely different model (Ng Kok Song, personal communication 28 February 2014). This was highlighted by a former director of GIC's economics and strategy department. The idea of creating a separate institution for managing surpluses was quite "revolutionary" because, at that time, the only examples of savings SWFs were countries of the Middle East such as Kuwait and Abu Dhabi (anonymous, personal communication, 20 August 2014). These countries' SWFs depended heavily on external fund management to account for most of their money. In stark contrast, Singapore's policymakers were determined to make Singapore's GIC differ from existing examples in the Middle East; from the beginning, Singapore developed in-house investment capacity (Braunstein and Tomba 2017).

Likewise, the case of financial institutions in Hong Kong offers little evidence for a diffusion-based argument. Given its high savings and the fact that its peer, Singapore, had created an SWF in the early 1980s, a diffusion argument might have predicted the creation of an SWF in mid-1980s Hong Kong. Although Hong Kong's policymakers had been actively observing peers, notably Singapore, they explicitly opted for private financial institutions (Nelson Chow, personal communication, 17 February 2015; OMELCO 1986; see SBR Harbour Department of Social Services, Confidential report, 1974–76). Surprisingly, official discussions about establishing a CPF and linked to that, an SWF, in Hong Kong took place in 1986–87, a period when Singapore's CPF, with its high contribution rates, was no longer considered an example of best practice by policymakers in Singapore itself (Hong Kong Hansard, 13 March 1987).[12] This would be surprising for proponents of a diffusion argument, because Hong Kong's debate about creating a CPF took place at a time when it was "unfashionable" to create such institutions.

5.3 Policy Network Account of Finance Institutional Choices in Hong Kong and Singapore

It is the cross-national comparison between Singapore and Hong Kong which indicates the effect of state-society relations on the choices of financial institutions. Decision-making structures were highly centralized in Hong Kong and Singapore, but linkages between state and private actors differed significantly, reflecting varying levels of state autonomy (e.g., see Hamilton-Hart 2003). Similar institutional choices were available and similar socioeconomic actors, though mobilized and structured differently, participated in public debates. In Hong Kong a number of powerful banks emerged, such as the Hong Kong Bank, Standard Chartered, and the Bank of East Asia. Likewise, Singapore saw the creation of a number of large banks, such the Overseas Chinese Banking Corporation, the Overseas Union Bank, and the United Overseas Bank (Ishihara and Kim 1982). However, these banks were structured differently within the policymaking processes of Hong Kong and Singapore.

In the 1970s and 1980s, the structural features of state-society relations in Hong Kong's savings domain were consistent with that of a clientele pluralist policy network (PN), allowing a segment of civil society to influence policymaking. This structure was characterized by a high concentration of decision-making power within the government's Finance Branch, which held strong linkages to highly mobilized domestic finance and commerce organizations (Ngo 1996; Chiu 1990; Leung 1990). It has been widely accepted in the literature that finance and commerce interests were overrepresented in Hong Kong's policymaking structures (Ngo 1996; Chiu 1994; Leung 1990). Up to the 1980s, nearly all of the Executive Council (ExCo)—Hong Kong's Cabinet—and the LegCo unofficials were successful businessmen. For example, in 1987, out of the ten unofficial members of the ExCo, seven were related to CEOs of organizations in trade, commerce, and banking. About 45 percent of all LegCo and ExCo members were businessmen or had direct links to business associations, and 48 percent of all LegCo and ExCo members were civil servants (Davies 1977, 78). In turn, Hong Kong's large commercial banks had close ties to its large merchant groups (Braunstein 2015, 184). The Hongs were not only connected via financial ties, notably cross-equity holdings, but also through cross-directorships (McCarthy 1982; Chiu 1994).[13]

Hong Kong's state apparatus enjoyed high levels of autonomy from its labor unions and welfare organizations, which were weakly mobilized and fragmented. This structure affected policymaking processes in Hong Kong's savings domain with regard to the types of finance institutions which were set up. It influenced the systematic overrepresentation of finance and business actors on important policy committees. While various socioeconomic actors—notably labor and welfare organizations—had a serious interest in this issue, only finance and business actors were directly involved in policymaking. Interestingly, Hong Kong's state apparatus also enjoyed high levels of autonomy from the London Colonial Office. With the abolition of the Imperial Restrictions in 1958, which required the strict monitoring of colonial budgets, Hong Kong was quasi-independent in economic policymaking from the United Kingdom (Ngo 1996; Goodstadt 2007). This status gave Hong Kong autonomy in finance and savings matters, such as the ability to raise loans without permission from the United Kingdom (Ngo 1996).

In contrast over the same period, the structure of state-society relations in Singapore's savings domain were consistent with that of a state-directed PN.[14] This was characterized by a high concentration of decision-making power in the Prime Minister's Office (PMO) and the Deputy Prime Minister's Office (DPMO); high levels of state autonomy, and low levels of mobilization among domestic producer groups. For example, the interest representation system of domestic finance and commerce was weak and fragmented. Singapore's government had not been penetrated by private interest groups, which followed their sector-specific goals (Ho 2000). On the contrary, Singapore's government held significant influence on civil society, notably local community organizations and trade unions (Lim and Pang 1986). Soon after the People's Action Party (PAP) came into power—with a moderate labor coalition—it began to foster the creation of the semi-governmental National Trades Union Congress (Rodan 1989).[15] Key positions of the National Trades Union Congress were filled with government representatives and PAP members. For example, in the late 1970s and the early 1980s Lim Chee Onn—minister without portfolio—was the secretary general of the National Trade Unions Congress (Rodan 1989). This structure affected policymaking processes and decisions about SWFs. While many different socioeconomic actors—particularly within domestic finance—had a substantive interest in this issue, only a small circle of state actors and international investment houses were directly involved in the policymaking processes which led to the creation of the Government Investment Corporation.

5.3.1 Singapore's 1981 Review on Reserve Management

The creation of the GIC in 1981 rose out of a "review" of how Singapore should reorganize its financial institutions. This review questioned how Singapore's reserve management had developed against earlier expectations (see Singapore Government Press Releases, statement from the Prime Minister's Office 1980, 1). It took place in a highly turbulent international financial environment. The question was whether to continue with existing financial institutions, or create an SWF with savings and international investment mandates. The review was influenced by Singapore's state-directed PN. A high concentration of decision-making power and high levels of state autonomy facilitated the pursuit of long-term transformative policies which were highly coordinated in Singapore's savings domain. The PN characteristics allowed for the exclusion of private finance actors, following their own short-term sector specific preferences, from the policymaking processes.

Different proposals were made regarding types of financial institutions, supported by particular socioeconomic actors. Preferences regarding SWFs and linked state finance institutions in Singapore's savings domain differed among these socioeconomic actors. From the late 1970s, Singapore's key government departments in the savings domain, notably the PMO, the DPMO, and the Ministry of Finance, were engaged with the search for an institutional way to enhance the returns on Singapore's savings. However, tensions emerged among these government departments. In the late 1970s there existed contradictory views on this topic, notably between the Ministry of Finance and the PMO, together with the DPMO. These tensions related to the question of whether to create a new financial institution (i.e., an SWF) for the management of Singapore's savings or continue with the existing mode via the MAS. Until 1980, the minister of finance was chairman of the MAS; as such, the Ministry of Finance supported the continuation of the existing institutional arrangement. According to Yeoh Lam Keong, former chief economist of the GIC, the Ministry of Finance was mainly concerned with responsibility and feasibility issues related to creating a new and separate financial institution (Yeoh Lam Keong, personal communication, 27 February 2014). Feasibility issues related to the question of stability in the flow of surpluses which could then be channeled into an SWF. Responsibility issues related to the risks associated with nonconventional asset classes and a long-term investment horizon. According to Yeoh Lam Keong, the Ministry of Finance may also have been uncomfortable with the attribution of responsibility in the case of losses (Yeoh Lam Keong, personal communication, 27 February 2014).

The deputy prime minister (DPM)—supported by the prime minister (PM)—called for a fundamental review of Singapore's existing financial institutions in the savings domain.[16] Both were highly supportive of creating an SWF with a savings mandate leading the flow of savings abroad. They were willing for the government to take responsibility because they considered it a "worthwhile endeavour" (Yeoh Lam Keong, personal communication, 27 February 2014). They noted that Singapore would have surpluses for many years, because it operated on the principle of budget surpluses and the mobilization of private savings via state savings vehicles (e.g., the CPF). According to a former GIC director, the DPM highlighted that, as of the early 1980s, Singapore was still a young country in demographic terms, where savings would be high in the future (anonymous, personal communication, 9 April 2014). As such, the DPM and PM believed that Singapore would have surpluses from private and public savings in the long-term (anonymous, personal communication 9 April 2014). Assuming that these would be accumulated over the long-term, the question arose of whether to continue managing them on a safe, short-term liquid basis, or on a more long-term risk basis via an SWF.

While international finance actors supported creating an SWF, which would channel domestic savings for long-term investments into international assets, domestic private finance actors were critical of the prospect. International finance actors had clear incentives for joint ventures and partnerships which focused on managing and allocating funds into international capital channels. They could benefit from the consultations in multiple ways (e.g., placement of funds under external management, and consultation fees). In contrast, private domestic finance actors did not support the creation of an SWF. Singapore's domestic commercial banks' criticism was very subtle; they indicated that they wanted to manage more money, and, like banks in other countries, provide comprehensive provident fund schemes, insurance schemes, and savings plans (*Straits Times*, 18 February 1979; *Straits Times*, 13 April 1985). As a result, they demanded that the government release part of these funds to the domestic private sector for management (*Straits Times*, 10 November 1989, 13). The domestic private finance sector "would like to see [Singapore's government] free a larger chunk of its funds for non-traditional investments" (*Asian Finance*,

15 February 1984, 21). Similarly, Singapore's private domestic insurance sector demanded less state involvement, and emphasized that more capital needed to be channeled through private domestic finance institutions.

Brief internal tensions and conflicts about the review of Singapore's reserve management were quickly resolved because of the high concentration of power within the structure of state-society relations. The execution of the review was delegated by the PMO to the DPMO. This was done through the appointment of the DPM as chairman of MAS (Singapore Government Press Releases 1980). Through this appointment the finance minister—traditionally the chairman of MAS—was pushed to one side in order to allow the DPM to review Singapore's reserve management (anonymous, personal communication, 9 April 2014). An official statement that "[t]he Prime Minister has charged Dr Goh Keng Swee with the responsibility of the Minister of Finance insofar as it relates to the function of the Minister under the provision of the MAS Act and the Currency Act" supports this (Singapore Government Press Releases 1980). Interestingly, apart from very few humorous comments in the parliament, there is no evidence of an internal struggle between the Ministry of Finance and the PMO (Singapore Hansard, 18 March 1981). Likewise, policy insiders, notably former MAS analyst Ng Kok Song—who later became GIC's chief investment officer—stated that due to the high level of authority in the hands of PM Lee Kuan Yew and DPM Goh Keng Swee, there was no internal struggle about this decision (Ng Kok Song, personal communication 28 February 2014). Although the Ministry of Finance had de jure power over savings policy, the ultimate decision-making power in the savings domain was in the hands of the PM. Together, the PM and DPM saw a need for fundamental reconsiderations about Singapore's reserve management (*Straits Times*, 6 October 2007).[17] According to a former GIC director, the relationship between the PM and DPM at that time was very close and firm (anonymous, personal communication 9 April 2014). Hence, if the PN network had been different in terms of power concentration, this might have resulted in competition for asset management among different state departments (i.e., the Ministry of Finance and PMO and DPMO). This in turn may have hampered the smooth creation of the GIC in 1981.

Exclusion of Domestic Finance

The mechanism whereby Singapore's state-directed PN operated to influence the kinds of financial institutions set up in the savings domain referred to exclusion. Due to the high level of power concentration and autonomy, Singapore's policymakers could bypass domestic finance actors. Reportedly no formal or informal consultation took place with private domestic finance organizations on the review (*Business Times*, 10 March 1981; *Asian Wall Street Journal*, 11 March 1981; Singapore Government Press Releases 1980). According to J. Y. Pillay—former managing director of the MAS and the GIC—at that time private domestic finance organizations were not part of policymaking in the savings domain, and thus not involved in the creation of the GIC (J. Y. Pillay, personal communication, 26 March 2014). Thereby, the PN prevented domestic private banking as well as private insurance actors, and later domestic fund management actors, from realizing their sector-specific preferences (i.e., managing a larger part of Singapore's private and public wealth). In turn, this allowed for the pursuit of long-term transformative policies in Singapore's savings domain and enabled high levels of coordination with other policy domains, notably monetary.

The exclusion of domestic private finance organizations in the 1980s was justified partly on the grounds of expertise. Former GIC chief investment officer Ng Kok Song attributes the exclusion of domestic private finance actors to "their lack of expertise" (Ng Kok Song, personal communication 28 February 2014; *Asian Banking*, December 1985). At the time of the GIC's creation, Singapore's private domestic actors in the savings domain had no fund management expertise (Ng Kok Song, personal communication 28 February 2014). Consequently, the DPMO began looking for international finance actors to support the development of the GIC's own investment capacity (*Financial Times*, 20 July 1981).[18] International finance actors had a strong expertise in the field of international fund management, and they were keen to participate in the review of Singapore's reserve management (*Asian Wall Street Journal*, 11 March 1981). However, from the late 1970s, Singapore's domestic finance sector had begun acquiring international banking skills and building expertise in modern fund management. By the early 1980s, Singapore's private banks had begun recruiting a number of experienced executives with international exposure, which key actors of Singapore's state-directed PN were aware of (S. Y. Lee 1981). For example, the DPM stipulated the secondment of senior representatives of the domestic private banking sector in order to provide a "back-up" for the GIC (*Straits Times*, 10 March 1981, 1–32). For example, the Overseas China Banking Corporation vice chairman had to be seconded to the GIC (*Business Times*, 10 March 1981, 1). Unsurprisingly, these secondments were disparaged by Singapore's domestic private finance organizations (*Business Times*, 7 August 1982). Its large private banks felt that they were deprived of their best people and had to compete with state finance institutions for talent.

Although large Singapore private banks, such as the Overseas China Banking Corporation, the Overseas Union Bank and the United Overseas Bank had been individually powerful economic actors, they remained very silent during the policy processes leading to the creation of the GIC.[19] None of Singapore's banks were involved in these processes (Richard Katz, personal communication, 31 April 2014). A former GIC director's statement that "[t]he banks leave it just to the government" draws attention to the passivity of private finance actors in policymaking (anonymous, personal communication 9 April 2014). Although in other circumstances, such passivity may have been due to acceptance of the kinds of finance institutions which were set up, occasional public comments indicate that domestic private finance actors, notably the Overseas Union Bank, were actually critical of the finance institutions set up in Singapore's savings domain (*Straits Times*, 10 November 1989). Private domestic finance actors preferred the development of private institutions in the savings domain, but the structure of state-society relations did not allow them to translate these preferences into policies (*Straits Times*, 10 November 1989, 13). Singapore's commercial banks were interested in managing part of Singapore's large reserves. For example, *Straits Times*' headline that "Singapore bankers want a slice of the MAS pie" draws attention to the banks' efforts in gaining higher exposure to the management of Singapore's reserves (*Straits Times*, 9 January 1986, 12). According to a former GIC director, they lobbied both the MAS and the GIC for such business (anonymous, personal communication 20 August 2014).

Inclusion of International Finance

The characteristics of Singapore's PN allowed policymakers to freely choose financial consultants. The PM entrusted the DPM with the responsibility of investigating and identifying adequate international finance actors regarding advice on creating an SWF (Ng Kok Song, personal communication 28 February 2014). The question posed to international finance actors was how Singapore should reorganize its reserve management function (Ng Kok Song, personal communication 28 February 2014). The DPM visited a number of international banks, including in the United States, Switzerland (e.g., UBS), and the United Kingdom (i.e., Rothschild & Sons) (Moser 2008). According to former Rothschild & Sons Vice Chairman Lord Claus Moser, Singapore's DPMO subsequently compiled a shortlist of four banks which included Rothschild & Sons (Moser 2008).[20] The final selection was made on a highly competitive basis, and was overseen by key actors of Singapore's PN, notably the DPMO, the Cabinet, and the PMO. During the final selection process, Rothschild produced a series of reports and held a number of interviews and meetings with the Cabinet, the DPM, and the PM. Lord Moser stated that this "was a very tough task [and] it was very tough competition" where Rothschild needed to present and justify its selection to all central organizations of Singapore's PN (Moser 2008). According to Lord Moser (2008), the meetings were not characterized by "friendship," and personal relationships did not matter in the selection process. Following the Cabinet's acceptance of Rothschild, PM Lee Kuan Yew needed to give the final assent. Lord Moser's testimony that this was "certainly the most frightening hour in my life" suggests how fierce the selection process was for Rothschild & Sons (Moser 2008). Finally, they were granted an initial appointment offer of six months, which would be only renewed on the condition of them "doing a good job" (Moser 2008).

Rothschild & Sons was appointed Singapore's official consultant on the "review" that led to the creation of the GIC in 1981. According to Lord Moser, their main task was "advising on what to do with [Singapore's] funds internationally" (Moser 2008). Rothschild's team in Singapore was led by the director of Rothschild's Government Advisory Division, Richard Katz, who was responsible for the international management of reserves of central banks (*Business Times*, 10 March 1981, 1; Richard Katz, personal communication 10 April 2014). Initially, Rothschild's small team in Singapore was supported by a big backup team in London (Moser 2008). Consultations took place between Rothschild's Claus Moser, Richard Katz, and Kate Mortimer and key representatives from the DPMO, notably DPM Goh Keng Swee (*Straits Times*, 9 April 1981, 12). The Singapore leadership demanded the creation of an SWF with an international investment mandate, and Rothschild suggested a concrete form of institution (Richard Katz, personal communication 10 April 2014). Rothschild formulated GIC's memorandum, which outlined the investment mandate and investment classes.[21] From the beginning, GIC's investment spectrum comprised shares, stocks, debentures, debenture stock, scrip, loans, bonds, obligations, notes, securities and investments by original subscription, tender purchase, and participation in syndicates in any part of the world (Memorandum GIC 1981). Furthermore, the GIC was allowed to invest in gold, silver, and commodities, to buy and sell currencies, property, and land, and to enter arrangements with other government authorities (Memorandum GIC 1981).

Beneficiaries of the GIC Creation

Over time the GIC's business partners included a select international group of financial organizations.[22] It is estimated that in the late 1990s, about

35 percent of the GIC's assets—equivalent to about S$ 30 billion—were outsourced to international finance houses (*Straits Times*, 14 April 1999). This has been well-appreciated by international finance actors. For example, Rothschild & Sons enthusiastically welcomed its 1981 appointment as GIC's official advisor. Lord Moser—then deputy chairman of Rothschild & Sons—describes this as the "biggest stroke of luck" in his career (Moser 2008). Soon after the GIC's creation under the auspices of the DPM and the chairmanship of the PM, it began to recruit external experts (Braunstein and Tomba 2017). In addition to scouting for official consultants, the DPM was also recruiting other staff during his March 1981 travels abroad in other financial centers (*Straits Times*, 10 March 1981, 1–32). The GIC hired a number of international managers in order to launch the department and train the young people the GIC was recruiting.[23] There is some evidence that the GIC outsourced funds to international fund managers in return for management expertise and staff training. For example, in 1983 the GIC approached Hagler Mastrovita & Hewitt Inc., which provided expertise and staff training in exchange for the management of discretionary funds from the GIC (*Fortune*, 21 March 1983).[24] However, the extent to which funds were allocated to external managers in exchange for expertise and in-house investment capacity development at the GIC remains unknown.

Because of its explicit policy of in-house investment capacity building, the creation of the GIC did not contribute to the development of domestic private insurance and provident fund sectors. Since its creation, the GIC has followed a strategy of in-house investment capacity-building via the strategic interaction and partnerships with third party managers. An official GIC statement that "[t]hese partnerships have helped [the GIC] to gain insights into high-quality investment ideas and research, as well as industry best practices in the areas of investments and operations" suggests that the GIC has greatly benefited from third party managers (GIC Report 2012, 20). A GIC report noted the strategic benefits of allocating funds to external managers. It stated that "[i]t diversifies the Government's portfolio, expands the investment opportunities available and deepens our understanding of financial markets" (GIC Report 2012, 20). The GIC also partnered with international financial organizations to develop its own asset management capabilities (Ng Kok Song, personal communication 28 February 2014). Ng Kok Song, a former GIC executive highlights that the goal was to develop a reserve management institution, which was distinct from existing reserve management institutions, notably the MAS, in terms of its "culture" (Ng Kok Song, personal communication 28 February 2014). According to Ng Kok Song, the MAS had a risk-averse culture, characterized by investments in highly secure and liquid international assets, whereas the GIC had a pure investment purpose, requiring a more risk-based approach characterized by long-term investments in riskier assets. Therefore, the GIC needed to be able to attract and retain funds and talent. Ng Kok Song's statement that "you need to compete against the private sector" indicates the tensions between the private domestic finance sector and the government (Ng Kok Song, personal communication 28 February 2014). As the GIC has upgraded its internal investment capabilities, "the role of external managers has become more nuanced" (GIC Report 2012, 20). Over the years the GIC has sought co-investment deals with firms operating in niche markets in which the GIC had not yet built capabilities or superior returns. The GIC has built up an in-house team, the "External Managers Department," responsible for appointing, monitoring, and reviewing external managers (GIC Report 2012, 20). As of the 2000s the GIC is one of the most respected funds in the SWF world with well above $300 billion of AUM. But little noticed there was also a real chance in Hong Kong to create a large CPF together with a Singapore style GIC.

5.3.2 Hong Kong's 1986 Central Provident Fund Review

This review was based on the question of whether Hong Kong should establish a large state-run mandatory central provident fund, and linked to that, an SWF that invests CPF funds into international financial assets. Preferences regarding the kinds of financial institutions set up in Hong Kong's savings domain differed among economic actors. Common to finance and commerce actors was their objection to the creation of a large state-run mandatory CPF, and creation of an SWF (Ngo 1996). They framed the creation of a CPF as an issue of inefficient state intervention, which would affect resource allocation and Hong Kong's role as a financial center. By collecting large "mandatory" amounts of domestic savings, financial actors viewed a large CPF as a direct competitor to their private schemes (Li 1988; *The Bulletin*, June 1985, 54). While different sectors of government, together with domestic finance and commerce, supported the option of private finance institutions, domestic grassroots/social-welfare actors and trade unions demanded a state-run CPF. Common to these actors was their lack of trust in private finance institutions, and their belief that a state-run CPF would present more benefits to the population (Hong Kong Hansard, 3 February 1993; *South China Morning Post*, 12 November 1987). Many associations, such as the Christian Industrial Committee, the Hong Kong

Council of Social Services, and the Hong Kong Social Worker's General Union, supported the creation of a state-run CPF. However, their actions in pursuit of this objective were poorly coordinated. Different but overlapping proposals and surveys were produced by various groups at similar times (see Li 1988; *South China Morning Post*, 17 August 1986).

The PN included only a small group consisting of public officials and finance/business organizations, serving on key policymaking bodies informing the decisions against state finance institutions. The financial secretary entrusted the realization of the CPF review in 1986–87 to the Education and Manpower Branch, specifically because the issue of creating a large CPF involved both employers and employees.[25] By then it was well known that the secretary of the Education and Manpower Branch was highly critical of the creation of a state-run CPF (Nelson Chow, personal communication 17 February 2015). The Education and Manpower Branch organized some research on the issue, and officials prepared a draft paper. According to Nelson Chow, former chairman of the Social Welfare Advisory Committee (SWAC), the officials of the Manpower Branch might have also consulted business associations, notably the HKGCC (Nelson Chow, personal communication 17 February 2015). Before the draft paper was forwarded to the relevant policy committees for further discussion and comment, convention in Hong Kong dictated discussing the draft paper with the financial secretary and the Star Chamber—a body of high-ranking officials (Scott 2010; Leo Goodstadt, personal communication 12 February 2015). The Star Chamber was chaired by the financial secretary (Leo Goodstadt, personal communication 15 November 2013). After a decision was reached, the Secretary of Education and Manpower appointed two policy committees (the Labour Advisory Committee and the SWAC) with the aim of discussing and commenting on the draft paper. Chow (personal communication 12 February 2015) noted that the draft paper prepared by the Manpower Branch had a 'negative tone' with regard to the creation of a CPF, and indeed advised against it.

Exclusion of Labor and Welfare

Out of the many consultative government committees, only two, namely the SWAC and the Labour Advisory Committee, were invited by the government to comment on the draft paper prepared by the Education and Manpower Branch (*South China Morning Post*, 26 November 1986; 18 December 1986).[26] Chow's statement that the "government made sure that only members [were] appointed who agree[d] with [the government]" indicates that a careful preselection took place (Nelson Chow, personal communication 17 February 2015). The actual composition of the committees in 1986 confirms that business representatives were systematically overrepresented

(Civil and Miscellaneous Lists Hong Kong Government, 1 July 1986, 103–11; Nelson Chow, personal communication 17 February 2015).

When social welfare and union representatives were appointed, they were systematically outnumbered by representatives of the finance and employer side. For example, the Labour Advisory Committee was a non-statutory consultative body, chaired by the commissioner for labor, with unofficial members. Out of these, five were supposed to represent employees and the other six to represent employers. On the employer's side, four representatives were elected from employer associations and two were appointed by the government, whereas on the employees' side, three representatives were elected from employee associations and two appointed by the government (Labour Advisory Board 2000). While the employee representatives of the Labour Advisory Committee supported creating a CPF, the employer representatives and business associations, such as the HKGCC, were opposed (see Li 1988, 39; *Hong Kong Standard*, 14 December 1986; Annual Report, Hong Kong General Chamber of Commerce, 1986). With six representatives on the employer side against a CPF and five representatives on the employee side pro-CPF, a decision was made to set up another working group (*Ming Po Daily*, 12 December 1986, highlighted by Li 1988, 56). This time, only finance associations were invited by the ExCo for comments on the consultation paper. These included the Life Insurance Council of Hong Kong, the Hong Kong Bank Association, and the Discussion Group on the Hong Kong Economy (*Hong Kong Standard*, 14 December 1986; Li 1988, 144). The Discussion Group on the Hong Kong Economy was an informal body of economists from Hong Kong's universities (Li 1988; *Hong Kong Economic Journal*, 16 May 1987). There was no formal appointment of a labor or welfare associate (Hong Kong Standard, 14 December 1986).

According to commentators, social welfare associations and trade unions were not included in the later stages of consultation (*Hong Kong Standard*, 18 May 1987; *South China Morning Post*, 12 November 1987; *Ming Po Daily*, 28 May 1987; *Mau Chi Wang*, 1 December 1986). The broad-scale exclusion of labor unions and welfare organizations was justified based on the complexity of the CPF issue (Li 1988). To business actors and state representatives, the issue of creating a large state-run CPF was multifaceted and had important wider economic implications (Li 1988). It was considered too important to allow unions and welfare organizations to make decisions on the topic. Consequently, government officials concluded that the issue of creating a CPF should be approached from an economics perspective and should not be mixed up with the "[w]ishes of the people" (*Hong Kong Hansard*, 13 March 1987, 1540).

Inclusion of Domestic Finance and Business

The second body involved with exploring the establishment of a CPF in Hong Kong was the Social Welfare Advisory Committee (SWAC). There were very few SWAC members, and only one representative of the Hong Kong Council of Social Services, who investigated the creation of a CPF (Civil and Miscellaneous Lists Hong Kong Government, 1 July 1986). The majority of the SWAC was against the creation of a CPF (Nelson Chow, personal communication 17 February 2015). Most of the members feared that a large single fund run by the government would disturb Hong Kong's financial sector (*South China Morning Post*, 17 August 1986).

Subsequently, a paper was released on the "Consultation on the Implications of Establishing a CPF in Hong Kong," reflecting the preferences of finance and business actors. Its focus was mainly on the downside, outlining eleven reasons against a CPF, and only six positive reasons, all of which were very vague (Hong Kong Hansard, 13 May 1987, 1592). For example, the paper suggested that "a CPF would remedy certain deficiencies" and thereby "improve Hong Kong's international image" (Hong Kong Hansard, 13 May 1987, 1592). However, this was not further specified. Out of these six "positive" reasons, at least three were formulated in a way that actually implied negative consequences. For example, the report mentioned that a CPF offered a potential pool of funding for the government, but at the same time emphasized that this might encourage government overspending, increasing the risks of a deficit. Regarding the risks and reasons against a CPF, the consultation paper was much more specific and detailed. It argued that a CPF is "economically damaging" because of the increase in labor costs that would destroy Hong Kong's competitiveness. Furthermore, the report highlighted that the creation of a state-run CPF was against the government's philosophy of noninterventionism. It would also pose a financial risk due to its "massive size." The paper concluded that "[t]he balance of the economic arguments is against the introduction of a CPF" (Hong Kong Hansard, 13 May 1987, 1605). In sum, a CPF would have a disturbing effect on financial markets in Hong Kong, and investment in foreign assets could also disrupt foreign exchange and money markets, which would affect the Exchange Fund and value of the HK$. However, according to Joseph Yam, former chief executive of the Hong Kong Monetary Authority, a large CPF would not have affected the Exchange Fund because a CPF, by definition, is managed centrally by the government. The government would obviously not do anything affecting monetary stability in Hong Kong (Joseph Yam, personal communication 19 November 2013).

The paper recommended "An Alternative Way Forward." It suggested relying on private banking and the financial sector for old-age security. It recommended the improvement of existing mechanisms such as long-service payment schemes, wage protection, and improved regulation concerning the protection of contributions to private funds, as well as social security benefits. These recommendations primarily reflected the preferences of the financial and commercial sectors. They supported allocating savings into deposits with licensed banks, and unit trusts investing in financial assets, life assurance, credit unions, real property through mortgages and the stock market (Hong Kong Hansard, 13 May 1987). The consultation paper was then used by the government to justify the dismissal of a state-run CPF (Hong Kong Hansard, 13 March 1987). The formal decision was made on 7 October 1987 in a policy speech by Hong Kong's governor (*Hong Kong Standard*, 8 October 1987). Policymakers referenced it to inform their decision about whether to create a CPF (Hong Kong Hansard, 13 May 1987).

Beneficiaries of the Absence of State-Finance Vehicles

The choice against creating a CPF favored domestic commercial banks, which began introducing private provident funds and life insurance schemes. Commercial banks started to enter the life insurance sector either directly or through alliances. For example, the Hong Kong Bank formed its own insurance subsidiary, Carlingford, which also uses the Hong Kong Bank's branch network (C. Yeung 1990). Another example is the Bank of China Group, which held alliances with Ming An, China Insurance, and Tai Ping. The Bank of China Group asked its mortgage customers to also insure with them (C. Yeung 1990). The Hong Kong Bank introduced a new provident fund in 1976 that was "open to all companies whether or not they [were] customers of the Bank" (*South China Morning Post*, 23 March 1976). The Hong Kong Bank and Swire formed a new partnership known as Wardley Swire Assurance, which provided services on retirement and pension schemes for Hong Kong, and managed these funds (*Hong Kong Standard*, 14 September 1976).

Conclusion

SWF variation is neither solely the outcome of macro-economic factors combined with efficiency considerations, nor the result of sweeping cross-national diffusion. This chapter finds that even small open economies within similar peer groups can make very different finance institutional choices. While Singapore created a number of highly coordinated state finance institutions, Hong Kong preferred short-term oriented private finance institutions and policies. The outcome was the creation of a state-run central provident fund and a sovereign wealth fund in Singapore, and the promotion of private insurance and the private pension fund sector in Hong Kong. This variation in finance institutions can be explained by the varying ways in which different structures of state-society relations have played out in the two city-states.

Hong Kong's clientele pluralist policy network (PN), characterized by high levels of coordination and state involvement, hampered the pursuit of policies and institutions with long-term investment mandates. State-society structures allowed policymakers to bypass domestic welfare organizations and labor unions, which demanded an CPF, and linked to that an SWF. The state-society structures influenced institutional choices—notably the promotion of private-pension and private-insurance schemes—structured around the immediate needs of Hong Kong's finance organizations. Contrastingly, Singapore's state-directed PN, also characterized by coordination and state involvement, facilitated pursuit of policies and institutions with long-term horizons. The hierarchical and autonomous structure of its PMO and DPMO allowed for exclusion of domestic private finance actors. High levels of autonomy enabled state actors to freely choose among international investment advisors.

The findings of this chapter emphasize the distributional struggles among socioeconomic actors in policymaking processes regarding the types of financial institutions set up. The existence of a strong and politically well-organized private sector in finance activities tends to suppress creation of state finance institutions within the savings and finance sector, notably large state-run pension funds, and linked to that, SWFs with savings mandates. The creation of SWFs and their mandates are conditioned by the state's relationship with the domestic private sector.

These findings have important implications for policymakers considering establishing SWFs. For other economies, notably Gulf countries, the stark differences in Hong Kong and Singapore delineate the vastly different potential outcomes regarding state finance institutions.

SIX

Capital Choices in Small Open Economies of the Middle East

Since the beginning of the twenty-first century, most of the small open economies of the Gulf region (i.e., Abu Dhabi, Kuwait, Bahrain, and Qatar) have a remarkable record of high and sustained growth.[1] In just a few decades they have emerged from pearl fishing outposts, marginally integrated into the world economy, to leading global trading and logistics hubs. As of 2019 they are among the richest countries in the world in terms of per capita income. They have produced regionally successful and highly profitable firms such as Emaar, the Kuwait Projects Company (KIPCO), and Etilsalat. They are home to large state-related companies that have become household names, such as Qatar Airways, Etihad, and Emirates.

The rise of these countries is strongly linked to the diffusion of SWFs in the region. Between the 1950s and 2000s, each of the Gulf states created SWFs. Over this period Gulf economies, such as Qatar, Bahrain, the United Arab Emirates (UAE), and Kuwait, became independent, and were confronted with windfall hydrocarbon revenues. The finite and volatile nature of these resources raise questions of diversification and securing future rents. SWFs translate windfall revenues during commodity booms into diversified global portfolios.

Despite geographical and cultural proximity, as well as close similarities in their export profiles, Gulf Cooperation Council (GCC) countries opted for different SWF types. Kuwait is the only economy—among the four— that has never created a development SWF, such as Mumtalakat (Bahrain) or Mubadala (Abu Dhabi); Bahrain is the only economy that has never created a savings SWF, such as the Kuwait Investment Authority (KIA) or the Abu Dhabi Investment Authority (ADIA).

An examination of formal institutional and informal linkages between government and private actors at the subnational level once again helps explain similarities and differences in capital choices. For example, in Abu Dhabi and Qatar, state-directed policy networks (PNs) allowed the pursuit of highly interventionist state strategies with SWFs that dominate the domestic finance and industrial landscapes. In Bahrain, in contrast, a centralized state and low levels of state autonomy from the highly organized domestic finance elite (i.e., a clientele pluralist PN) led to state intervention supporting the domestic private finance sector. State assets were mobilized to the advantage of private finance and created a private equity type SWF, Mumtalakat. Contrastingly in Kuwait, a centralized state with weakly mobilized private finance actors, but a strongly organized commerce merchant class, led to state action benefiting the commerce and merchant sector and in the creation of the KIA.

The chapter begins by examining the small open GCC economies' common historical and macroeconomic background. Four subsections then outline Kuwait's, Abu Dhabi's, Qatar's and Bahrain's state-society relations in the savings and industrial policy domain, and the types of financial institutions they set up from the 1960s to the 2000s.

6.1 Common Background and SWF Choices

Kuwait, Bahrain, Abu Dhabi, and Qatar share a common historical experience with the British Empire and a number of similarities in terms of macroeconomic features—most notably size and dependency on oil/gas, as well as their exposure to international business and commodity cycles (see table 6.1). Between the 1960s and '70s these economies became independent and were confronted with windfall hydrocarbon revenues. They have all been governed by strong rulers from wealthy and powerful domestic tribal clans, including the Al-Thani family in Qatar, the Al-Sabah family in Kuwait, the Al-Khalifa family in Bahrain, and the Al-Nahyan family in Abu Dhabi. In Kuwait, Abu Dhabi, and Qatar, resource wealth has been controlled by the ruling families, and natural resources have significantly contributed to public finance (Said Zahlan 1989).

However, state-private sector relations differ among the four countries, shaped by location and reaching back to the pre-oil era. The absence of an entrepôt economy, poor harbors, and an inhospitable climate set Qatar and Abu Dhabi apart from Kuwait and Bahrain. Bahrain emerged as a major trade center and pearling spot in the Persian Gulf, leading to the emergence of a powerful commercial class (Field 1985). Likewise, Kuwait's location on a strategic trade route to Aleppo and Baghdad and its natural harbors ushered in a powerful domestic merchant elite (see Crystal 1990). While Kuwait had two economic pillars—entrepôt trade in the winter and pearl fishing in the summer—economic activity in Abu Dhabi and Qatar was dominated by highly mobile foreign traders in the pearl fishing sector (Crystal 1990; Davidson 2009). The collapse of global pearl trade in the 1920s drove traders from Abu Dhabi and Qatar (Crystal 1990; Davidson 2009). This collapse combined with a lack of easily accessible ports significantly weakened Qatar's merchants, who played a mostly negligent role in economic policymaking (Crystal 1990; Mehran 2013). The rulers of Qatar distanced themselves very early from domestic merchants. Instead, they formed an alliance with Britain and the national population of Qatar through distributive policies (Crystal 1990).

Before independence, the rulers of these territories held British bank accounts or created investment boards, through which they channeled their oil/gas royalties. Bahrain had the Government Reserve Fund, which allocated half of its assets into British stocks and half in fixed deposits with the Eastern Bank and the British Bank of the Middle East (British Treasury 1963). Under British influence, Abu Dhabi created the Abu Dhabi Investment Board in 1967 and Kuwait the Kuwait Investment Board in 1953. The latter was highly unpopular with Kuwait's leadership, because of

TABLE 6.1, Macro-characteristics Bahrain, Qatar, Kuwait, and the United Arab Emirates in 2007

	Bahrain	Qatar	Kuwait	UAE*
GDP (bn)	17.4	71.0	112.1	198.7
GDP per head	16,699.0	53,12.0	32,98.0	37,687.0
GDP per head (PPP)	23,934.0	56.15	38.34	27,837.0
Consumer price inflation (average %)	3.3	13.7	5.5	13.3
Current-account balance (bn)	2.9	11.4	47.5	36.4
Current-account balance (% of GDP)	16.7	16.0	42.3	18.3
Exports of goods fob (bn)	13.8	42.0	63.7	180.9
Imports of goods fob (bn)	−10.9	−19.6	−20.6	−116.6
External debt (bn)	8.6	39.9	33.6	66.5
Debt-service ratio, paid (%)	3.7	6.7	3.3	2.6

Source: Economist Intelligence Unit (EIU, 2009a, 2009b).
*There are no precise data available for Abu Dhabi

Britain's influence on Kuwait's asset allocation and "a perceived" low return (Eastern Department 1954). This was well-known among British leadership. An official statement that "[the Kuwait Investment Board's] investment policy is widely thought to be directed by the United Kingdom and is bound to be unpopular with the Kuwaitis, who expect at least 12 percent [return]" draws attention to the motivation behind Kuwait's creation of an SWF (Eastern Department 1954).

SWF Choices Following Independence

In the years following independence (the period between the 1960s and 1970s), small open economies in the Gulf demonstrated interesting sectoral variation in their SWFs and domestic state-private sector structures (see table 6.2). A comparative analysis of SWF variation in GCC economies reveals systematic deviation among state-private sector structures across policy domains that mirror different designs and uses of SWFs. The creation of large SWFs with savings mandates (e.g., the Qatar Investment Authority, the Abu Dhabi Investment Authority, and the Kuwait Investment Authority) reflected concentrated state structures with high levels of autonomy from a weakly organized domestic private finance sector. Cross-temporal variation in SWFs is in line with the sequences of change in state fragmentation/domestic structures. Following the mid-1990s, the organization of the state in Qatar's industrial domain shifted from a fragmented to a highly centralized decision-making structure. This was accompanied by the creation of SWFs with development mandates in the 2000s. Interestingly, Kuwait decided against creating a large Mubadala-type SWF with a development mandate. Yet the Kuwait Investment Authority (KIA) and the Kuwait Investment Company hold a smaller strategic developmental subsidiary, which decreased substantially in size following the Iraqi invasion (anonymous, personal communication, 23 September 2014).

Unlike Abu Dhabi and Qatar (from the mid-1990s onwards), state-society relations in Kuwait's industrial domain were characterized by a highly mobilized merchant elite and a fragmented state apparatus with low levels of autonomy. In contrast to all three others, Bahrain did not create a savings-oriented SWF but relied instead on private finance institutions.

6.2 Kuwait's Savings Policy: The Kuwait Investment Authority

While preparing for independence from Britain in 1960, the Kuwait government established the General Reserve Fund as its main treasurer. It

TABLE 6.2, Structure of state-private sector relations in GCC states and corresponding SWFs

		SAVINGS/FINANCE DOMAIN				INDUSTRIAL DOMAIN			
		Kuwait	*Abu Dhabi*	*Bahrain*	*Qatar*	*Kuwait*	*Abu Dhabi*	*Bahrain*	*Qatar*	*Qatar*
Period		1960s–2000s	1970s–2000s	1970s–2000s	1970s–2000	1960s–2000s	1970s–2000s	1970s–2000s	1970s–mid1990s	mid 1990s–2000s
State	Concentration	*High*	*High*	*High*	*High*	*Low*	*High*	*High*	*Low*	*High*
	Autonomy	*High*	*High*	*Low*	*High*	*Low*	*High*	*High*	*Low*	*High*
Private	Mobilization	*High*	*Low*	*High*	*Low*	*High*	*Low*	*Low*	*Low*	*Low*
SWFs created after independence		KIO KIA	ADIA	n/a	QIB QIA	n/a	Mubadala, IPIC, ADIC	Mumtalakat	n/a	Qatar Holding, Qatar Diar

"received all revenues (including all oil revenues) from which all state budgetary expenditures were paid" (Yi-Chong 2009, 287). Immediately after independence, Kuwait established a separate investment committee in the Department of Finance, and created the Kuwait Investment Office in London to replace the British-run Kuwait Investment Board (Bazoobandi 2013). Following nationalization of oil companies in 1974–75, reserves increased substantially from about $3 billion at the end of 1973 to about $12 billion at the end of 1975 (Johns 1976, 21). In 1976, the deputy emir issued Decree Law No.106, the legal basis for the creation of the Future Generations Fund. Article 2 of the law stated: "A special account shall be opened for creating a reserve that would act as an alternative to oil wealth." According to this law, 50 percent of the assets of the General Reserve Fund were transferred to the newly created Future Generations Fund. In addition, the Future Generations Fund annually receives 10 percent of all state revenues, and the entire fund investment income (Bahgat 2010; Bazoobandi 2013, 35). The Future Generations Fund keeps all its assets outside Kuwait, and part of the Fund is managed by the Kuwait Investment Office in London (Roberts 2011). Following the second oil shock in the late 1970s and the drop in oil prices in the early 1980s, Kuwait began consolidating separate government funds and investment entities (i.e., the Kuwait Investment Office, the General Reserve Fund, and the Future Generations Fund) under the umbrella of a newly created entity, the Kuwait Investment Authority.

State decision-making structures in Kuwait's savings domain are highly centralized and segments of the business sector are highly mobilized. Formed in 1961, the Kuwait Chamber of Commerce is hierarchically organized and functions as a lobbying, expertise, and coordination platform for private business organizations. It remains the only chamber in Kuwait, dominated by well-organized merchant families and representing all private companies in the country. In strong contrast to the other small open Gulf economies, notably Qatar, the ruling family is absent from the Kuwait Chamber of Commerce (Crystal 1990). According to a highl level official of the Chamber, it is represented on all major economic policy bodies via appointments to committees (anonymous, personal communication, 23 September 2014). These committees allow private business to interact with the state (Moore 2002). The interaction between the Kuwait Chamber of Commerce and Industry and the KIA is also facilitated through personal ties. For example, Kuwait's deputy prime minister Anas Khalid Al Saleh was a member of the Kuwait Chamber of Commerce and Industry board of directors between 2006 and 2012 before he became oil minister and chairman of the KIA (Anas Khalid Al Saleh 2018).

In turn, these structures influenced the logic of policymaking, facilitating direct negotiations between the state and the business sector, through which the state seeks to accommodate the interests of a particular group within its broader agenda. Different preferences among socioeconomic actors towards the KIA indicate distributional conflicts—for example, between the commerce and finance communities. While the Kuwait Chamber of Commerce and the country's merchants broadly supported the creation of an SWF, domestic private investment houses and finance firms were highly critical (anonymous, personal communication, 23 September 2014). They claim that the KIA competed with the private domestic finance sector for talent. They also complained that Kuwait's SWF was crowding out domestic fund management, and, as a result, they repeatedly demanded that the KIA invest more in the Kuwait Stock Exchange in order to support or reinforce the domestic market.[2] The extent to which the SWF actually crowded out domestic fund management, especially in terms of talent, remains unknown.

The Finance Department, later renamed the Ministry of Finance, was Kuwait's dominant state agency, and had significant autonomy from the private finance sector (Moore 2002). The National Bank of Kuwait was established by domestic merchants with the support of the ruler, while other banks were created with significant state involvement (National Bank of Kuwait 2015). The state's dominance was reflected in the Kuwait Banking Association—formerly the Kuwait Banking Committee (established in 1981)—which served as a coordination body with direct representation from the ruling family. Its principal objective was the coordination of members' activities "within the framework of the state's plans, and economic and monetary policies" (Kuwait Banking Association 2014).

Kuwait's Industrial Policy

Kuwait's industrial policy choices were characterized by short-term strategy, low levels of coordination, and low levels of intrusion for private socioeconomic actors. With the exception of the oil sector, policy choices were structured around the immediate preferences of private producer groups (Johns 1976). The government only entered sectors in which private merchants had little interest (Crystal 1990). Kuwait's merchants were heavily involved in the construction and logistics sector, such as the Kuwait Oil Tanker Company and Kuwait Airways (Crystal 1990).[3] Al-Kandari's statement that "[m]ost industry in Kuwait other than oil and natural gas is based on simple processing and largely depends on imports of primary [and], intermediate goods and materials" indicates a link between Kuwait's merchants and manufacturers (Al-Kandari 1982, 39).

Although the Industrial Development Board (established in 1961) was officially charged with outlining long-term anticipatory policy, most of its five-year plans emphasized short-term reactive policy and institutional choices (Al-Dekhayel 2000). They produced reports stressing short-term goals and the need to expand the private sector's role in manufacturing and trade, and recommending that the state supports this via tariff protection, tax exemptions, cheap loans at low subsidized interest rates, industrial estates and by granting monopolies (Al-Dekhayel 2000). For example, merchants were allowed to maintain their monopolies in trade and services (Crystal 1990, 90). The Kuwait Chamber of Commerce and Industry regulated permits for foreigners, who were their major competitors. Another form of subsidization of domestic entrepreneurs was the creation of joint stock companies with preferential treatment of Kuwaitis in case of government sales. The state bought shares in order to avoid losses to Kuwaiti shareholders. Large amounts of public funds were transferred to the private sector via overpriced government land purchases (Al-Dekhayel 2000). In addition, by law, Kuwait's private industrial sector was given preference in government purchases. Policies and institutional choices strove to protect the immediate interests of local merchants (Al-Dekhayel 2000).

Between the 1960s and 2000s, the state apparatus in Kuwait's industrial domain was highly fragmented and diffused, with multiple state agencies possessing overlapping jurisdictions. Khouja and Sadler (1979, 120) estimate that since the 1970s Kuwait has had ten government agencies tasked with industrial development. These include specialized departments, such as a joint office with the United Nations Industrial Development Organization, the Ministry of Planning (which replaced the Kuwait Planning Board), and the Ministry of Commerce and Industry. The private domestic sector is strongly represented in all of these agencies (Al-Dekhayel 2000). For example, out of the Development Planning Board's sixteen members, ten were drawn from the private sector (Al-Dekhayel 2000). Likewise, the Kuwait Chamber of Commerce was especially influential in the Ministry of Commerce Trade and Industry, which served as an important platform for state-business interaction (Moore 2002). As a result, the degree to which these departments could act autonomously from domestic merchants and traders was low (Khouja and Sadler 1979).[4] These agencies lacked a clear conception of their mandate and role, resulting in incoherent policy (Khouja and Sadler 1979).

Private commercial organizations were able to influence industrial policymaking directly through their positions in the state apparatus (e.g., membership in the Cabinet) (Chrystal 1990; Al-Dekhayel 2000). Each of the leading merchants was represented on an average of five boards of shareholding companies.[5] Together they held directorship positions in ninety-five of Kuwait's shareholding companies. This number is high, given that by 1977 there were only about 109 privately-owned public shareholding companies and forty privately owned public shareholding companies with government participation (Khouja and Sadler 1979, 128). While Kuwait's business elite had little interest in the creation of SWFs with development mandates, the populist nature of parliamentary politics from the 1960s onwards also hindered the creation of such a fund. In his seminal article "Defying the Resource Curse: Explaining Successful State-Owned Enterprises in Rentier States," Steffen Hertog highlights the lack of regime autonomy in economic policymaking, imposed by popular electoral politics from the 1960s onward. Hertog (2013) links this absence of state autonomy to Kuwait's National Assembly.

Unlike other parliaments in the region, Kuwait's National Assembly has important authority in policymaking (e.g., the power to remove confidence in individual ministers and override the emir's veto). This is relevant to the domestic deployment of oil revenues. The members of the National Assembly are elected in free and fair elections, which are structured around popular politics (Herb 2014). In turn Kuwait's ruling family is responsive to the parliament by supporting a welfare state that provides a comfortable life for every Kuwaiti citizen (Tetreault 1991). As such, Kuwait's political system discourages ambitious diversification projects, such as were undertaken in Qatar and Abu Dhabi, which have a direct impact on the immediate benefits of Kuwaiti citizens (Herb 2014).

Apart from affecting the creation of SWFs, state-society relations also impact the oversight of such funds. Unlike those of Abu Dhabi and Qatar, Kuwait's parliament frequently challenges the ruling family in economic policy (Herb 2009). This helped unmask a major investment scandal in Kuwait's SWF in the early 1990s.[6]

6.3 Abu Dhabi's Savings Policy:
The Abu Dhabi Investment Authority

The Abu Dhabi Investment Authority (ADIA) was created as a means of managing the country's surpluses, in step with the British-run Abu Dhabi Investment Board, which had been in existence since 1967. The motivation behind the ADIA's creation in 1971 was very similar to Kuwait's when creating the Kuwait Investment Office ten years prior. It was a means of achieving more independence (from Britain) in managing Abu Dhabi's savings, which multiplied rapidly in the 1970s due to a number of oil discoveries and high oil prices. Three years later in 1974, the ADIA took over the management of all wealth—including that of the Abu Dhabi Investment Board—and in 1976 its name was changed to the Abu Dhabi Investment Authority (Bazoobandi 2013, 73).

Although formally independent, the ADIA has strong links to the government. All of its senior officials and board members are senior government officials appointed by an emiri decree. For example, half of the board members come from the Al-Nahyan family, who simultaneously occupy positions in the Executive Council. According to Davidson (2009), the chairman, together with a former banker from Paribas, who joined the Investment Authority in the early 1980s, are in full control (see Landon 2008). In the mid-1990s, its holdings reached about $100 billion, invested internationally in equities, bonds, and real estate (Davidson 2009, 73; ADIA 2009). The ADIA receives most of its assets under management from the Abu Dhabi National Oil Company (ADNOC) (Abdelal 2009). With its fourteen subsidiaries, the ADNOC accounts for about 80 percent of Abu Dhabi's national income (Abdelal 2009).

Between the 1970s and the 2000s, state-society relations in Abu Dhabi's savings and industrial domains were characterized by highly concentrated decision-making structures with high levels of state autonomy from weakly mobilized domestic private producer groups. This allowed pursuit of long-term-oriented policies, with high levels of coordination and state involvement. Unlike Kuwait's parliament, Abu Dhabi's appointive council holds only advisory power (Herb 2009). In the absence of parliamentary constraints, Abu Dhabi's state enjoys autonomy from popular pressures, which in turn is reflected in the types of economic policy and financial institutions it fosters. This autonomy affected policymaking processes in Abu Dhabi's savings domain over this period. Reflecting this, Abu Dhabi created an SWF with a savings mandate immediately after British independence in 1971.

The UAE Constitution specified that resources and wealth were the property of the respective emirate (Bazoobandi 2013). As such, from 1971 onwards, the government of Abu Dhabi has had full authority over the allocation and management of its natural resources and wealth. The Executive Council is the central economic policymaking body and was led by the emir (Davidson 2009; Executive Council Abu Dhabi 2015). It consisted of thirteen members, drawn mostly from the Bani Yas Tribe, which has around twenty subsections (Sheikh Mohammed 2014). Of them, the Al-

Nahyan family was the most powerful. Over the years, this ruling family co-opted a small number of families from these subsections into a firm political-economic network.[7] Apart from the ruling Al-Nahyan family, important subsections of the tribe, which were on the Executive Council, were the Al-Mazroui, the Al-Suwaidi, the Al-Romaithi, and the Al-Qubaisi. As of this writing, these five subsections were in control of the Executive Council. Out of the thirteen members on the Executive Council in 2014, nine were related to those five families (Gulf News 2014). According to Davidson (2009), inclusion and exclusion from the Economic Council is a barometer for influence and prestige among Abu Dhabi's tribal elite. Economic posts in the savings domain have been distributed among factions of the tribes within this network. Members have occupied cross-directorships in important state bodies, such as the Executive Council, the Finance Department, the Development Department, and banking and financial organizations. Banking organizations in Abu Dhabi's savings domain have had especially strong connections to the state. For example, the royal family is represented on the Board of Directors in Abu Dhabi's major banks such as the Abu Dhabi Commercial Bank, First Gulf Bank, Abu Dhabi Islamic Bank, the National Bank of Abu Dhabi, and the Union National Bank. Unsurprisingly, there has never been a private banking association in Abu Dhabi, and the state is a major shareholder in almost every bank.

State-society relations also matter with regard to the control and oversight of SWFs. Similar to Kuwait, Abu Dhabi had its own SWF scandal in the early 1990s involving the Bank of Credit and Commerce International (BCCI). Founded in the early 1970s, the BCCI became the fastest growing global bank at the time with the help of Abu Dhabi (*Wall Street Journal*, 11 March 1992). The ADIA together with Sheik Zayed—the ruler of Abu Dhabi—owned around 77 percent of the BCCI (Prokesch 1991). The BCCI was involved in a number of illicit activities including money laundering in Europe, Africa, Asia, and the Americas; bribery of officials in most of those locations; support of terrorism, arms trafficking, and the sale of nuclear technologies (Congressional Research Service 1992). In contrast to Kuwait, fraud and mismanagement allegations were initiated from the outside by countries in which the BCCI was active, notably Luxembourg and the United States through a congressional investigation (Farah 1991; Congressional Research Service 1992). Following these accusations in the late 1980s Abu Dhabi continued to inject money into the BCCI in an attempt to limit losses (Brooks 1991; Congressional Research Service 1992). The comparison with Kuwait suggests that PNs also affect patterns of control and oversight of SWFs.

Abu Dhabi's Industrial Policy: ADIC, IPIC, and Mubadala

Between the 1970s and 2000s Abu Dhabi created a number of state finance institutions with development mandates.[8] Following windfall oil revenues in the 1970s, policy decisions were made leading to the creation of the Abu Dhabi Investment Company (ADIC) in 1977 (Davidson 2009, 74). ADIC's highest authority was its Board of Directors, whose members were appointed by the emir. Historically, it has been under the control of the ruling family and the Al-Suwaidi section of the Bani Yas tribe (Davidson 2009). The ADIC came under the umbrella of the Abu Dhabi Investment Council, established in 2007 and also under the control of the Al-Nahyan family (InvestAD 2015). It has invested actively in international as well as domestic assets (Abu Dhabi Council 2015a). Its domestic holdings have included stakes in the National Bank of Abu Dhabi, the Abu Dhabi National Insurance Company, and the Abu Dhabi Aviation Company (Abu Dhabi Council 2015b).

The ADIC created the International Petroleum Investment Company (IPIC) in 1984 as a joint venture between the ADIA and the ADNOC. The IPIC was established by an emiri decree with a mandate "to secure end markets for Abu Dhabi crude" (IPIC 2015a). Since the 2000s, IPIC's investments have spanned the entire international hydrocarbon value chain. Between the 1980s and 2000, it acquired controlling stakes in upstream companies (e.g., CEPSA, OMV, and COSMO Oil) midstream companies (e.g., PARCO, Gulf Energy Maritime, ADCOP, Emirates LNG, and OMV CEPSA), and downstream companies (e.g., OMV, COSMO Oil, Borealis, ChemaWEyaat, Oasis International Power, Duqm Refinery, NOVA Chemicals, Fujairah Refinery, EDP, PARCO, and CEPSA) (IPIC 2015a). IPIC fell under the umbrella of the Supreme Petroleum Council, which is responsible for the petroleum industry of Abu Dhabi and is controlled by the ruling family. Out of its nine directors, five are from the ruling Al-Nahyan family, and three are from the Al-Suwaidi section of the Bani Yas tribe (Abu Dhabi National Oil Company 2015). The IPIC's chairman is a member of the ruling family as well as deputy prime minister of the UAE, and its managing director is from the Al-Qubaisi section of the Bani Yas tribe (IPIC 2015b).

Mubadala was established in 2002 by the government with the main objective of facilitating Abu Dhabi's diversification and transformation process (Mubadala 2015). With an asset volume of approximately $60.8 billion, Mubadala is involved in various economic sectors, such as aerospace, semiconductors, real estate, and health care. It is exposed to these sectors via its subsidiaries, international partnerships, and joint ventures. In 2016, Abu Dhabi announced plans to merge Mubadala and IPIC with the aim of streamlining investment operations across the two SWFs. According to Schena (2017) concerns about inter-fund rivalry and competition, leading to suboptimal investment outcomes, were also linked to this decision. Abu Dhabi's crown prince is the chairman of Mubadala's Board of Directors (Mubadala 2015). The Al-Suwaidi section of Bani Yas is also represented on Mubadala's Board of Directors. For example, as of 2014, the Al-Suwaidi member is simultaneously a member of the Abu Dhabi Executive Council and the chairman of Abu Dhabi's Department of Finance. The remaining five directors of Mubadala are successful technocrats who made careers within the state enterprise sector, and who hold important positions in the state apparatus, such as chairmanships of regulatory authorities and government departments, government enterprises, government banks, and the Abu Dhabi Executive Council.

Over this period, there was no independent association representing private organizations in Abu Dhabi's industrial domain. As of 2014, there were around 80,000 business entities operating in Abu Dhabi (Ahmad 2014). It is mandatory for all commercial, industrial, vocational, or professional entities with offices in Abu Dhabi to join the Abu Dhabi Chamber of Commerce and Industry. However, it had weak research capacity and there were no sector-specific committees within the chamber (Hertog 2013). Because there is only one chamber, which comprises all businesses registered in Abu Dhabi, there is no competition for members. Furthermore, the Chamber is a government body set up to help coordinate the interests of the private sector with the interests of the state (ADCCI 2015a). Its mission is to advocate policies that "contribute to Abu Dhabi's sustainable economic development" (ADSG 2015). The Chamber has strong connections to the Department for Economic Development. Both consider each other official partners (ADCCI 2015b). This relationship becomes visible in terms of recruitment patterns between the two entities. Officials who start their career in the Chamber often proceed to the Department of Economic Development. Via the Chamber, the state has co-opted the private sector into the state apparatus. Until 2014, when elections were introduced, nearly one-third of the twenty-one members on the chamber's board were appointed by the emir (ADCCI 2013). This gave him the opportunity to include members with close connections to the state. For example, the vice-chairman of the Chamber was on the Board of Directors of Mubadala and began his career in the ADNOC, while also having held membership positions in the state-related National Bank of Abu Dhabi (National Bank of Abu Dhabi 2015; Mubadala 2015).

As in Abu Dhabi's savings domain, the Executive Council is at the center of decision-making in the industrial realm. Directly subordinate to it are the Department of Finance and the Department for Economic Development. The Department for Economic Development's as well as the Finance Department's chairmen are simultaneously members of the Executive Council. Both play a key role in formulating long-term industrial policy. The Department for Economic Development, for example, introduced the Plan Abu Dhabi 2030 infrastructure projects worth more than $400 billion, including tramlines and metro as well as a select range of high-technology heavy industry (Davidson 2009, 81). The chairman of the Department of Economic Development also chairs the Abu Dhabi Council for Economic Development, which has a close relationship with the Urban Planning Council (ZonesCorp 2010; Abu Dhabi Council 2015a).

The state-directed PN in place facilitated the pursuit of capital choices with high levels of state involvement and coordination. In the industrial realm this resulted in the creation of ADIC, IPIC, and Mubadala, aimed at long-term industrial transformation. In the financial realm this involved the creation of the ADIA. Similar types of SWFs can be found in Qatar.

6.4 Qatar's Savings Policy: Qatar Investment Board and Qatar Investment Authority

Shortly after Qatar's independence, the emir established the Qatar Investment Board in 1972. It was created with the purpose of coordinating the "overall investment strategy of Qatar" (El-Mallakh 1979, 131). The Qatar Investment Board can be described as the predecessor of the Qatar Investment Authority created in 2004-05. From 1972 onward, reserves were channeled via the Qatar Monetary Agency to the Qatar Investment Board, which managed and coordinated these assets. The Qatar Investment Board was led by the minister of finance, and its Board of Directors included an advisor to the emir, as well as the director of the emir's private office, the director of finance, and a Swiss banker. In addition, the Qatar Investment Board also drew on a group of international financial experts, notably representatives from Manufacturers Hanover (a bank holding company based in the United States), the First National Bank of Chicago, Morgan Grenfell, and Deutsche Bank (El-Mallakh 1979, 131).

There is a direct link between the 1972-created Qatar Investment Board and the 2005-created Qatar Investment Authority (QIA). An official statement that "[the Qatar Investment Authority] builds on the heritage of Qatari investments dating back more than [three] decades" draws direct attention to the connection between these two entities (Qatar Investment

Authority 2014). The QIA was created with the purpose of diversifying Qatar's wealth across asset classes and regions through return-oriented investments (Qatar Investment Authority 2014). Its mission, defined in Article 5 of the State of Qatar Emiri Decision No (22) of 2005 (the QIA Constitution) is to "develop, invest and manage the state reserve funds and other property assigned to it by the Supreme Council in accordance with policies, plans and programs approved by the Supreme Council" (Qatar Investment Authority 2014). This demonstrates the centrality of the Supreme Council to QIA's funding and investment structure. Again the Supreme Council was directly subject to the emir, and consisted of the minister of energy and industry, minister of finance, minister of economy and trade, the governor of the Qatar Central Bank, the economic advisor of the emir, and representatives from the Qatar Investment Authority and the Qatar Development Bank (Doha News 2013; General Secretariat for Development Planning 2011). The QIA's Board of Directors had full control over its business and its members were appointed in accordance with the emir's decision. It was chaired either by the prime minister or by the emir himself. The board also included members simultaneously sitting on the Supreme Council (Qatar Investment Authority 2014).

Between the 1970s and the 2000s, the structure of state-society relations in Qatar's savings domain was highly centralized and autonomous from a weakly organized private banking sector (i.e., a state-directed PN). There was no banking association representing the private banking-finance sector. During the 1970s and '80s, apart from regional Arab Banks (e.g., Bank Al-Mashrek and Bank of Oman) and large foreign international banks (e.g., Standard Chartered Bank, British Bank of the Middle East, Citi Bank, Banque Paribas), there were only smaller, privately-run money exchange companies (e.g., Al-Fardan Exchange and Finance Co, Al-Basry Exchange) (Qatar Monetary Agency 1985). This structure enabled the government to pursue long-term-oriented policies with high levels of state involvement. Reflecting this, Qatar's government created an SWF with a savings mandate.

The emir (Khalifa Al-Thani, 1972–95; Hamid Al-Thani, 1995–2012) chaired the Supreme Council of Economic Affairs and controlled policy-making in Qatar's finance and savings domain (Mehran 2013; Ibrahim and Harrigan 2012). Qatar's banking system had been controlled by the state via direct shareholdings and appointments on the banks' Board of Directors. For example, the Qatar state holds a 50 percent ownership stake in Qatar's oldest bank, the Qatar National Bank, established in 1964. Its chairman is the minister of finance, who is appointed by the emir. Two other members of the Qatar National Bank's Board of Directors also belong to the ruling family (Qatar National Bank 2015). The chairman of the 1975-created Commercial Bank of Qatar was also from the ruling family. Although this bank is "formally" Qatar's first private bank, the ruling family occupies central positions on the bank's Board of Directors. Likewise, the 1982-created Qatar Islamic Bank was chaired by a member of the royal family, with other royal family members sitting on its Board of Directors (Qatar Islamic Bank 2015). Among Qatar's largest banks, not one has been genuinely private (see Qatar Monetary Agency 1985). The institutional choices of Qatar support the hypothesis that state-directed PNs in the finance domain lead to the creation of SWFs with savings mandates.

Qatar's Industrial Policy (1970s–1990s)

Over this period, oil and gas revenues were low and volatile, which was reflected in the magnitude of spending in Qatar's industrial policy domain.[9] Particularly in the 1980s and early 1990s, Qatar was highly exposed to external shocks in the energy market and the construction sector. For example, Qatar's newly established cement industry was badly affected by the early 1980s recession and by intense international competition pressures (Ministry of Information 1985). It had to make significant price cuts (reducing its prices three times) and reduce its original cement output by two-thirds, from 330,000 to 110,000 tons (Ministry of Information 1985, 23). Likewise, falling steel prices and high production costs, which were three times more than in other regions, created further problems for Qatar's public sector (Moore 2002). In addition, Qatar faced significant challenges in the oil sector in the 1980s and early 1990s, as oil fields aged and prices dropped (Ibrahim and Harrigan 2012). Qatar responded with austerity programs to reduce public spending and suspend public/private infrastructure projects (Moore 2002). Furthermore, it embarked on partial privatizations in order to relieve the fiscal burden on the government (EIU 2009a).

Between 1972 and 1995, decision-making structures were highly fragmented. During this period, the system of private interest representation was characterized by low levels of mobilization. Despite the existence of a light manufacturing industry, (in 1983 there were around 1,195 establishments in the manufacturing area, such as clothing, furniture, or packaging manufacturing), there existed no business association representing these organizations (Ministry of Information 1985, 27). Secondary literature highlights that in contrast to other GCC economies, notably Kuwait, Qatar had a weak domestic merchant and business class (Crystal 1990; Mehran 2013). There existed no formal state agency or planning institution in

Qatar's industrial domain. According to El-Mallakh (1979), this role was pursued by the Council of Ministers. But until the mid-1990s, the Council of Ministers was characterized by high levels of factionalism. Despite high levels of autonomy from domestic merchants, there was intense competition among members of the ruling family over power and influence in social and industrial policymaking (Crystal 1990; Mehran 2013).

Qatar's Industrial Policy (1990s–2000s): Qatar Holding and Qatar Diar

Between the late 1990s and the 2000s, Qatar created a number of state-finance institutions with development mandates under the auspices of the Qatar Investment Authority. Qatar Holding was created in 2006 as a direct investment arm of the QIA. It was a global investment house that "invests internationally and locally in strategic private and public equity as well as in other direct investments" (Qatar Holding 2013; Katara Hospitality 2015). Another example is the QIA's real estate and infrastructure investment arm, Qatari Diar, established in 2005. Among Qatar Diar's international investments are more than forty-nine projects in twenty-nine countries, and among its domestic projects are infrastructure projects such as the Qatar Railways Development Company and real estate projects, most notably Lusail City (Qatari Diar 2014).

Almost all specialist state agencies and bureaus in Qatar's industrial domain were created in the early 2000s. For example, the Ministry of Municipality and Urban Planning established the Central Planning Unit to coordinate national infrastructure projects (Ibrahim and Harrigan 2012, 10). In addition, the government created the General Secretariat for Development Planning in 2007, with the objective of strategic planning and formulating Qatar's National Vision 2030. This was followed by forming the Supreme Committee for Development planning in 2011 to implement the Qatar National Vision 2030 (General Secretariat for Development Planning 2011).

From the mid-1990s on, Qatar experienced windfall gas revenues combined with centralized decision-making structures in the industrial domain. The ascension of Hamad Al-Thani in 1995—through a palace coup—triggered a process of centralization and institutionalization among state agencies in the industrial domain. Beginning in 1995, internal factionalism in the royal family was ended by replacing the "old guard" from the Council of Ministers with like-minded members of the ruling family (Mehran 2013).[10] Qatar's first permanent constitution in 2003 and its amendment in 2004 ascribed near absolute power to the emir (Qatar Constitution 2004, Article 64–75). From the mid-1990s, the inner circle of top policymakers included only a handful of people, notably the emir, the emir's son, his second wife, the emir's maternal and childhood friend who was the deputy prime minister, and the prime minister (Mehran 2013, 117). This circle, under the leadership of the emir, was tied to a strong kinship network consisting of between fifty and sixty members (Mehran 2013). It included members from the royal family and other key families, with intimate links to the top policymakers, and technocrats occupying central positions. Their main tasks were information-gathering, policymaking, and policy implementation via the chairmanship of specialist agencies (Mehran 2013).

This centralized and institutionalized decision-making affected the logic of policymaking in Qatar's industrial domain from the late 1990s onward. According to a representative of the Qatar Chamber of Commerce, the 2000s were marked by increasing competition between the state via its SWFs and the private domestic sector, especially in domestic construction (anonymous, personal communication, 25 September 2014). The government has been involved in almost every economic sector via the Qatar Investment Authority and its investment arms. Unlike in Kuwait and similar to Abu Dhabi, there has been no direct or indirect relationship between Qatar's SWFs and its Chamber of Commerce, which "formally" represents the private sector. According to a Chamber official, between 1995 and 2012, the Qatar Chamber of Commerce tried "unsuccessfully" to convince the government to consult the Chamber before major projects were commenced (anonymous, personal communication, 25 September 2014). A representative at the Qatar Chamber of Commerce admitted that the Chamber had little influence on policymaking and that the government generally did not listen to it in economic policymaking (anonymous, personal communication, 25 September 2014). Yet the extent to which Qatar's SWFs led to a crowding out of the domestic private sector remains unknown.

6.5 Bahrain: Mumtalakat

In 2006 the government of Bahrain created Mumtalakat with a view towards more active and coordinated management of the country's non-oil assets. Although Mumtalakat is involved in a number of different sectors including aluminum production, telecommunications, real estate, tourism, and transportation, with AUM of $9 billion, it is one of the GCCs smaller SWFs (Mumtalakat 2017). These assets were the result of Bahrain's diversification plans of the 1970s and 1980s, which built on Bahrain's proximity to oil-rich countries and the availability of oil and gas (IMF 1983; *Financial Times*, 1 June 1982). The strategy was to leave enough space for smaller local private enterprises which receive government assistance for selective projects, while undertaking large capital intensive projects in cooperation with neighbor governments, such as Kuwait and Saudi Arabia (IMF 1983; Lawson 1991). Large-scale projects included the petrochemical complex (e.g., Arab Petroleum Services Company, established 1977), aluminum rolling plants (e.g., Aluminium Bahrain, in operation since 1971), ship building and repairing (e.g., Arab Shipbuilding & Repair Yard, established in 1977), transport (e.g., Arab Maritime Petroleum Transport Company, established in 1973) and telecommunications (e.g., Arab Satellite Communications Organization, established in 1976; Bahrain Telecommunication Company, established in 1981) (IMF 1983; Mumtalakat 2017).

Despite high levels of oil revenues—at least in the early 1980s—Bahrain is the only GCC country that has never created a savings SWF, such as the KIA or the ADIA. In 1981 Bahrain's official reserves stood at around $1.6 billion, equivalent to eight months of non-oil imports (IMF 1983). The traditional "rules of thumb" used to inform reserve adequacy suggest that countries should hold reserves equivalent to three months' worth of imports (IMF 2011). This suggests that Bahrain had some surplus available, which could have been used for the creation of a KIA-like SWF. Instead, Bahrain's government relied on private finance institutions, and since the early 2000s Bahrain has emerged as the leading conventional as well as Islamic finance center in the region (IMF 1983). This in turn was the result of Bahrain's diversification strategy—following the 1970s oil shock—to become the region's financial service hub (Hussein 2004). Through a combination of preferential tax treatment and nearly total freedom from normal banking regulation, the Bahraini government encouraged the creation of offshore banking units and regional offices from foreign companies (Hussein 2004). Corresponding to this, the share of services and trade in its GDP increased from 25 percent in 1973 to 33 percent in 1979 (IMF 1983). Bahrain became a window for banking, and neighboring countries with closed banking systems, notably Saudi Arabia, increasingly recycled their oil surpluses via Bahrain (*Financial Times*, 1 June 1982).

By the time of British withdrawal from the Gulf in 1971, a powerful coalition had emerged between rich merchants and the ruling family/central administrative officials (Lawson 1991). Executive power and decision-making structures remained concentrated within the ruling Al Khalifa family (EIU 2007). Most of the key cabinet posts are held by members of the ruling family, and the king appoints the members of the Consultative Council, which offsets the power of the elected parliament (EIU 2007). Bahrain's merchant elite was especially influential and well-organized in commerce and finance affairs (Lawson 1991). With nearly 200 financial institutions, Bahrain now has "the largest concentration of banks in the Arab world" (Hussein 2004, 12). Banks are represented by the Bahrain Bank Association, which is one of the oldest finance associations in the Gulf, originating in the 1970s (BAB 2009).

The Bahrain Chamber of Commerce and Industry (established in 1939) is one of the oldest and most established chambers of commerce in the region and represents the private sector (Bahrain Chamber 2017). The chamber is especially strong on trade and services. While most of its committees are led by private sector members, the industrial committee mainly consists of state officials (Bahrain Chamber 2017). State-private sector relations in which state decision-making structures are highly concentrated and segments of the private sector are highly organized facilitate the interaction between both. In turn this shapes the content of policy.

Conclusion

The chapter found similarities between the configurations of state and private actors in the savings domain of Abu Dhabi, Qatar, and Kuwait. Between the 1960s and the 2000s, all of these economies established SWFs with savings mandates, channeling significant proportions of domestic savings into international assets. Over this period, the savings domains of Abu Dhabi and Qatar were characterized by strong and autonomous states and weakly mobilized domestic private-finance actors. For example, there was no banking association in Qatar and Abu Dhabi. As a result, the state was the dominant player in the banking systems across these economies, responsible for the appointment of key positions in the banking sector. Kuwait's savings domain was characterized by a centralized state with a highly mobilized segment of business in the form of a strong merchant elite that was well-organized in the Kuwait Chamber of Commerce. Unlike Qatar and Abu Dhabi, however, Kuwait had a strong parliament that was central to influencing economic policymaking. In stark contrast, Bahrain did not create an SWF with a savings mandate, despite periods of surpluses. Instead, Bahrain relied on the expansion of private finance institutions.

Second, the chapter discovered similarities between the configuration of state and private actors in the industrial domains of Abu Dhabi, Bahrain, and Qatar (1990s to the 2000s). These are cases of a centralized and autonomous state and a weakly mobilized private sector in the industrial domain. There was no merchant elite independent from the political or royal/tribal elite in Abu Dhabi or Qatar. The ruling families were themselves the commercial elite (Herb 2014). In Qatar, as well as Abu Dhabi, both the chamber of commerce and industry had been quasi-government departments. The rulers of both Abu Dhabi and Qatar held strong influence over the appointment of members in the domestic business chambers. In contrast, state-society relations in Kuwait's industrial domain were characterized by a fragmented state and a highly mobilized private sector. While short-term ad-hoc policies in Kuwait were reflected in the fact that it did not create an SWF with a development mandate, SWFs with development mandates were created in Qatar (e.g., Qatar Holdings and Qatar Diar), Abu Dhabi (e.g., Mubadala and IPIC), and Bahrain (e.g., Mumtalakat).

The chapter has implemented a cross-country and cross-sectoral comparison to assess the effects of policy networks on the development and uses of SWFs in four otherwise similar economies. Looking at SWFs in OECD and BRIC economies offers another avenue to expand the range of cases in investigating the role of state-private sector relations on capital choices.

SEVEN

Capital Choices in OECD and BRIC Countries

While debates on the appropriate role of the state in the economy have long occupied academics and policymakers, the dispute has reached new heights since the 2007–8 global financial crisis. The phenomenal growth of BRIC economies after the Western financial system's collapse raised a number of questions about the future direction of capitalism (Bremmer 2009). In this context SWFs have symbolized the redistribution of wealth and financial power from the United States and Europe to non-OECD countries and the increasing role of governments in managing this wealth (Setser 2008; Truman 2010a).

SWFs have become significant actors in both BRIC and OECD countries. The largest SWF, with one trillion $ assets under management can in fact be found in the OECD country of Norway. The total number of SWFs and their total assets has grown significantly over the 1990s and 2000s in both OECD and BRIC economies. We can also observe OECD countries that established SWFs despite difficult public finance positions. For example, France created a large SWF in 2008 while entering a recession. The Fonds Stratégique d'Investissement managed a volume of $25 billion, with a mission of supporting domestic small and mid-cap enterprises with strong innovation potential and protecting strategic French companies from hostile foreign takeovers. In 2011 Italy established the Fondo Strategico Italiano, which manages a much smaller amount between $1–$4 billion, also as a vociferous statement against unwanted foreign takeovers. This was again a period where Italy experienced a debt crisis against the backdrop of sluggish economic growth. As such, it is even more surprising that some OECD countries with huge surpluses and reserves, notably Germany and Switzerland, have repeatedly resisted calls for the creation of an SWF.

This chapter investigates whether the expectations of state-society structure impacts on capital choices—derived in previous chapters from small open economies in Asia and the Gulf—are also applicable to other countries. This helps determine whether further analysis in this area is warranted. The chapter begins with a short overview of SWF debates. That is followed by an short introduction of some of the domestic structures in OECD countries, specifically Switzerland and BRIC economies, and their corresponding SWF choices.

7.1 SWF Variation in OECD Countries

Discussions about SWF creation have occurred in twenty-two out of thirty OECD countries, and fourteen of these have effectively created SWFs. In all cases discussions have preceded the creation of SWFs (see table 7.1). For example, in 2017 the Swedish finance minister initiated a debate about establishing an SWF in order to solve Sweden's illiquid bond market problem (Reuters, 18 April 2017). Thanks to a solid public finance situation, Sweden does not need to issue bonds to finance budget deficits. The minister of finance suggested issuing special government bonds and placing their proceeds into an SWF, which could then be used for international investments (Reuters, 18 April 2017).

Similarly, a debate on creating an SWF has reemerged in the United Kingdom in the context of the "Brexit" vote, when Britain opted to leave the EU. Brexit spurred a fundamental question about Britain's structural deficit, long-term planning capacity, and lack of infrastructure. Parties of diverse ideologies have begun considering the potential of wealth funds. Conservative member of parliament John Penrose suggested creating an SWF, which would be managed through a fully independent, stand-alone National Insurance Trust. This was reflected in the 2017 Conservative Manifesto, which pledged to create a number of "Future Britain Funds." In 2016 the Conservative government had proposed a "shale gas wealth fund" to ensure "that the benefits of shale developments are shared by communities in which the resource is developed." The Labor Party also holds a strong interest in a national investment fund. London's City University "Citizens' Wealth Funds Project," led by the financial journalist Stewart Lansley, proposes pooling publicly-owned wealth in permanent trust funds that are collectively owned and managed in pursuit of alleviating societal inequalities (Lansley 2016, 2017). Lansley explores the potential of a UK Social Wealth Fund—its principles, governance, and purposes. One way of capitalizing a UK SWF is mobilizing Britain's public estate: land and property owned by central and local government, and bodies such as the National Health Service and transport authorities (Lansley 2016, 2017). Thus far these holdings have remained fragmented and have not been managed in a coordinated or efficient manner.

The increase of development SWFs in OECD countries following the global financial crisis of 2007-08 is strongly associated with state-owned enterprise reforms. This wave of SWFs is not focused on securing future rents; rather, they are used as mechanisms for fundraising or public sector restructuring. As vehicles to regulate state-owned enterprises, SWFs allow states to remain in control of firms while introducing market forces (Braunstein and Caoili 2016). Countries such as Turkey and Slovenia aim to follow in Singapore's earlier footsteps. In 2014 Slovenia established the Slovenian Sovereign Holdings with a mandate to actively manage state assets. The state transferred its stakes from ninety-eight companies, including energy, finance, transport, and infrastructure, into the Sovereign Holding (Slovenian Sovereign Holdings 2018). In Austria there was a brief informal debate about restructuring Austria's existing state holdings, OEIAG, along the lines of Singapore's Temasek (*Die Presse*, 7 July 2011). In 2016 Turkey created the Turkiye Wealth Fund with AUM of approximately € 200 billion (Bossart 2017). It was capitalized with key public assets, such as Ziraat Bank, Halkbank, Borsa Istanbul, and Turkish Airlines, which were previously held by the Treasury or the Privatization Administration (Bossart 2017). The Turkiye Wealth Fund's mandate is developing strategic assets and providing funding for priority projects (IFSWF 2018a).

Other strategic investment funds and development SWFs in OECD countries have been capitalized with fiscal resources or endowments of existing funds. For example, France's Strategic Investment Fund—now Bpi France—was created in 2008 by transferring assets previously held by the Caisse des Dépôts et Consignations and the French government. Its primary aim is to support the development of small and medium enterprises with strong potential for innovation and sector leadership, and to stabilize the capital companies deemed strategic to the French economy (Fiechter 2010). Similarly, the Italian Fondo Strategico Italiano—renamed CDP Equity—was created in 2011 with an endowment from the Cassa Depositi e Prestiti, an Italian investment bank owned by the Ministry of Finance. Its directive is undertaking investments in "companies of significant national interest" (Annual Report FSI 2015). It does this primarily through minority or co-investments with other SWFs, such as the Kuwait Investment Authority, Qatar Investment Authority, Korea Investment Corporation, the Russian Direct Investment Fund, and China Investment Corporation (IFSWF 2018b). In a similar fashion, in 2014 Ireland created the Ireland Strategic Investment Fund with a discretionary portfolio of € 8 billion, and an objective of generating returns and economic impact for the country. The fund was sourced through a transfer of assets from the National Pension Reserve Fund (Inderst 2016).

The idea to use a portion of tax revenues to create an SWF has been pursued by a number of countries, notably Luxembourg and Israel. The notion of introducing a special tax for future generations has been promoted by the current government of Luxembourg, the Bettel–Schneider ministry (a coalition between the Democratic Party, the Luxembourg Socialist Workers' Party, and the Greens), which in its 2015 budget set up a "Wealth Fund for Intergenerational Generations." Its aim is to gather at least €50 million per year from an e-commerce VAT and another portion from excise duties to reach €1 billion. The Luxembourg government intends to follow the example of Norway, a country that through its sovereign wealth fund turned nonrenewable resources, specifically its deposits of oil, into diversified financial assets for future generations (Braunstein et al. 2016). In a similar fashion, in 2013 the Israeli cabinet approved the creation of an SWF, which will hold and invest between $50 billion and $70 billion. The government aims to capitalize this fund with the revenue it expects to earn from its natural gas finds over the coming twenty-five years. Its goal is for the SWF to absorb 34 percent of total government revenue from gas windfall in order to avoid the Dutch Disease. It plans to introduce a special tax on oil and gas exploration firms (EIU 2013). A few years ago Iceland discussed the creation of an SWF that could be financed through a resource tax on fishing and energy companies, which generate a huge portion of Iceland's export revenues (*Financial Times*, 24 April 2008).

Similarly, the Australian Future Fund was created in 2006 to use surpluses from the cyclical housing and commodity boom to meet long-term budget liabilities, such as pension liabilities for public servants and military personal (Eccleston 2010). Another reason for the creation of the Future Fund was related to the credibility of the conservative government of former Prime Minister John Howard toward sustainable economic management. It aimed to create an institutional mechanism sustaining Australia's long-term spending power vis-à-vis short-term electoral cycle. When the Labor government lead by Kevin Rudd came

TABLE 7.1 Debates on SWF creation and characteristics of OECD and BRIC SWFs

OECD	SWF	Debate	Type created	Reserves (in billion USD)	GDP 2016 (in billion USD)	Reserve/ GDP in %	Total reserves in month of imports
Australia	yes	yes	saving	55	1,204	5	2
Austria	no	yes	n/a	23	386	6	1
Belgium	no	no	n/a	23	466	5	1
Canada	yes	yes	saving	82	1,529	5	2
Chile	yes	yes	saving	40	247	16	6
Czech Republic	no	no	n/a	85	192	44	6
Denmark	no	no	n/a	64	306	21	5
Estonia	no	no	n/a		23	2	0
Finland	no	no	n/a	10	236	4	1
France	yes	yes	dev	145	2,465	6	2
Germany	no	yes	saving	184	3,466	5	1
Greece	no	no	n/a	6	194	4	1
Hungary	no	no	n/a	25	124	21	3
Iceland	no	yes	n/a	7	20	36	10
Ireland	yes	yes	dev	3	294	1	0
Israel	yes	yes	saving	95	318	30	11
Italy	yes	yes	dev	135	1,849	7	3
Japan	no	yes	n/a	1,216	4,939	25	17
Korea	yes	yes	saving	370	1,411	26	8
Luxembourg	yes	yes	stab		59	2	0
New Zealand	yes	yes	saving	17	185	10	n/a
Norway	yes	yes	saving	60	370	16	5
Poland	no	yes	n/a	114	469	24	5
Slovak Republic	no	no	n/a	2	89	3	0
Slovenia	yes	yes	dev		43	2	0
Spain	no	no	n/a	63	1,2320	5	2
Sweden	no	yes	n/a	59	510	12	3
Switzerland	no	yes	n/a	678	659	103	17
Turkey	yes	yes	dev	105	857	12	6
United Kingdom	no	yes	n/a	134	2,618	5	2
BRIC							
Brazil	yes	yes	dev	364	1,796	20	17
Russia	yes	yes	saving, stab, dev	377	1,283	29	13
India	no	yes	dev	361	2,263	16	8
China	yes	yes	dev, saving	3,097	11,199	28	17

Sources: Compiled from World Bank database (2017), individual SWF sites.

into power in 2007, the Future Fund was complemented with the Education Investment Fund, the Health and Hospital Fund, and the Building Australia Fund, which invested in education, health, and other infrastructure projects (Eccleston 2010).

Switzerland

Switzerland is the most puzzling example of non-SWF creation among OECD countries, and proponents of standard explanations would expect the creation of a Swiss SWF. By late 2016 Switzerland had accumulated around CHF710 billion, which is equivalent to 110 percent of its GDP. As of 2017, Switzerland's reserves were equivalent to seventeen months of imports. This is far above the rule of the thumb of three months of imports (IMF), and is more than what is needed for the monetary operations of the Swiss National Bank. Switzerland began accumulating massive reserves after September 2011 when the Swiss National Bank decided to fix the Swiss franc to the euro at 1.2 percent and intervened accordingly (*Finanz und Wirtschaft*, 27 February 2017). This was in the aftermath of the global financial crisis 2007–8 and in the context of the euro crisis. Switzerland experienced massive capital inflows from foreign investors and from Swiss residents, who invested in the Swiss franc as a means of hedging against the financial crisis (WTO 2013; IMF 2015c).

After Switzerland had created the currency peg with the euro in 2011, the idea of creating a Swiss SWF—to use part of its massive reserves for investments—was born (Senner and Sornette 2017). It was suggested that the country should follow Singapore's model (i.e., Singapore's GIC), where a Swiss SWF would issue a special bond and swap them for a part of Swiss National Bank's reserves (Senner and Sornette 2017). According to Senner and Sornette, these operations would have not affected the balance sheet of the Swiss National Bank. Part of the bank's foreign assets would have been replaced with bonds issued by the SWF (Senner and Sornette 2017).

Different SWF options for Switzerland were discussed, ranging from an SWF with a strategic investment mandate to one with a savings mandate. Regarding the latter it was suggested that a Swiss SWF could be used to pool domestic funds. The Swiss financial sector could use their excess sight deposits (which are liabilities on the Swiss National Bank balance sheet) to purchase special bonds that the Swiss National Bank would have acquired from the SWF. Thereby the Swiss National Bank would sell special bonds to domestic finance institutions, which would sterilize the sight deposits and further reduce the Swiss National Bank's balance sheet. In turn this would offer Swiss pension funds attractive investment opportunities (Senner and Sornette 2017). Another SWF option promoted by the center-left Social Democrats was the creation of a private equity type SWF that invests in technology start-ups and protects against hostile takeovers of strategic firms (Sornette 2015).

While Swiss banks are in favor of international SWFs that invest in Switzerland, they oppose the creation of a Swiss SWF (*Swiss Banking*, May 2008). The Swiss Bankers Association supports a free market approach toward investments by international SWFs (Swiss Bankers Association, May 2008). It warns that "a hasty or unjustified political response would threaten capital inflows into Switzerland and raise the prospect of retaliatory actionably foreign government, for instance against Swiss investment in their countries" (Swiss Bankers Association, May 2008, 9). This reflects Switzerland's financial system, which has close ties to the international community. "Most Swiss banks act as financial turntables by attracting funds from external (i.e. foreign) sources, mingling them with domestic savings, and investing the net funds abroad" (Meier et al. 2012, 52).

Swiss banks have voiced heavy resistance to the creation of an SWF (*Swiss Banking*, May 2008). They argue that the state is not able to make better investment decisions than the private sector (Foellmi 2015; Brunetti 2015). Likewise, Thomas Jordan, the governor of the Swiss National Bank, is critical of the idea of carving out money from the National Bank to create an SWF. This could lead to unintended consequences for Swiss monetary policy and might interfere with the independence of the National Bank (*Swissinfo*, 14 June 2017). Furthermore, it is often argued that parts of the Swiss National Bank's assets have already been managed similarly to an SWF (Brunetti 2015). It should also be mentioned that the Swiss National Bank is privately owned, with the majority held by cantons and cantonal banks (SNB 2017). Cantonal banks—stemming from the desire of every Swiss member state to have its own bank—operate like commercial banks but also provide cantonal financing (Fehrenbach 1968). The outsourcing of part of the Swiss National Bank's reserves for a national SWF would lead to reduced assets, which in turn would reduce the profit potential of the Swiss National Bank. By law Swiss cantons receive two-thirds of the Swiss National Bank's profits. As such, the creation of a Swiss SWF would reduce their revenues (Bundesrat 2016).

Swiss banks have a central role in Switzerland's policymaking structures. The structural features of state-society relations in Switzerland's savings domain are consistent with those of an industry dominant pressure pluralist policy network (PN). This type of PN describes state-society relations where decision-making structures are fragmented and state officials have low levels of autonomy, while the business sector is highly mobilized. The essence of this PN is that it allows an asymmetry in the representation of private interests. The Swiss finance sector is strongly organized (Katzenstein 1987). A small number of large banks are strongly interlinked internationally, together with insurance and reinsurance companies associations converging in a small number of peak associations. All of these play a strong role in pre-parliamentary bargaining (Katzenstein 1987). In contrast to standard explanations an analysis of the organizational characteristics of policy making help make sense of the absence of a Swiss SWF.

Norway and Alaska

Norway's Government Pension Fund Global was set up in 1990 to invest Norway's proceeds from petroleum into international assets, notably equity and fixed income instruments. However, the word "pension" is misleading since the fund has neither liabilities nor an explicated pension mandate. The fund receives all petroleum revenues and is an integrated part of the government's annual budget (Skancke 2003). The Ministry of Finance owns the fund on behalf of the Norwegian people and outsources the management to Norges Bank Investment Management. Following the advice of Norges Bank Investment Management and discussions in parliament, the Ministry of Finance determines the fund's investment strategy (Norges Bank 2018). For example, in November 2017 the Norwegian SWF announced that it will divest from earlier investments in oil and gas stocks, which were equivalent to $ 60 billion (*Financial Times*, 16 November 2017).

When Norway discovered oil in the late 1960s, it had a well-established corporatist polity. Political scientist Bent Tranøy's statement that "one must grasp the domestic politics of handling petro-wealth in a corporatist state" underlines the importance of understanding the political context in which particular SWF types emerge (Tranøy 2010, 198). Using Peter Katzenstein's terminology (1985), Tranøy suggests that the Government Pension Fund Global is a means of flexible adjustment in a highly globalized environment and a tool to address external pressures and domestic compensation in supporting Norway's welfare model. Considerations on Norway's SWF variation were influenced by public debates as well as a corporatist polity and a small number of bureaucrats in an iron triangle, comprising of the Ministry of Finance, the Statistics Norway, and the Central Bank. Tranøy (2010) identifies the combination of a corporatist polity and strong technocrats as the key shapers of how oil wealth is managed in Norway. Tranoy's central argument that Norway's SWF variation is a result of the domestic "effort to integrate rent-based revenues into an established domestic order with an older governance, production and distributional structure" indicates the role of domestic institutions and path dependency (Tranøy 2010, 178). At the point when oil was discovered, Norway was a mature democracy and already had a set of established corporatist institutions. Knowing the potential harm of windfall oil revenues, the government looked for an institutional mechanism to address the question of how to preserve the old order—with only gradual change—in an international economic context.

In a similar fashion, the Alaska Permanent Fund (APF) was established in 1976 in the context of Alaska's oil pipeline construction. Due to the state's high exposure to commodity price cycles, the APF was created to save in good times and spend in bad times. However, its creation necessitated a constitutional amendment. Alaska's population voted in broad support of the constitutional amendment and the creation of the Fund (Brown and Thomas 1994). The constitutional amendment stipulated that at "least 25 percent of all mineral lease rentals, royalties, royalty sales proceeds, federal mineral revenue-sharing payments and bonuses received by the state [should be placed with the Alaska Permanent Fund]" (APF 2015). To manage the investments of the APF, the Alaska legislature established the Alaska Permanent Fund corporation. As of 2015 the AUM of the APF were estimated at around $50 billion. High levels of political freedom in Alaska's political system within the US federal system are reflected in Alaska's economic policymaking and the APF's creation. According to Brown and Thomas (1994, 44), this makes it very difficult to "promote any common goal on a long-term basis" with regard to the APF and Alaska's fiscal policy. Another factor relates to the APF's unique incentive structure. Its founder, Governor Jay Hammond, followed the idea of giving Alaska's residents a direct stake or interest in the Fund by paying them an annual dividend out of its earnings (Brown and Thomas 1994, 41). This is an unusual practice among SWFs. Brown and Thomas's statement that the so-called APF dividend "soon became a sacred political cow" suggests that it is very risky for politicians to change the investment framework of the SWF (Brown and Thomas 1994, 43). The adoption of ethical investment guidelines implies a trade-off for the APF's return. It is widely acknowledged that extensive exclusion based on ethical principles could harm the return and risk profile of funds (*Financial Times*, 3 November 2014). Three decades after the establishment of Alaska's APF a new group of countries (i.e., BRIC economies) started to create SWFs.

BRIC Economies

The abbreviation BRIC was coined in 2001 by Jim O'Neill—chief researcher at Goldman Sachs—to describe the largest emerging economies (O'Neill 2001). The first BRIC Foreign Ministers Meeting took place in 2006 and eight summits have been held since then, with the 2010 addition of South Africa changing the acronym to BRICS. BRIC countries together account for about 43 percent of the world population, 23 percent of the global GDP, and more than half of world economic growth over the last decade (BRIC 2017). During the early years BRIC economies shared a number of important similarities, such as large foreign exchange reserves and very strong state presence in their respective financial markets.

The creation of SWFs, especially in BRIC economies, has been closely associated with "turf battles between central banks and finance ministries over foreign exchange policy, investment policies for international reserves, or the extent to which earnings on reserves should be used to finance the government" (Truman 2010b). Some of the BRIC countries' SWFs, especially China's, are very large. For example, the China Investment Corporation has AUM of approximately $800 billion, followed by China's SAFE Investment Company with AUM $440 billion (Sovereign Wealth Fund Institute 2017). Russia's National Welfare and Reserve Funds have combined AUM of approximately $90 billion (Sovereign Wealth Fund Institute 2017).

Russia is frequently referred to as an instance where self-interested elites in the central organization shape policy choices and SWF variation. Political scientist Fortescue draws attention to the role of interest clashes in domestic debates and their consequences on SWF variation over time. Without explicitly referring to a theoretical frame, Fortescue (2010) maps out a number of different actors responsible for Russia's SWF variation. The dominant actors in the controversial debate on SWF variation include the Central Bank, the Ministry of Finance, the Ministry of Economic Development and Trade, and to some extent the Ministry of Industry and Energy. While the preferences of Russia's Central Bank and Ministry of Finance vis-à-vis SWF variation were particularly influenced by experiencing high inflation in the 1990s, the motivations of other ministries relate to developing domestic infrastructure. In contrast to the Ministry of Finance, the latter two did not want SWF resources to be invested in international financial assets but rather spent on domestic projects. This idea of spending on domestic development and infrastructure projects was also supported by a domestic industrial lobby.

The debate on whether to spend SWF resources domestically or abroad involved different ministries with varying interests. Each ministry proposed a perspective on how to restructure Russia's Stabilization Fund. Initially the SWF was under the very conservative management of the Central Bank, investing mainly in government bonds. It was used as a sterilization vehicle to manage the excessive inflow of oil money and tame inflation. Later, Russia's Stabilization Fund was split into two branches by creating a separate investment portfolio for future pension liabilities and repaying foreign debt.

A similar debate took place in China about the management of its massive currency reserves. The contest over the creation of an SWF was between China's central bank, the People's Bank of China, and the Ministry of Finance. According to Lieu and He (2012), this contest has been a derivative of the larger battle between them for influence over broad economic policy and control of the country's financial assets. In 2007, China, with $1,400 billion, held the largest foreign exchange reserves worldwide (Setser 2008, 206), much more than it would have needed for its balance of payments purposes (El-Erian 2008, 195). Until 2007—in other words, before China established its SWF—the bulk of this money was conservatively invested in low-yielding US treasury bonds. Chinese assets abroad have earned very poor returns, and with the depreciation of the dollar, to some extent they have even performed negatively (Martin 2008; Elwell 2012). However, the holding of large sums of foreign exchange reserves is costly because of the "difference between the return on reserves and the return on more profitable alternative investment opportunities" (Jeanne 2007).

The conflict over the management of China's reserves reflected a similar, earlier contest in neighboring South Korea. Although South Korea is not a BRIC economy, its SWF, the Korean Investment Corporation, illustrates the typical conflicts that emerge between the ministries of finance and central banks over the creation of an SWF (Kim 2012). The Korean Investment Corporation was created by the Ministry of Finance in order to manage foreign exchange reserves from the Bank of Korea. The Bank of Korea initially opposed the idea. Conflicts between the Bank of Korea and the Ministry of Finance were mediated by the Presidential Office and the National Assembly (Kim 2012).

Brazil created the Fundo Soberano do Brasil in 2008 after the discovery of a large oil and gas field. Initially the fund creation experienced resistance from private actors, notably banks, and the parliament (Reinsberg 2009). Given the lack of initial legislative approval, Brazil's president Lula de Silva created the SWF via decree. Finally, the parliament approved the SWF creation but the fund was only endowed with a relative small amount of about $6 billion (Reinsberg 2009). Following Brazil's recession the government systematically drew on the fund in order to shore up public accounts (*Bloomberg*, 23 December 2015). This led to an alleged depletion of the fund in 2016 (Seeking Alpha, 24 May 2016).

India created an SWF, the National Infrastructure Investment Fund, in 2015 with the purpose of catalyzing capital into India's core infrastructure, including airports, railways, roadways, waterways, and ports. However, the SWF's creation faced strong domestic opposition especially from the Reserve Bank, the Security and Exchange Board, and business associations like the Federation of the Indian Chambers or the Confederation of Indian Industry (Reinsberg 2009). India's Narendra Modi administration planned a core funding of Rs 40,000 crore—about $6 billion—which would be used to further leverage international capital and leading infrastructure operators (NIIF India 2017). According to media reports, by June 2017 India's National Infrastructure Investment Fund has only received Rs 15 crore—$2.4 million—from the Ministry of Finance for administrative purposes (*Indian Express*, 3 June 2017). In October 2017 the National Infrastructure Investment Fund announced the signing of an investment agreement worth $1 billion with a subsidiary of the Abu Dhabi Investment Authority (NIIF India 2018).

The "New" BRICS: Next Eleven and CIVITS

Soon after BRICS became a mainstream acronym for emerging economies, the question arose of which country will be the group's next member. Attempting to answer this question, in 2005 Jim O'Neill together with his Goldman Sachs team, identified the "Next Eleven" growth markets— Vietnam, South Korea, Turkey, the Philippines, Pakistan, Nigeria, Mexico, Iran, Indonesia, Egypt, and Bangladesh. Robert Ward from the Economist Intelligence Unit introduced in 2007 the rival acronym CIVETS, standing for Colombia, Indonesia, Vietnam, Egypt, Turkey, and South Africa (Financial Times, 8 June 2012; Lawson, Heacock, and Stupnytska 2007). These countries have been identified as the next group with the potential to become important economies during this century by using a set of variables including education, taxation, demographics, and consumption levels (*Financial Times*, 8 June 2012; Reuters, 13 July 2007).

Common to all of these economies is that they have either created SWFs, such as Egypt, Turkey, Vietnam, Nigeria, Mexico, and Iran, or at least considered the creation of SWFs, notably Bangladesh, Colombia, and Indonesia (see Schena, Braunstein, and Ali 2018; *Reuters*, 17 July 2018). But interestingly many of these nations are neither endowed with oil wealth nor otherwise enjoy large export surpluses (see Schena, Braunstein, and Ali 2018). Many of the new funds have been created since the global financial crisis, and more recently in the wake of commodity price declines and slowing growth in emerging economies (see Schena, Braunstein, and Ali 2018). One of the key objectives of these newly created funds has been the promotion of domestic investment to restart economic growth, promote economic diversification, and advance national competitiveness.

Conclusion

SWF variation in the OECD and BRIC country cases of this chapter call for further analysis of the impact of state-society relations on capital choices. The chapter has shown how debates about SWFs have arisen in almost every country. In addition, these debates illustrate the array of preferences regarding capital choices, in terms of whether an SWF is created and, if so, what type.

The emergence of many new funds affirms the need for further studies on the impact of state-society relations on capital choices, and the wider implications thereof. As highlighted in previous chapters, SWF creation relates to choices concerning the accumulation and allocation of resources. This chapter has shown that even in countries with substantial surplus wealth, such as Switzerland, these are challenging questions. As such, political contests and the structures should be especially influential in newly emerging economies that create SWFs with limited resources.

EIGHT

Conclusion

Domestic Politics and Capital Choices

The central theme of this book has been the varying effects of domestic politics on capital choices. Key questions have arisen as a result: If surplus alone does not lead to the creation of SWFs, which other factors contribute to their creation? Why do some countries with large current account surpluses create SWFs while others do not? What drives these choices? Relatedly, why do countries with similar macroeconomic features, such as Kuwait, Bahrain, Qatar, and Abu Dhabi, or Singapore and Hong Kong, choose very different types of SWFs? Related to this but often neglected are issues of distributional implications. Choices about SWF creation are choices about massive capital allocation on the sectoral or macro level. What are the implications of SWF choices for other economic actors?

To answer these questions, this book has distinguished among state-society structures, notably state-directed policy networks at one extreme and pressure pluralist networks at the other. It has investigated capital choices in the savings and industrial policy domains. The effects of state-society structures at the sectoral level have been compared across small open economies. This has allowed addressing of standard arguments, because small open economies are extremely exposed to international diffusion and efficiency pressures. Hence this book has examined the effects of state-society structures comparatively across sectors and countries.

This comparative approach showed that sectoral structures have an independent effect on SWF variation both across and within countries.

The analytical framework developed in this study adds value even to cases that have already been analyzed in depth, such as the small open GCC economies and East Asian city-states, because it focuses on the sectoral level, which has been overlooked in many studies (e.g., Shih 2009; Abdelal 2009). The policy network analysis shows that similar players were involved but were organized differently, and that these differences had a critical effect on SWF creation.

This chapter reviews the analytical starting point and research design. It then outlines empirical findings, arguments developed and their wider theoretical implications.

A Policy Network Analysis of Capital Choices

SWF variation across and within small open economies seems puzzling to standard explanations, because they ignore domestic politics. Responding to this, an increasing number of inside-out approaches integrate the role of domestic politics. But again most of the inside-out approaches focus on the macro-institutional environment, which makes within-country variation confusing. Policy outcomes can be difficult to explain in purely veto player or macro-institutional terms. Such is the case when actors with a great deal of resources exercise little influence in the policymaking process, while those with scant resources exercise greater influence.

Existing inside-out approaches overemphasize the insulation of the state from civil society, and thereby fail to account for the role of non-state actors or remain vague in their definitions of civil society and nonstate actors. An investigation of the characteristics of a single actor may not be sufficient in understanding their influence on policymaking processes and outcomes (see Montpetit 2005). Whether business will be able to influence decisions on SWFs depends on their mobilization and state access. In turn, state access depends on the level of state autonomy. Even highly mobilized private producer groups may find it very difficult to influence policymaking processes if there is a concentrated and autonomous state structure in place. In contrast, when the state structure is fragmented, characterized by low levels of autonomy, or both, then highly mobilized domestic private groups may have more of an effect on policymaking processes and policy choices.

The book opens the "black box" of SWF creation—in terms of the roles of different political actors within countries and cross-country—through its policy network (PN) analysis. Different types of PNs relate to different organizational maps of state-society relations. The influence arising from these maps depends on the centralization of decision-making power, autonomy of state actors, and mobilization of civil society. These maps can be systematically linked to differences in policymaking processes, and as such to different policy choices. For example, the notion of a clientele pluralist PN describes a state-society relationship where decision-making structures are highly concentrated, state officials have low levels of autonomy, and there are high levels of business mobilization. Such structures permit an asymmetry in the representation of private interests, and business can follow their sector-specific preferences in the policymaking process. Policy choices consequently are structured around the immediate needs of particular firms and private sector interests, which often result in short-term-oriented, ad hoc solutions uncoordinated with previous policies. In contrast, anticipatory policies, such as the creation of an SWF, require PNs that allow for a long-term view of economic policymaking. Due to their central role in the accumulation and allocation processes of domestic savings, the creation of SWFs can be intrusive for domestic financial actors. They manage a country's excess savings and surpluses through investment and diversification into international assets. SWFs can also be crucial for a country to implement and coordinate its saving policy within a context of high capital mobility and openness. By withdrawing liquidity from the domestic market and channeling surpluses abroad, SWFs are also important for addressing inflation pressures.

Research Design and Case Selection

Cross-country and cross-domain comparison allow the investigation of the effects of political structures on capital choices. Each of the empirical chapters has examined the policy choices discussed in the respective policy domain, the PNs in place, and the policy choices made. To assess the effects of various PNs on policy choices, close attention has been paid to the debates and policy preferences of different socioeconomic actors. An examination of archival data and interviews has identified policymaking processes among the cases, which has allowed for the assessment of the effect of PNs on policy choices with regard to the creation of different SWF types and to the question of who benefited and who suffered due to the particular choices made.

Hong Kong and Singapore were selected because they had similar values in the variables highlighted by the standard efficiency- and diffusion-based explanations. Efficiency-based approaches would lead us to predict that Hong Kong and Singapore would have created similar SWF types because both were very open, both were confronted with similar external pressures (e.g., competition and inflation), and both had high levels of domestic savings. Likewise, constructivist approaches would predict that both economies would adopt similar types of SWFs because they belonged to the same peer group (i.e., they shared similar structural profiles), were highly exposed to international pressures, and were confronted with similar, but separate, challenges. The factor that efficiency- and diffusion-based accounts omit is domestic politics.

This book has used the selected cases to inductively develop hypotheses whereby PNs may have influenced the creation of different SWF types. Between the 1960s and the 1980s, Hong Kong and Singapore exhibited important variations in terms of the independent variable (state-society relations) and the dependent variable (the creation of different state finance institutions). This makes both cases particularly useful for investigating mechanisms whereby state-society relations may have influenced institutional choices. The book has investigated these through systematic observation of the actors involved in debates and policymaking processes. The effects of different PNs have been compared across domains (i.e., the savings and the industrial policy domain) and across small open economies (i.e., Hong Kong and Singapore between the 1960s and the 1980s). The research has compared the types of PNs with the choices made (i.e., the creation of different SWFs and other related state finance institutions, such as CPFs and development banks). It has looked at the alternative choices that were available and discussed at the time. In addition, it has provided a plausibility probe for the hypotheses developed in earlier chapters by looking at SWF types in small open Gulf economies (i.e., Kuwait, Abu Dhabi, Bahrain, and Qatar) and OECD as well as BRIC economies.

For example, between the 1960s and 1980s, Hong Kong and Singapore had similar chambers of commerce, manufacturing associations, and large commercial banks, but were organized very differently. While large commercial private banks had little influence on policymaking in Singapore, they had a great influence on policymaking and institutional choices in Hong Kong. This book has argued that this divergence was due to the presence of different PNs. Organized interests not part of the particular PN were systematically excluded from policymaking and from advisory committees in Hong Kong and Singapore. This had important implications for policymaking processes and for the kinds of finance institutions set up. The structure of state-society relations has a key influence on policymaking and policy choices regarding SWFs. The organization of the state and businesses in policymaking processes is closely linked to policies about the creation of different SWFs. Because of the massive capital involved in such decisions, SWF choices have large distributional consequences for the private sector.

Empirical Findings

Cross-National Variation in Hong Kong's and Singapore's Savings Domain (1960s–80s)

From the 1970s on, high levels of domestic savings in both economies were increasingly exposed to similar external pressures, notably inflation in an environment of high capital mobility. The 1970s witnessed unprecedented levels of commodity price hikes, translating into rising worldwide inflation. Increasing inflation, combined with heightened capital mobility, put significant pressure on the high levels of domestic savings in Hong Kong and in Singapore. Through high import ratios and high capital flows, these pressures were directly transmitted into the domestic economy of Hong Kong and Singapore, thereby affecting purchasing power (see Krause 1988).

Confronted with external pressures, policy choices began to diverge dramatically in Hong Kong and Singapore from the late 1960s on and resulted, in the 1980s, in the establishment of very different kinds of finance institutions (see table 8.1). While in Hong Kong, savings continued to be allocated through private savings vehicles (e.g., private commercial banks and private pension funds), in Singapore a significant portion of domestic savings were channeled into state finance institutions, most notably the state-run Central Provident Fund (CPF) and the state-owned banks, notably the Post Office Savings Bank. Singapore's government created an SWF—the Government Investment Corporation (GIC)—to manage these savings abroad in order to acquire a better return on large levels of accumulated wealth. The GIC's international investment mandate also had the effect of mitigating domestic inflation pressures.

The decision to create an SWF with a savings mandate in Singapore was linked to earlier decisions about other state finance institutions and driven by a state-directed PN, which was able to exclude domestic finance and commerce organizations from policymaking processes—at least in the early formation stage. Due to high levels of power concentration and autonomy, Singapore's decision-makers could freely choose among international investment houses. In contrast, in Hong Kong the decision against creating state finance institutions with a savings mandate, notably a state-run CPF, affected the potential to create an SWF with a savings mandate like in Singapore. This decision was driven by a clientele pluralist

PN in Hong Kong that included domestic finance and business organizations from important policy bodies and excluded weakly mobilized labor and welfare organizations.

Cross-National Variation in Hong Kong's and Singapore's Industrial Domain (1960–80s)

By the early 1960s, Hong Kong and Singapore had embarked on labor-intensive industrialization as a consequence of the significant decline in their role as regional entrepôts. Confronted with similar external pressures (i.e., increasing international competition and protectionism), policy choices in Singapore and Hong Kong began to diverge from the late 1960s onward, and resulted in different types of finance institutions in their industrial domains. Despite similarities in terms of their high openness and small domestic markets, Hong Kong's and Singapore's policymakers made very different policy choices regarding state finance institutions (see table 8.1). While Hong Kong's policymakers chose not to enlarge its state sector and not to create a state development bank or a state development fund, Singapore's government embarked on a comprehensive industrial upgrading program and chose to enlarge the state sector. They first created a development bank, and later an SWF with a development mandate (Temasek). Through this SWF, Singapore's government obtained direct stakes in a variety of unrelated sectors (e.g., technology, finance, manufacturing, and infrastructure) and in joint ventures that were considered crucial for Singapore's diversification into higher value-added industries.

Between the 1960s and the 1980s, industrial policy in Singapore was formulated within a state-directed PN. It was characterized by weak and fragmented manufacturing associations, a weakly mobilized and passive banking and commerce sector, and a centralized and autonomous state dominated by its Ministry of Finance. The PN operated via inclusion and exclusion. Only high-level bureaucrats and politicians from the Ministry of Finance, as well as a small number of external economic advisors from the World Bank, were part of the policymaking process, leading to the emergence of a fledging state enterprise sector, the creation of the DBS and the creation of Temasek. The creation of Temasek was aimed at structural transformation through industrial upgrading and increased coordination among government-linked companies. Specifically, domestic private entrepreneurs viewed the government's policies as highly intrusive, mainly because of competition and crowding out aspects. However, the extent to which SWFs, such as Temasek, had a crowding out effect on the private sector remains unknown. In stark contrast, MNCs did not perceive Singapore's SWFs as intrusive, because Singapore's SWF and its companies were cooperating with MNCs. They provided important infrastructure and operated in areas complementary to MNCs, creating joint ventures with them. Members of PNs benefit from capital choices accruing from these PNs.

Over the same period, industrial policy in Hong Kong was formulated in a clientele pluralist PN. It was characterized by weakly mobilized industrial associations, and by a highly centralized state with close links to strongly mobilized domestic finance and commerce organizations. An arrangement was in place encouraging interaction between bureaucrats and policymakers from the Finance Branch, the Commerce and Economic Development Bureau, and finance as well as commerce organizations. Because of this arrangement, there was a low level of differentiation between the state apparatus and finance and commerce actors. This made finance and commerce actors influential in economic policymaking. These actors had diametrically opposed preferences to the manufacturing sector in terms of finance institutions in the industrial domain. They had a strong preference for low levels of state involvement in the lucrative industrial financing area. As such, they strongly opposed proposals for the creation of state finance institutions, notably a state-run development bank or a development fund. Clientele pluralist PNs in the industrial policy domain lead to the noncreation of state organizations leading the flow of industrial capital.

Cross-National Variation in GCC Countries and Beyond

In line with previous findings, SWF choices in GCC economies are consistent with their respective formal institutional and informal linkages between governmental and private actors at the subnational level. For example, in Abu Dhabi and Qatar, the centralized state, weakly mobilized private finance, and high levels of state autonomy allowed the pursuit of highly interventionist state strategies with SWFs that dominate the domestic finance and industrial landscape. In Bahrain, by contrast, the centralized state and low levels of state autonomy from a highly organized finance elite led to state intervention supporting the activities of the domestic private finance sector. In such cases we observe the mobilization of state assets to the advantage of private finance and the emergence of private equity type SWFs such as Mumtalakat. In contrast, in the absence of a strong private finance elite, we see state action that is highly coordinated in the finance sector and the creation of SWFs with savings mandates. For example, in countries such as Kuwait, a centralized state with a weakly mobilized pri-

TABLE 8.1. External pressures and financial institutions set up in Hong Kong and Singapore between the 1950s and the 1980s

Period	Similar External Pressures		Different Responses	
	Hong Kong	*Singapore*	*Hong Kong*	*Singapore*
1950s–early 1960s	Decline in entrepôt trade following the Korean War in the early 1950s.	Decline of entrepôt trade following the emancipation of Singapore's neighbours in the late-1950s.	Noncreation of a state industrial bank.	Establishment of the MFI and the EDB.
1960s–early 1970s	Loss of Commonwealth preferences; tensions with neighbouring China; increasing competition with NIE (Taiwan, South Korea); protectionism in OECD markets.	Expulsion of Singapore from Malaysian Union (i.e., loss of common market); tensions with neighbouring Indonesia and Malaysia; increasing competition pressure with NIE; protectionism in OECD markets.	Expansion of private commercial banks' activities in industrial financing.	Creation of the DBS; expansion of state sector.
1970s	Increasing competition pressures with Malaysia, Thailand in labor intensive light manufacturing; 1970s oil shock; protectionism (e.g., Multi Fibre Agreement).	Increasing competition pressures with Malaysia, Thailand in labor intensive light manufacturing; 1970s oil shock; protectionism.	Noncreation of industrial bank and development fund.	Reorganization of the state sector and the creation of Temasek.
1980s	Effective opening of China's industrial zones leading to increased outsourcing of labor intensive industries to China; partial revival of Hong Kong's role as entrepôt trade hub.	Opening of Malaysia and Indonesia and outsourcing of labor intensive industries. Recession in the United States in 1983, especially in the electronics sector; translation of the US recession into Singapore's first recession in 1985.	Noncreation of a development fund for small and medium enterprises.	Restructuration of Temasek and its international expansion.

Note: NIE = newly industrializing economies

vate finance sector but strongly organized commerce merchant class led to the creation of the Kuwait Investment Authority and state actions benefiting the commerce and merchant sector.

SWF variation in OECD and BRIC countries warrants further analysis of the impact of state-society relations. Debates about SWFs have occurred in almost every OECD and BRIC country, suggesting different preferences regarding capital choices. For example, different SWF options for Switzerland were discussed, ranging from an SWF with a strategic investment mandate to one with a savings mandate. However, Swiss banks voiced heavy resistance to the creation of an SWF. The structural features of state-society relations in Switzerland's savings domain are consistent with that of an industry dominant pressure pluralist PN. This type of PN describes state-society relations where decision-making structures are fragmented and state officials with low levels of autonomy are positioned vis-à-vis a highly mobilized banking sector.

Out of the book's key developments is the argument that state-society structures are key in explaining choices about SWFs. The structure of state-society relations matters because it allows the inclusion and exclusion of actors in policymaking processes that concern the allocation of wealth. This is especially crucial during times of economic growth, windfall revenues, and export surpluses. Allocating capital—even with substantial surplus wealth—is challenging and contested, especially for many developing countries with no or only little surpluses. Such surpluses certainly have competing uses.

Capital choices, and as such, SWF choices are products of policymaking. In turn policymaking is a collective enterprise that involves state as well as private actors. Because of the massive size of these funds, SWF choices have important implications for private actors and can create winners as well as losers.

Out of the entire range of actors interested in a policy issue, often only a few are actually involved in the policymaking process. While some actors are directly involved in policy processes, other actors can merely voice their ideas and advocate positions in hope of influencing the policymaking process (Montpetit 2005; Howlett 2002). Policy networks offer a structural analysis of civil society and state actors in the policymaking process, by which different structures create different policy logics.

Decisions about creating SWFs are long-term policy choices requiring high levels of coordination and cooperation with other policy instruments aimed at comprehensive structural transformation. The state engages in economic projects with repercussions for the investment decisions of the private sector—at least in the early stages of SWF creation. To be able to implement such choices effectively, the state needs to enjoy high levels of autonomy combined with high levels of concentration in state decision-making structures. Hence, SWFs are more likely to emerge in state-directed PNs.

Between the 1960s and 1980s, external developments (e.g., increasing international competition, inflation, and currency volatility) put pressure on socioeconomic actors in Hong Kong and Singapore. Similar issues were discussed, similar policy choices were available, and similar actors were involved in the debates, but organized differently. Various socioeconomic actors favored particular policy choices, and they were aware of alternatives.

Different PNs lead to different strategies and institutional choices. There is a systematic linkage between the type of PN and the kinds of financial institutions set up. Variation concerning types of SWFs is systematically related to variation in state-society relations. The case outcomes show variation, which runs counter to observable expectations of the dominant explanations (i.e., efficiency- and diffusion-based explanations)

Implications for Theories of Sovereign Wealth Funds

This book has drawn upon a different theory and demonstrated its contribution. It has analyzed the effects of state-society structures on the kinds of financial institutions set up in policy domains. It posed the following research question: Do differences in domestic state-society structures influence the choice and type of state finance institution, and, if so, how and why?

This book complements existing inside-out literature on SWFs by integrating socioeconomic actors, such as the finance and commerce sectors. Understanding the organizational characteristics of these actors and their access to policymaking bodies is vital to explaining within-country variation in SWF choices. A meso/sector-level focus permits a disaggregated perspective, which accounts for within-country SWF variation. In turn, within-country SWF variation also implies distributional aspects and different preferences, which can be linked back to the actors included and excluded in policymaking.

A PN analysis of SWF variation improves the understanding of how and why domestic structures influence the form and content of policy choices, which has until now remained underdeveloped in the SWF literature. Only a few studies have systematically investigated the effects of PNs on policy outcomes (e.g., Dunn and Perl 1994; Daugbjerg 1998, 1998a;

Howlett 2002; Montpetit 2005). PN structure affects policymaking and the form of finance institution implemented, via inclusion and exclusion (see fig. 8.1). The insights derived from this PN analysis allow development of more precise predictions of cross-country and within-country variation in policy outcomes. This book treats different types of SWFs as policy outcomes. In line with this conceptualization, SWFs can be seen as state strategy tools in the international political economy with roots in domestic politics. In turn, this conceptualization makes this book compatible with other inside-out studies as well as with standard SWF approaches.

This book has advanced an understanding of the role of distributional aspects of SWFs, which until now has remained underdeveloped. Understanding distributional consequences helps clarify the role of policymaking mechanisms in terms of network effects and winners and losers of particular types of SWFs. Overlooking these distributional aspects, without establishing socioeconomic actors' preferences towards particular policy choices in debates and proposals may lead scholars to underestimate the role of organizational state-society linkages. For example, in Singapore's savings domain, overlooking state-society structures could lead to the incorrect conclusion that the policy outcome of creating the GIC mirrored an underdeveloped domestic private finance sector.

A domestic politics approach focused on state-society structures offers a complementary perspective—within established analytical frames—for analyzing unexplained SWF variation across countries. Efficiency approaches would benefit from the insights of a domestic-politics perspective in two crucial ways. First, a domestic-politics perspective would assist an understanding of why similar economies confronted with similar macro challenges make different decisions about SWFs. Similarly, such an approach may help establish a greater degree of accuracy for constructivist explanations. For ideas to be influential, they must be translated into the policymaking processes. A domestic politics perspective would help to assess why ideas—the "fad" of having an SWF—have dissimilar impacts on economies within similar peer groups facing similar challenges. For political accounts of SWFs, the focus on state-society structures provides a mediating variable that shapes debates and links actors to policymaking processes regarding state finance institutions.

Where Do We Go from Here?

The insights of this book also have observable implications for capital choices in other policy domains, such as infrastructure and trade policy. While Hong Kong did not create state finance institutions in the trade

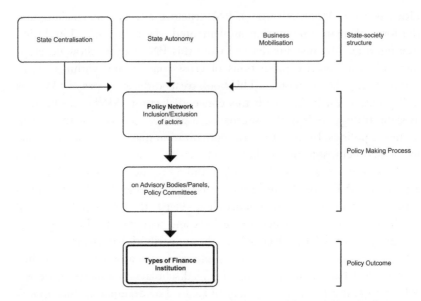

Figure 8.1. Factors shaping policy networks and types of financial institutions

domain between the 1960s and the 1980s, Singapore created the International Trading Company (INTRACO) in 1968 with the aim of marketing Singapore in overseas markets. One of INTRACO's main purposes was sourcing cheaper supplies overseas and developing Singapore's export markets. INTRACO did this partly through its holdings in companies operating in the transport/logistics sector (e.g., INTRACO Ports Pte Ltd, Transport Services Gatx Terminals Pte Ltd) and the material supply sector (e.g., Goodwin Timbers Pte Ltd and Seasonal Garments Manufacturing Co Pte Ltd) (Lee 1978).

Another area in which to develop the findings of this book would be through the monetary-policy domain, with the purpose of determining whether the meso-level insights of this thesis hold on the macro level. In strong contrast to other policy domains, both Hong Kong and Singapore[1] established similar state finance institutions in the monetary domain. In the 1970s, both Hong Kong and Singapore had long-established SWFs with stabilization mandates (i.e., the Hong Kong Exchange Fund and the Singapore Currency Fund). Hong Kong's Exchange Fund and Singapore's Currency Fund share many similar features. Both had their origins in the 1930s, a period of high currency volatility. Each of them had a liquid coin/

notes portfolio as well as an investment portfolio. Similar to the Hong Kong Exchange Fund, the majority of the liquid component of the Singapore Currency Fund was held by Crown agents as deposits in London, most notably as British treasury bills. Like the Hong Kong Exchange Fund, the Singapore Currency Fund was required to provide a 105 percent backing of its currency in order to fully guarantee convertibility into silver, and later into the British pound (Lee 1974). In Singapore, the Currency Fund was managed by the Board of Currency, while in Hong Kong it was managed by the Exchange Fund Committee. Until the late 1960s and early 1970s, both funds were also very similar in size.

Summing Up

The aim of this book was to show that formal and informal linkages are of consequence in explaining the kinds of financial institutions set up; hence, the question of whether differences in domestic state-society structures influence choice and type of SWFs, and, if so, how and why.

This final chapter takes a wider view of the empirical studies and discusses the theoretical and empirical implications of the cases. It first outlined the puzzle of different types of sovereign wealth funds in small open economies. It then presented competing explanations of the drivers of different SWF types, and introduced a policy network (PN) perspective as the adopted approach. The chapter highlights that PN analysis provides an important contribution to existing approaches to SWFs based on "efficiency" and "diffusion." Furthermore, it indicates potential avenues for integrating PN analysis with other theoretical approaches.

It has examined the creation of SWF types and their different consequences for socioeconomic actors. The major finding was systematic variance among PNs, policy processes, causal mechanisms, and policy outcomes. Out of these findings it generated hypotheses that SWFs with development mandates, as well as SWFs with savings mandates, are more likely to be created in countries with state-directed PNs. This relates to the more general hypothesis that PN structures affect the kinds of financial institutions set up, and that different institutions favor different kinds of interests. This book asserts that sovereign wealth funds should be seen as an outcome of policymaking, where actors with different preferences compete for the allocation of resources, and where the organizational characteristics of policymaking play a central role.

Afterword

Capital Choices in a Post-Covid-19 Environment

States will emerge from the Covid-19 shock as more dominant and prominent actors in markets and business.[1] At a time when the private sector is hesitant to invest, governments around the globe are stepping up at an unprecedented scale to limit economic damage from Covid-19.[2] Governments are leaving their traces in markets by initiating more rigorous investment restrictions designed to protect domestic companies from hostile foreign takeovers, and by implementing exceptional measures to stabilize domestic markets.[3] Major central banks have been resorting to unorthodox, expansionary monetary policy—even more so than during the aftermath of the 2008 global financial crisis. In a similar, novel manner, governments around the globe have started and will continue to pursue expansionary fiscal policies while running up ever-higher budget deficits. In their annual communiqué for 2020, the G20 leaders noted that, as of November 2020, "on a global scale, [G20] members injected over $11 trillion so far to safeguard the economy and protect livelihoods, secure the continuity of businesses, and protect the most vulnerable segments of the population" (G20 2020).

The visible hand of the state in markets is reflected in governments' increasing involvement in the allocation of capital via mechanisms that include sovereign wealth funds (SWFs). A key driver of government action is the concern for how to prevent liquidity problems among industries and businesses from becoming solvency problems. In light of this concern, many countries have responded by creating Covid-19 emergency funds. For example, Norway created a $5 billion fund to buy bonds issued by Norwegian companies, so as to increase liquidity in primary and secondary markets, and then to sell them as bonds mature and as the market normalizes. Other measures include deferred payments, guaranteed credit facilities, and government-backed loans. Additional government initiatives contribute state capital to fund credit platforms operated by local banks and private financial intermediaries that have sufficient capacity to assess credit risk and manage funding requests.[4] For example, Australia created in April 2020 a structured finance support fund with assets of $15 billion to assist smaller lenders, thereby helping to maintain liquidity and issue loans to consumers and small businesses during the Covid-19 pandemic (Commission 2020).

The Covid-19 shock could be one of those events for which SWFs were designed: a systemic economic shock that calls for large, patient, and stable pools of capital that can be activated for macroeconomic stabilization. A number of news agencies, notably Reuters, declared that "sovereign wealth funds are having their rainy-day moment" (Galani 2020).

Countries' SWF responses to Covid-19 have been varied, ranging from drawdowns designed to stabilize public budgets, to undertakings in the financing and development of vaccines, to corporate assistance packages. The latter effort reflects earlier instances when a number of countries used their SWFs to support key players in domestic economies.[5] The question of whether SWFs in the Middle East and Africa are engaged in a liquidation race remains unclear. News outlets, such as Reuters, point to a liquidation race—of up to $225 billion—in equities to support those regions' public finances. If that is occurring, it could ultimately lead to a depletion of the Gulf region's net financial wealth by the mid-2030s. IFSWF State Street research suggests that no large-scale liquidation has occurred (IFSWF 2020; Arnold 2020). Singapore's SWF Temasek helped to recapitalize—with $1.5 billion—Sembcorp Marine, a shipbuilding and repairing conglomerate that was hard hit by the downturn in the marine sector. Temasek also underwrote a funding package of $13 billion for Singapore Airlines due to downturns in the global airline industry (Galani 2020). Beyond corporate assistance packages, a number of governments with SWFs, such as Nigeria and Norway, have announced withdrawals from their SWFs to help their economies deal with the effects of Covid-19. Out of all SWFs, the Ireland Strategic Investment Fund made the most explicit step in addressing the corporate consequences of Covid-19 measures. Within the fund there is a sub-portfolio called the Pandemic Stabilization and Recovery Fund with a total of €2 billion in capital for helping large and medium-size companies (ISIF n.d.)

While some SWFs might disappear in a post-Covid-19 environment—as a direct consequence of fulfilling their mandates—there are also signs of increased demand for new SWFs.[6] For example, economists from the Asian Development Bank's research unit promote the idea of creating remittance stabilization funds for lower- and middle-income economies that rely to a significant extent on remittance inflows (Lanzafame and Qureshi 2020).[7] Remittances refer to personal funding flows from expatriates to their friends and families back home. Around 247 million people, or 3.4 percent of the world's population, according to the latest World Bank figures, live in a different country from that of their birth. Historically, remittances have remained stable and even countercyclical during economic downturns, but their exposure during the Covid-19 pandemic raises great concerns for countries that have relied on them to shield against fluctuations in foreign direct investments. Global remittances were projected to decline by approximately 20 percent to US$445 billion in 2020 due to Covid-19 (World Bank n.d.). This is the sharpest decline in recent history.

New forms of SWFs have frequently emerged out of policy responses that were shaped and informed by economic shocks. For example, the oil shocks in the 1970s led to the first waves of SWF creation among oil-exporting economies in the Middle East. To insulate their capacity-constrained domestic economies from the negative externalities of the so-called resource curse, capital was gathered into investment pools. These pools channeled surplus funds into the well-established financial markets of developed economies in order to avoid the Dutch Disease. (The concept of Dutch Disease was described in Chapter 2, titled "Global Review.") In a similar fashion, the Asian Financial Crisis (AFC) in 1997–1998 revealed the risks of volatile, short-term capital flows of "hot money," and led to "profound changes in the demand for international reserves" and the wider introduction of SWFs throughout Asia (Aizenman and Lee 2007, 192). The hoarding of international reserves and the subsequent creation of SWFs after the AFC was particularly driven by a realization among Asian governments that self-insurance in the form of large reserve buffers was preferable to IMF conditionality and the associated loss of sovereignty (Higgott 1998).

Reflecting earlier examples of SWF creation, government responses to Covid-19 have led to new types of state-owned equity funds with expiration dates: expiry date funds (EDFs). In contrast to traditional SWF structures, EDFs are temporary agencies. Unlike traditional SWFs, which usually recycle excess reserves from natural resources or noncommodity revenues (i.e., balance-of-trade or budget surpluses), the capitalization sources of

EDFs relate to state budgets, state guarantees, national development banks, and legislation that creates special-purpose vehicles with credit authorization. By mid-2020, governments around the globe—France, Germany, Italy, Poland, Argentina, Colombia, and the Philippines—had announced the creation of EDFs (BakerMcKenzie 2020). Some of these funds, notably Germany's Economic Stabilization Fund, are comparable in size with the world's largest SWFs, such as the Abu Dhabi Investment Authority or the Kuwait Investment Authority.[8] That said, the majority of these new funds are smaller—between $1 billion and $20 billion—making them comparable with the Vietnam Investment Corporation or Chile's Stabilization Fund.[9]

The idea behind EDFs was to translate state aid into equity that could then be allocated into a portfolio under a SWF-type vehicle. Then, in times after the pandemic, governments could start selling back the stakes to the private sector. Many debt and equity investments were directed into sectors such as the automotive, energy, or aviation industries. These sectors will face increasing pressure in the future due to structural and policy-induced changes (e.g., decarbonization efforts to reduce climate change). Another idea behind these new funds was to intervene against the risk of international hostile takeovers or asset sales of national companies at depressed valuations during an economic crisis, which might add to further downward pressures in national equity markets. The funds' expiry dates ensure the eventual transfer of equity stakes to private ownership, either structured or unstructured. Expiry dates ranging between two and five years for state guarantees and funds, and the inclusion of clauses that emphasize the divestment process, should be in line with market conditions. Through recapitalization, the funds' assets grow during periods when capital injection is needed. The funds shrink during periods of economic recovery. The idea behind EDFs is to permit the use of market mechanisms to preserve public interest while contributing to economic recuperation.

However, the idea of having a state fund that acquires shares and silent partnerships, or that takes over other components of companies in a situation of economic distress, is not entirely new. For example, Hong Kong's Monetary Authority used its large foreign exchange reserves during the Asian Financial Crisis of 1997 to 1998 to sustain the fixed exchange rate. To avoid a complete collapse of the Hong Kong stock market between 1997 and 1998, when the Hang Seng Index of stock prices fell by around 50 percent, the Hong Kong Monetary Authority used the Exchange Fund to acquire substantial parts of Hong Kong's equity market. Between mid- and late August 1998, the Hong Kong Exchange Fund acquired around US$15 billion worth of blue-chip stocks.[10] Subsequently, the Hong Kong government opted for an unorthodox disposal strategy with an aim of minimizing market disruption. The key mechanism in the disposal strategy of the acquired shares was the Tracker Fund of Hong Kong, an exchange traded fund (ETF) created in 1999 (Hong Kong Monetary Authority 2009). The Tracker Fund of Hong Kong's initial public offering, with a size of approximately US$4.3 billion, was the largest IPO ever in Asia, excluding Japan, at the time of the launch. By 2002, Hong Kong's Hang Seng Index of constituent stocks had been returned to the market (TRAHK n.d.). Moreover, Hong Kong's emergency scheme later turned out to be the midwife for the Asian ETF sector by encouraging investment in unit trusts (TRAHK n.d.).

Beyond Hong Kong's 1990s experience, another example, from the early 1930s, offers additional salient parallels. In the wake of the Great Depression, the Italian state created, in 1933, a public financial holding company, the Instituto per la Ricostruzione Industriale (IRI). Initially, the IRI was set up as a temporary agency to allow the state to intervene during an economic shock without jeopardizing free market competition. The IRI became the majority shareholder of companies in the telecommunications, steel, shipping, engineering, and energy industries, thereby becoming the owner of Italy's biggest industrial complex. It eventually owned 21.5 percent of Italian joint stock company shares (Saraceno 1955; Skidelsky 2020). However, soon after the creation of the IRI, it became clear that its liquidation would be difficult, partly because of its enormous size and the limited absorption capacity of the Italian capital market (Saraceno 1955). Over the next five decades the scale and scope of the IRI expanded to include not only motorways, telephone networks, the national airline carrier Alitalia, but also aerospace, microelectronics, complex systems engineering, telecommunication technologies, marketing, and food and beverage sectors (Megginson and Scannapieco 2006; Skidelsky 2020). However, by the early 1990s the IRI's losses and inefficiencies worsened—losses rose to 4.2 trillion Italian lire (about 0.3 percent of GDP) and consolidated debt reached 72 trillion Italian lire (around 4.5 percent of GDP)—owing to its noneconomic goals and heavy investments in declining sectors (Karantounias and Pinelli 2016). While the Hong Kong experiment with an EDF, following the rescue of Hang Seng Index companies, was a successful case of EDFs, Italy's IRI highlights the propensity for permanent institutionalization of EDFs and their long-term risks.

The recent emergence of new state fund structures in the form of EDFs together with anecdotal historical evidence affirms the need for further studies on the impact of state-society relations on capital choices, and the wider implications thereof. As highlighted in previous chapters, the creation of state fund structures relates to choices concerning the accumulation and allocation of resources. Cross-national and cross-sectoral differences in government responses and capital choices related to Covid-19 allow for further analysis of the impact of state-society relations. Beyond that, the creation of new fund structures, which are capitalized with budgetary sources, raises the question: Do rising government deficits reduce or "crowd out" private investments?[11]

The rapidity and deep socioeconomic impact of the Covid-19 crisis have starkly highlighted the severity of impacts of global shocks that result in market breakdowns and failures. Under such conditions, capital choices by governments become more focused, but also more urgent, placing a premium on adaptability and innovation. To the extent that state fund structures, such as expiry date funds, are effective in stabilizing the effects of severe economic shocks while avoiding externalities, such as crowding out, they will be an important addition to government toolkits in confronting future shocks.

REFERENCES

Aizenman, Joshua, and Jaewoo Lee. 2007. "International reserves: precautionary versus mercantilist views, theory and evidence." *Open Economies Review* 18, no. 2: 191–214.

Arabian Business. 2017. "Qatar Wealth Fund ais to inject dollar deposits in local banks". June 20. https://www.arabianbusiness.com/qatar-wealth-fund-said-inje ct-dollar-deposits-in-local-banks-678263.html

Arnold, Tom. 2020. "Oil-Rich Wealth Funds Seen Shedding Up to $225 Billion in Stocks." *Reuters*, 29 March. https://www.reuters.com/article/us-health-coronav irus-swf-analysis-idUSKBN21G05K

BakerMcKenzie. 2020. "COVID-19: Government Intervention Schemes Guide | Insight | Baker McKenzie." Accessed 4 January 2021. https://www.bakermck enzie.com/en/insight/publications/2020/03/covid19-government-intervention -schemes

Bortolotti, Bernardo, and Veljko Fotak. 2020. "Sovereign Wealth Funds and the COVID-19 Shock: Economic and Financial Resilience in Resource-Rich Countries." SSRN Scholarly Paper ID 3665993. Rochester, NY: Social Science Research Network. https://doi.org/10.2139/ssrn.3665993

Braunstein, Juergen. 2017. "Understanding the Politics of Bailout Policies in Non-Western Countries: The Use of Sovereign Wealth Funds." *Journal of Economic Policy Reform* 20, no. 6: 46–63. https://doi.org/10.1080/17487870.2016.12477 05

Braunstein, Juergen, and Asim Ali. 2019. "New Frontiers in Sovereign Wealth Fund Capitalization." In *Development in Turbulent Times: The Many Faces of Inequality within Europe*, edited by Paul Debrescu. Cham: Springer International Publishing.

CDP. n.d. "Liquidità Covid-19 | CDP." Accessed 12 December 2020. https://www.cdp.it/sitointernet/en/liquidita_covid_19.page

Commission, Australian Competition and Consumer. 2020. "Co-operation on Funding to Aid Smaller Lenders during COVID-19." Accessed 7 April 2021. https://www.accc.gov.au/media-release/co-operation-on-funding-to-aid-smaller-lenders-during-covid-19

Cutler, David M., and Lawrence H. Summers. 2020. "The COVID-19 Pandemic and the $16 Trillion Virus." *JAMA* 324, no. 15: 1495. https://doi.org/10.1001/jama.2020.19759

Galani, Una. 2020. "Breakingviews—Sovereign Funds Are Having Their Rainy-Day Moment." *Reuters*, 23 June. https://www.reuters.com/article/us-sovereign-wealthfund-economy-breaking-idUSKBN23U0DN

G20. 2020. "G20 Leaders Unite to Enhance Pandemic Preparedness." 22 November. https://g20.org/en/media/Documents/G20%20Leaders%20Unite%20To%20Enhance%20Pandemic%20Preparedness_EN.pdf

Higgott, Richard. 1998. "The Asian Economic Crisis: A Study in the Politics of Resentment." *New Political Economy* 3 (3): 333–56. https://doi.org/10.1080/13563469808406364.

Hong Kong Monetary Authority. 2009. "Hong Kong Monetary Authority—10th Anniversary of Listing of TraHK." 12 November 2020. //www.hkma.gov.hk/eng/news-and-media/insight/2009/11/20091112/

IFSWF. 2020. "Sovereign Wealth Funds and Institutional Investors Maintain Exposure to Risk Assets in the Face of Covid-19 | International Forum of Sovereign Wealth Funds." 14 May. https://www.ifswf.org/general-news/sovereign-wealth-funds-and-institutional-investors-maintain-exposure-risk-assets-face

IMF. 2020. "Policy Responses to COVID19." Accessed 15 November 2020. https://www.imf.org/en/Topics/imf-and-covid19/Policy-Responses-to-COVID-19

ISIF. n.d. "Pandemic Stabilisation and Recovery Fund." Ireland Strategic Investment Fund. Accessed 20 January 2021. http://isif.ie/

Karantounias, Vassilis, and Dino Pinelli. 2016. "Local State-Owned Enterprises in Italy: Inefficiencies and Ways Forward." Economic Brief 010. Brussels: European Commission.

K&L Gates Hub. 2020. "COVID-19: Measures under the Economic Stabilization Fund Act and the Law on the BayernFonds to Mitigate the Economic Consequences of the COVID-19 Pandemic." 28 April. https://www.klgates.com/covid-19-measures-under-the-economic-stabilization-fund-act-04-28-2020

Lanzafame, Matteo, and Irfan A. Qureshi. 2020. "Protecting the Remittance Lifeline from COVID-19's Economic Fallout." Asian Development Bank. 24 August. Accessed 14 December 2020. https://blogs.adb.org/blog/protecting-remittance-lifeline-covid-19-s-economic-fallout

Megginson, William L., and Dario Scannapieco. 2006. "The Financial and Economic Lessons of Italy's Privatization Program." *Journal of Applied Corporate Finance* 18, no. 3: 56–65. https://doi.org/10.1111/j.1745–6622.2006.00098.x

PFR. 2020. "Polski Fundusz Rozwoju (Grupa PFR)—Inwestycje Dla Polski." 2020. Accessed 04 January 2021. https://pfr.pl/

Rodrik, Dani. 2020. "Making the Best of a Post-pandemic World." Project Syndicate, 12 May. https://www.project-syndicate.org/commentary/three-trends-sha ping-post-pandemic-global-economy-by-dani-rodrik-2020–05

Saraceno, Pasquale. 1955. "IRI: Its Origin and Its Position in the Italian Industrial Economy (1933–1953)." *The Journal of Industrial Economics* 3, no. 3: 197–221.

Schena, Patrick J., Juergen Braunstein, and Asim Ali. 2018. "The Case for Economic Development through Sovereign Investment: A Paradox of Scarcity?" *Global Policy* 9, no. 3: 365–76. https://doi.org/10.1111/1758–5899.12549

Skidelsky, Robert. 2020. "The Crowding-Out Myth." Project Syndicate, 24 August. http://www.project.syndicate.org/commentary/public-investment-private-capi tal-crowding-out-myth-by-robert-skidelsky-2020–08

Thomson Reuters. 2009. "Kuwait Sovereign Fund takes Stake in Gulf Bank". 26 January. https://www.reuters.com/article/gulfbank-kiaidUKLNE50P0622009 0126?edition-redirect=uk

TRAHK. n.d. "History of the Fund—the Tracker Fund of Hong Kong (SEHK: 2800)." Accessed 25 December 2020. https://www.trahk.com.hk/eng/Fund/hi storyFund

World Bank. n.d. "World Bank Predicts Sharpest Decline of Remittances in Recent History." World Bank. Accessed 26 December 2020. https://www.worldbank .org/en/news/press-release/2020/04/22/world-bank-predicts-sharpest-decline -of-remittances-in-recent-history

Appendix 1

Relationship between SWF Type and Funding Sources

In order to test the relationship between SWF type and funding source we use information on the fifty-six SWFs listed in the SWF Institute ranking from thirty-six countries across the globe, including the United States, China, the United Arab Emirates, Russia, Singapore, and Mexico, to mention a few. The relationship between the main types and funding sources of SWFs was estimated with help of multinomial logistic regression analysis using SPSS statistical software. Based on the model fitting information in table 1, the sigma value of 0.005 is less than the p-value of 0.05 (at 5 percent significance level), thus, the model fits the data significantly better than the null model. Proceeding with the interpretation of parameter estimates, the four funding sources (i.e., fiscal, financial, commodity, and foreign exchange) were set as predictor variables, while three main types of SWFs were chosen as dependent ones. The stabilization fund type was set as a reference category. Tables A1 and A2 below illustrates the relationship between SWF types as a function of the funding sources. The results from multinomial regression analysis revealed:

- For the savings fund relative to the stabilization fund, the regression coefficient for commodity has not been found to be statistically different from zero given that fiscal, financial, and forex are in the model. The same conclusion applies to other sources of funding for savings relative to stabilization funds.

- In contrast, for the development SWF relative to the stabilization SWF, the regression coefficient for commodity and fiscal funding sources have been found to be statistically significant, given that other predictors are in the model.
- An odds ratio > 1 indicates that the risk of the outcome falling in the development fund group relative to the risk of the outcome falling in the referent group (stabilization fund) increases as the commodity and fiscal variable increases. Thus, the outcome is more likely to be in the development fund group.

TABLE A1 Model fitting information and parameter estimates

	Model fitting criteria	Likelihood ratio tests		
Model	–2 Log Likelihood	Chi-Square	df	Sig.
Intercept Only	33.871			
Final	15.099	18.772	6	.005

Source: SPSS output.

TABLE A2

Type[a]		B	Std. Error	Wald	df	Sig.	Exp(B)	95% Confidence Interval for Exp(B)	
								Lower Bound	Upper Bound
Saving	Intercept	-1.099	1.155	.905	1	.341			
	Commodity	1.424	1.211	1.383	1	.240	4.154	.387	44.566
	Fiscal	2.197	1.633	1.810	1	.178	9.000	.367	220.927
	Financial	19.863	11875.381	.000	1	.999	4.231E8	.000	.[b]
	Forex reserves	0[c]	.	.	0	.	.	.	.
Development	Intercept	-19.562	1.054	344.392	1	.000			
	Commodity	*18.788*	*1.164*	*260.578*	*1*	*.000*	*1.445E8*	*14756821.139*	*1.414E9*
	Fiscal	*21.759*	*.000*	*.*	*1*	*.*	*2.817E9*	*2.817E9*	*2.817E9*
	Financial	38.326	11875.381	.000	1	.997	4.414E16	.000	.[b]
	Forex reserves	0[c]	.	.	0	.	.	.	.

[a]The reference category is: Stabilization.
[b]Floating point overflow occurred while computing this statistic. Its value is therefore set to system missing.
[c]This parameter is set to zero because it is redundant.
Source: SPSS output.

Notes

CHAPTER 1

1. According to Harvard Professor Lawrence Summers (2007) "[t]he logic of the capitalist system depends on shareholders causing companies to act so as to maximi[z]e the value of their shares." Yet, the state as a shareholder might may not necessarily be motivated by share value maximization of companies but by strategic means, such as extracting technologies (e.g., see Bremmer 2009; Summers 2007).

2. For a detailed overview of these controversies, see Hufbauer, Wong, and Sheth (2006).

3. Within the SWF literature it is widely agreed that SWFs have been in existence at least since the 1950s.

4. For an overview of different SWF characteristics, see Truman (2008, 2010a), the IMF (2008), Gilson and Milhaupt (2008), Aizenman and Glick (2008), and Beck and Fidora (2008).

5. According to some estimates, by 2015 the size of global SWFs could reach a volume of between $12 trillion to $14.4 trillion (Jen 2007; Aizenman and Glick 2008; Lyons 2007).

6. E.g., for case studies, see Helleiner (2009), Yi-Chong and Bahgat (2010), Bazoobandi (2013); for regression analysis and modeling, see Aizenman and Glick (2008), Chwieroth (2014), and Wang and Li (2016).

7. E.g., see Pekkanen and Tsai (2011) and Clark, Dixon, and Monk (2013).

8. The general resurgence of state finance institutions refers to the recent creation of the Asian Infrastructure Investment Bank in January 2016, and the rise in bilateral state investment funds and sector-specific development funds.

CHAPTER 2

1. For example, see Bortolotti et al. 2009; Barbary et al. 2010; Rose 2012; Lopez 2015; Aguilera et al. 2016; Hussein 2019.

2. For an overview of the different definitions and conceptions of SWFs, see Braunstein (2013).

3. Examples of SWFs with savings mandates include the Australian Future Fund, the Kuwait Investment Authority, the Abu Dhabi Investment Corporation, the New Zealand Superannuation Fund (see Orr 2017), and the Government Investment Corporation Singapore.

4. It should be mentioned that some public pension funds, notably the California Public Employees' Retirement System, take more active investment approaches by investing internationally into various asset classes, such as public equity and real estate. This let them make look similar to SWFs with savings mandates (see annual ESADEgeo reports and Sovereign Wealth Fund Institute 2015).

5. Examples of SWFs with development/diversification mandates include Mumtalakat (Bahrain), Mubadala (Abu Dhabi), Temasek (Singapore), the China Investment Corporation, Khazanna Nasional (Malaysia), and the Vietnam State Investment Corporation.

6. Other examples not mentioned include the International Petroleum Investment Corporation, the Abu Dhabi Investment Corporation, and Qatar Diar (see Behrendt 2008).

7. Examples for SWFs with stabilization mandates include the Hong Kong Monetary Authority, the Monetary Authority of Singapore, the Stabilisation Fund Portfolio Trinidad, the Revenue Equalisation Fund (Kiribati), the Petroleum Fund (Timor Leste), and the Economic Stabilisation Fund (Chile).

8. Academics, such as Gilson and Milhaupt (2008), as well as international organizations, notably the IMF (2008), have followed these classifications.

9. See the appendix for the model and data on the relationship between SWF type and funding sources.

10. It should be noted that Saudi Arabia, with its Public Investment Fund, has an SWF that has been in existence for a while.

11. E.g., see Herb (2016) on the implications of lack in transparency among Asian SWFs.

CHAPTER 3

1. However, the distinction between the two approaches is not always clearly made. Authors, such as Pekannen and Tsai (2011), are vague in terms of whether they are interested in SWF behavior or SWF creation.

2. See Fortescue (2010), Liew and He (2012), Shih (2009), and Lee (2010).

3. Allison's seminal book *Essence of Decision* (1971) looks at the processes and characteristics of government organizations and policy outcomes.

CHAPTER 4

1. While in 1967 there were an estimated 42,000 local civilians employed in the British Armed Forces, this decreased to 32,000 in 1968, and dropped to 19,000 in 1970 (Seng and Yah 1971, 29).

2. Another reason for the increase in wages was Singapore's high wage policy (see Low 2005). Drawing on the US Bureau of Statistics Survey, Chiu, Ho, and Lui

(1997, 83) calculate that the hourly labor cost was higher in Singapore (i.e., $2.67) than in other countries, notably South Korea ($2.46). According to an expert on Singapore and former deputy CEO of the Hong Kong Monetary Authority, wage increases hit particularly small and medium enterprises in Singapore and not so much MNCs. MNCs were mostly in the high value added business so they don't mind the high wage (anonymous, personal communication, 30 October 2013).

3. However, the government provided basic infrastructure, including drainage network, sanitation, roads, public housing, education, health services, and provision of some public goods; it also exercised control over franchised public utilities, especially after Governor Murray Maclehose's arrival.

4. Between the 1960s and the 1980s, the Hong Kong and Shanghai Banking Corporation was commonly referred to as the Hong Kong Bank.

5. In the year 1965 a new Banking Ordinance required banks to publish statistics on their loans.

6. However, there are some exceptions, notably Goodstadt 2005, 2007.

7. A statutory board refers to a government economic institution that is established by an act of parliament and is charged with a specific task (Krause et al. 1987, 113).

8. Major statutory boards established in this period included the Jurong Town Corporation (established 1968), the National Productivity Board (1972), the Sentosa Development Corporation (1972), the Singapore Institute for Standards and Industrial Research (1973), the Telecommunication Authority of Singapore (1974), the Urban Redevelopment Authority (1974), the Vocational and Industrial Training Board (1979), the International Enterprise Institute (1983), and the Construction Industry Development Board (1984).

9. Until the late 1990s Temasek invested primarily in domestic equity.

10. The creation of the CMA in 1934 was an outcome of Hong Kong's manufacturers' attempts to organize themselves in a context of import tariffs imposed by China on Hong Kong products (Ngo 1996, 78).

11. But according to O'Rear there have been very few industrial members of the HKGCC (David O'Rear, personal communication, 23 October 2013).

12. Mahjong is a traditional Chinese board game.

13. The organizational density ratio varies across subsector organizations ranging from 0.02 (this means that two out of 100 potential members are members in an association) to 0.80 (i.e., eighty out of 100 potential members are actual members in a particular association). Although there is a broad range, most of the business associations in Singapore have had a low-density ratio (see Braunstein 2015, 75–76).

14. An observer's testimony that "[w]hile many successful Chinese entrepreneurs today may well continue to subscribe to the SCCCI, this may be no more than a symbolic and atavistic ritual, while they may simultaneously be far more active and functional in other bodies, such as the Singapore Manufacturing Association" indicates increasing levels of competition for members between the SCCCI and the SMA (*Business Times*, 20 January 1978, 6).

15. The Ministry of Finance called for a single Chamber of Commerce to be formed in order to represent Singapore's business community regionally and internationally. Furthermore, the minister of finance urged the private sector to present

itself more coherently to the Singaporean government (*Straits Times*, 6 June 1976, 6). The SFCCI replaced the former Joint Standing Committee of Commerce and Industry, which had been an informal body of Singapore's four Chambers.

16. Internally the SMA was organized along product groups, such as food, drugs, drinks, tobacco, wood, paper and printing, chemicals and oil, metals and engineering, and electronics. Each of these groups was headed by a chairman, and the problems of each group were presented to the SMA committee, which then carried out studies and presented them to the authorities (*Business Times*, 3 February 1978, 6). The SMA also employed full-time staff for data collection (SMA 2012, 11). The SMA collected statistics and information concerning trade, manufacturing and industry, and it organized trade exhibitions and trade missions (S. Y. Lee 1976; SMA 2012).

17. Goodstadt highlights that there is one important exception, namely the annual budget (Leo Goodstadt, personal communication, 12 February 2015).

18. Until 1979, when the Ministry of Trade and Industry was created, the Ministry of Finance had combined responsibilities of the treasury and economic development (Chew and Kwa 2012).

19. Lim and Pang's statement that "[t]he ruling party, in power since 1959, wields complete political power, through its exclusive representation in parliament, and its de facto control of the government bureaucracy, the labour movement (through the National Trades Union Congress) and local community organisations (through the People's Association)" highlights the PAP's dominance in Singapore (Lim and Pang 1986, 15).

20. These also included representatives from the judiciary, paramilitary, big business organizations, the bureaucracy, and academics (Ho Khai Leong 2000, 32).

21. Tan Jake Hooi's statement that "[t]here is no local government authority in Singapore, and all activities of government are carried out by centralized government departments and Statutory Boards" highlights the high levels of concentration in decision making (Tan Jake, Hooi 1972, 2).

22. Ho Khai Leong's statement that "[permanent secretaries] carry very heavy responsibilities in determining almost completely all administrative, professional, technical and service policies, and to carry them out in the most efficient manner; they are also responsible for reviewing the organisation, function and activities of the ministry concerned and have ultimate discretion on policy implementation" highlights the central position of permanent secretaries in Singapore (Ho Khai Leong 2000, 166).

23. Chen's quote that "[c]onsequently, the Government can usually achieve a high level of efficiency and effectiveness in planning and implementing projects and activities for national development" indicates a link between high levels of autonomy and smooth policy implementation (Chen 1976, 79).

24. For example, a Hong Kong industrialist's statement that "[i]t should be pointed out that not all factories are members of the CMA, and therefore it is not fair to penalise our entire industry on account of the CMA's failure to supply information" highlights industrialists' critique vis-à-vis the CMA (*Star*, 20 January 1968).

25. Singapore's economy had a large exposure to the global oil shocks of the 1970s (Nyaw 1991, 201–2).

26. Companies included Sembawang Holdings, National Engineering Services, International Development and Construction, Singmanex, Singapore General Aviation Service, Neptune Oriental Lines, the Development Bank of Singapore, Singapore Airlines, and Jurong Bird Parks (*Straits Times*, 16 February 1977).

27. The number of employees refers to the people employed by the firms that are controlled by Temasek. Initially, in 1974, Temasek was set up to hold S$345 million equity invested in thirty-six government-linked companies (*Straits Times*, 25 June 1999, 74).

28. Sheng-Li Holding was established in the same year as Temasek in order to reorganize the twelve defense and strategic sector companies, such as Chartered Industries of Singapore and Chartered Ammunition Industries, and to coordinate the rapid growth in Singapore's defense industry in an environment of increasing international competition (*Straits Times*, 20 April 1989, 27). At the beginning, Sheng-Li Holding's investment focus was primarily concentrated on the technology and defense sector. Shortly after the creation of Temasek, in 1976 the Ministry of Development delegated its equity stakes to MND Holding. It transferred government-linked companies in the infrastructure and housing sectors, such as the Resources and Development Corporation and the Housing and Urban Development Company, to MND Holding. Its official mandate was to make direct investments in companies in order to develop domestic infrastructure.

29. In 1974 the Ministry of Finance transferred its entire equity portfolio to the newly created Temasek. It transferred its equity stakes from government-linked companies, such as Singapore Airlines, Sembawang Holdings, National Engineering Services, International Development and Construction, Singmanex, Singapore General Aviation Service, Neptune Oriental Lines, the Development Bank of Singapore, and Jurong Bird Park to Temasek (*Straits Times*, 16 February 1977).

30. In the early 1960s, Albert Winsemius and I. F. Tang were dispatched from the United Nations to lead the UN mission for Singapore's industrial development. Soon after the UN report was completed in 1961, I. F. Tang became a high-level civil servant in Singapore, and Winsemius became an independent economic advisor to Singapore's government (Ngiam and Tay 2006). From the 1960s onward Winsemius spent between two and three weeks in Singapore every year advising key civil servants, such as Ngiam Tong Dow, on economic development and institutional policy (Ngiam and Tay 2006). Most of these civil servants later occupied central roles in the Ministry of Finance and Temasek as well as its key enterprises, such as the DBS.

31. They included J. Y. Pillay, at that time an official at the Ministry of Finance and later permanent secretary at the Ministry of Finance and founding chairman of Temasek; Heng Hong Ngoh, administrative officer; Hon Sui Sen, at that time a senior civil servant and first EDB chairman and later finance minister and chairman of DBS; Ngiam Tong Dow, at that time a civil servant who later served as permanent secretary in the PMO and in the Ministry of Finance and chairman of DBS, EDB, and SingTechnologies (former Sheng-Li Holding); and S. Dhanabalan, at that time assistant secretary at the Ministry of Finance, who became later CEO of a firm owned by Temasek and CEO of Temasek (Ngiam and Tay 2006). All these people have played a central role in the design and implementation of institutional policy. For example, Dhanabalan, who was at this time Finance Minister Goh's

assistant, prepared a draft on the EDB for the Cabinet for approval for the initial S$100 million funding (Schein 1996, 38). EDB's first chairman, Hon Sui Sen, was sent to the World Bank for six months' training (Schein 1996).

32. Prasad—the former director of the Budget Division in the Ministry of Finance—remembers a story concerning the name of Temasek. According to Prasad, a number of names, such as Colossal Holding and Singlaboran Holdings (Singapore Safeharbor in Malay) were suggested. Finally, Pillay highlighted that Temasek Holding should be elegant enough (Ajith Prasad, personal communication, 21 March 2014).

33. In an interview, Albert Winsemius—head of the UN delegation in Singapore—said: "Generally speaking, the members of the Chinese Chamber of Commerce have almost always been against the threat of foreign enterprise. It's our island, it's our island. We will never give in to that. But the medical doctors and the lawyers also took this stand" (Winsemius 1982d, 23–24).

34. The EDB's focus was on MNCs rather than on domestic enterprises. The pioneer status legislation, including concessionary tax rates and economic expansion incentives, were specifically addressed for large exporting firms (i.e., MNCs). Frederic Deyo's statement that "[w]hile government industrial policy has not explicitly favored foreign firms over local investors, it has nevertheless had this effect" draws attention to the structural bias in favor of MNCs (Deyo 1981, 65). For example, until the 1980s promotional activities for local enterprises in the EDB (i.e., the local industries desk) were carried out by only one person (Deyo 1981, 65).

35. Kunio Yoshihara's statement that "domestic entrepreneurs were unknown outside Singapore and foreign companies preferred the government as their partner, the government may have got involved in their ventures" indicates that MNCs had a preference for cooperating directly with the state (Yoshihara 1975, 162). Singapore's government took equity positions in foreign companies, and there were joint ventures between later SWF subsidiaries and foreign companies, such as Jurong Shipyard's joint venture with Japan's Ishikawajima Harima Heavy Industries (Yoshihara 1975). Singapore's government "accounted for nine per cent of the paid-up capital of the foreign-controlled companies (Yoshihara 1975, 161).

36. Small manufacturers have usually operated from rented premises, and as such they were lacking in collateral. As a consequence, banks were not keen on lending to them, because of the lack of guarantees (Drake 1969). In Singapore half of bank credit went to commerce, export/import businesses, as well as to the rubber industry, whereas only a small proportion went to manufacturers (Drake 1969). Small-scale domestic business and construction relied on local banks for credit. A large number of local banks catered specifically to particular dialect groups, including the Chinese Commercial Bank (Hokkien), the Ho Hong Bank (Hokkien), the Lee Wah Bank (Cantonese), and the Sze Hai Tong Bank (Teochews) (Drake 1969).

37. For an overview of Temasek's subsidiaries and related enterprises, see the *Directory of Subsidiaries and Related Companies of Temasek Holdings (Pte) Ltd, Sheng-Li Holdings Co Pte Ltd, and MND Holdings (Pte) Ltd* (Temasek 1982).

38. For an in-depth view of this debate, see Koh (1987a, 1987b) and Lee Tsao and Low (1990).

39. The Economic Committee had eight subcommittees (*Business Times*, 19

December 1985). The Business Enterprise Committee was chaired by the parliamentary secretary and its members included the head of the civil service, the permanent secretary of Home Affairs, the permanent secretary of environment, the permanent secretary of National Development, the director of the Revenue Division, the director of the Management Service Department, the director of planning from the Ministry of National Development, and the director of the Ministry of Trade and Industry (*Business Times*, 19 December 1985). Further committees included the Local Business Subcommittee (*Straits Times*, 31 December 1985) and the Entrepreneurship Subcommittee (*Straits Times*, 24 December 1985). The Manufacturing Subcommittee was chaired by the chairman of Hewlett Packard, General Electrics, National Iron and Steel Mills, Sembawang (MNCs and GLCs) (*Straits Times*, 19 December 1985). The Services Subcommittee was further subdivided into eighteen working groups.

40. The subcommittee was also concerned with Sheng-Li Holding and MND Holding.

41. An international financial expert's statement that "[t]hese foreign companies could set up here and subsequently float the company on the Singapore stock market, thereby allowing Singaporeans to buy- into them, and eventually move overseas from here" highlights the need for a well-established stock exchange (*Straits Times*, 6 September 1986, 21).

42. It also included officials from Sheng-Li Holding and MND Holding, which were already part, or became later part, of Temasek.

43. The similar was the case for Sheng-Li Holding.

44. These included the Resources and Development Corporation, the Housing and Urban Development Company, the Development and Construction Pte Ltd., the Primary Industries Enterprise Pte Ltd, the Construction Technology Pte Ltd., the International Development and Consultancy Corporation Pte Ltd., the Urban Development and Management Co Pte Ltd. (see *Straits Times*, 20 April 1989, 27; 5 December 1986, 33; 15 January 1980, 11).

45. Prasad's statement that "MND holding is largely a shell company, to get around legal hurdles" highlights the strategy behind the decision to retain MND Holding (Ajith Prasad, personal communication, 21 March 2014).

46. As in the case of Singapore Technologies, some of the equity stakes of MND Holding were already integrated into the portfolio of Temasek in 1984.

CHAPTER 5

1. This chapter draws on Braunstein 2017b. Gross domestic savings are calculated as GDP less final consumption expenditure (total consumption).

2. In absolute numbers, $71 billion in 1980.

3. In absolute numbers, nearly $8 trillion in 2015.

4. Total reserves comprise holdings of monetary gold, special drawing rights, reserves of IMF members held by the IMF, and holdings of foreign exchange under the control of monetary authorities.

5. This estimation was made in 1986, based on the following calculation: given 2,600,000 people in the local labor force, a 5 percent contribution, and an average

worker income of HK$3,000 per month, each year would mean an accumulation of between HK$8,000 and 9,000 million net (excluding interest earned) (Hong Kong Hansard, 5 November 1986, 327).

6. Calculated with data from Hong Kong Hansard, 5 November 1986, 327; FedPrimeRate 2015.

7. Some public pension fund schemes, such as the California Public Employees' Retirement System, invest part of their assets abroad. If CPFs manage their assets actively in international assets, then they are very similar, apart from their liability structure, to SWFs with a savings mandate.

8. This had the important effect of mitigating inflation pressures (see Low 2005).

9. According to Chow, assistance schemes in Hong Kong were only for the very poor and it was only a very small amount of money. There was nothing in place for those who retire, unless they were very old (i.e., seventy years and above) (Nelson Chow, personal communication, 17 February 2015).

10. The risk referred to high levels of volatility in Hong Kong's domestic market (i.e., reoccurring speculation and domestic banking crises).

11. As such, the Hong Kong government already had experience (though on a very small scale) of state finance institutions with a mandate of investing domestic savings abroad (see Li 1988). However, it only covered teachers (Li 1988). Every teacher had to contribute 5 percent of his or her salary to the Subsidized Schools Provident Fund, which was managed by government officials under the Education Department (see EDB Hong Kong 2012).

12. It was then in 1985 when Singapore went into its first severe recession, partly because of its high mandatory CPF contribution rates (up to 50 percent of income).

13. The notion of "hongs" refers to large business houses, such as Swire, Jardine Matheson, Butterfield and Swire, Dent & Co, and Wheelock Marden.

14. The saving domain relates to the policy domain, which is concerned with the allocation of public and private savings.

15. Lim and Pang's statement that "[f]rom the 1950s through the early 1960s, Singapore was characterized by a politically active and radical, confrontationist labour movement with left-wing leadership" indicates the existence of an active labor movement before the mid-1960s (Lim and Pang 1986, 20).

16. These considerations took place in a context of rumors that the MAS had lost millions in currency transactions caused by a dive in the Deutschmark (*Straits Times*, 13 March 1981). DPM Goh Keng Swee was reportedly not happy with how reserves were managed in Singapore (*The Straits Times*, 13 March 1981).

17. PM Lee Kuan Yew was paraphrased by the *Straits Times* on 6 October 2007: "In the 1960s and 1970s [b]ecause of inflation, a share could be bought, and it could drop in value, and the dividends of 5 percent, 5.5 percent were not equal to the inflation that was taking place. So we were losing money. And that was when Dr Goh Keng Swee came to see me and said, 'We can't leave this just alone to the Minister of Finance. He's got so many other duties. We need a body that would just study asset transfers, different assets, stocks, bonds, properties, equities, commodities, steel, corn, whatever, and preserve our core value,' because at that time inflation was raging 7, 8, 9, 10 percent. [. . .] That was when GIC was formed in 1981 and we had lost millions of dollars" (*Straits Times*, 6 October 2007).

18. For example, a former executive partner in Salomon Brothers (James D. Wolfensohn), a former real estate specialist at Prudential Insurance (Theodore M. Garhart), and a former stock specialist form College Retirement Equities Fund (Douglas C. Salmond) were recruited to train seventeen Singaporeans at the GIC (*Straits Times*, 15 March 1983).

19. Because of the oligopolistic position of large banks, it is often assumed that representatives of these firms have direct contact with policy makers, and as such the ability to influence policy in a critical way (Coen 1997).

20. For Lord Claus Moser the shortlisting of Rothschild & Sons was the direct result of the personal relationship between him and Singapore's DPM Goh (Moser 2008). Lord Moser noted in an interview: "Dr Goh had been my student as an undergraduate at LSE and he had done his PhD under me. He considered me as his great man. And he got in touch with Rothschilds formally because of me. So we got a tender to get shortlisted with the other banks" (Moser 2008).

21. Preceding the creation of the GIC, Rothschild & Sons had already been actively involved in the creation of the Venezuelan Investment Fund (Richard Katz, personal communication, 31 April 2014). Katz's statement that "this was what we suggested to Dr Goh and followed up with a full presentation and memorandum" highlights the important influence of Rothschild & Sons (Katz 2014). Although this looks like diffusion, the thesis can exclude emulation as a potential explanation for the creation of the GIC, because Venezuela's structural characteristics differed significantly from those of Singapore. As such, Venezuela cannot be considered as a peer of Singapore.

22. GIC's network of international business partners has included a highly select group of individuals, notably Barton M. Biggs (managing director at Morgan Stanley Investment Management), Rolf E. Breuer (chairman, Deutsche Bank), Raymond T. Dalio (chairman, Bridgewater Associates), David I. Fisher (chairman, Capital Group International), Maurice R Greenberg (chairman, American International Group), William H. Gross (managing director of Pacific Investment Management Company), Yoshinari Hara (president, Daiwa Securities Group), David H. Komansky (chairman, Merrill Lynch & Co), Duncan M. McFarland (president, Wellington Management Company), John Olcay (vice chair, Fischer Francis Trees and Watts), Ramon De Oliveira (chairman, J. P. Morgan Fleming Asset Management), Marcel Ospel (President, UBS), and Henry M. Paulson (chairman, Goldman Sachs) (GIC Yearbook 2001).

23. In addition, Rothschild & Sons provided long-term staff training. For example, each year two people from the GIC or the MAS were appointed to a two-year training program. Furthermore, there was an agreement with Wharton Econometric Forecasting Associates from Wharton Business School to train twelve Singaporeans in computerized systems of modelling and forecasting at the National University of Singapore.

24. *Fortune*'s comment that "[Hagler Mastrovita's] compensation includes management of discretionary fund" suggests that the GIC placed out funds in return for staff training (*Fortune*, 21 March 1983).

25. The question of whether it was the financial secretary, the chief secretary, or the governor who delegated the issue to the Education and Manpower Branch cannot be completely clarified. However, it would have involved the financial sec-

retary, because he was at the center of any decision making in Hong Kong's savings domain.

26. The government could have also chosen other policy bodies, such as the Consumer Council, District Boards, and Pensions Assessment Board (see Civil and Miscellaneous Lists Hong Kong Government, 1 July 1986).

CHAPTER 6

1. This chapter draws on Braunstein 2019.

2. These points were specifically highlighted by high level representatives from private Kuwait finance houses such as KFH Investment and the Kuwait Economic Society (anonymous, personal communication at the LSE Kuwait Programme Workshop in Kuwait, 22 September 2014).

3. Until the mid-1970s, the Kuwait Oil Tanker Company was fully owned by Kuwait's private sector (KOTC 2015). Kuwait National Airways was founded in 1954, but the government took full ownership only in 1962 (Kuwait Airport 2015).

4. A 1971 World Bank Mission report on the "Promotion of Manufacturing in Kuwait" highlighted the lack of coordination and autonomy among these agencies (see Khouja and Sadler 1979).

5. Calculated by using data from Al-Dekhayel, 2000, 52.

6. Following the Gulf War, a relatively strong Kuwaiti parliament uncovered a major fraud including a number of members of the ruling family, such as the emir's cousin Sheik Fahad Mohammed al-Sabah, former chairman of Kuwait's SWF (Cohen 1993). In the late 1980s, the KIA invested more than $5 billion via a Spanish middleman (Cohen 1993). Kuwait's Parliament Finance Committee found evidence of corruption and gross mismanagement in these investments and called for legal action against former managers (Cohen 1993).

7. Apart from the ruling Al-Nahyan family, important subsections of the tribe, which were on the Executive Council, were the Al-Mazroui, the Al-Suwaidi, the Al-Romaithi, and the Al-Qubaisi.

8. Up until 2013, Abu Dhabi disposed of at least three SWFs with development mandates including the International Petroleum Investment Corporation (established in 1984), Mubadala (2002), and the Abu Dhabi Investment Council (2007).

9. In 1977, the state allocated around 35 percent of its total budget to industrial development, but by 1978 the share had declined to 23 percent (Mallakh 1979, 69). During this same period, housing expenditures increased from 10.2 percent in 1977 to 17.8 percent in 1978 (El-Mallakh 1979, 69).

10. Through his status of successor, Hamad Al-Thani had already started Cabinet reforms in 1992 by reshuffling and replacing the old guard with like-minded development-oriented family members (Mehran 2013, 113).

CHAPTER 8

1. In *The Political Economy of Exchange Rate Policy* (2014) Harvard Professor Jeffrey Frieden makes a compelling case for the relevance of domestic politics to explain policy choices in the monetary domain.

AFTERWORD

1. I would like to thank Pat Schena and Adam Dixon for their valuable input and feedback. Harvard Professor Dani Rodrik provides an outline of the emerging relationship between markets and states in a post-pandemic world (Rodrik 2020).

2. Cutler and Summers (2020) provide an excellent overview of the potential costs of Covid-19.

3. Governments that tightened foreign investment restrictions in a series of strategic sectors include Austria, Belgium, Czech Republic, France, Germany, Hungary, Italy, Luxembourg, Netherlands, Poland, Spain, Sweden, UK, EU, Canada, Australia, and Japan (BakerMcKenzie 2020).

4. Countries that created guaranteed credit facilities, government-backed loans, and government initiatives that contribute state capital to fund platforms include Austria, Bahrain, Belgium, Czech Republic, Egypt, France, Germany, Hungary, Italy, Kazakhstan, Morocco, Saudi Arabia, Turkey, UAE, Luxembourg, Netherlands, Poland, Russia, South Africa, Spain, Sweden, Switzerland, Ukraine, UK, Argentina, Brazil, Canada, Chile, Colombia, Mexico, Peru, United States, Australia, China, Hong Kong, Indonesia, Japan, Malaysia, Philippines, Singapore, Taiwan, Thailand, and Vietnam (BakerMcKenzie 2020).

5. For example, during the 2008 global financial crisis, the Kuwait Investment Authority supported the Kuwait bourse and helped to bail out the Gulf Bank (Thomson Reuters 2009, January 26). In a similar fashion, the Qatar Investment Authority injected more than US$3 billion into Qatar's four largest banks to keep them solvent (Arabian Business 2017, June 20). Likewise, Abu Dhabi's SWF helped to rescue Dubai World, a major Dubai real estate investment company, and the Russian SWF helped to support the ruble during the 2015 currency crisis by injecting money into local banks (*New York Times*, 9 March 2015).

6. Especially SWFs of some commodity-exporting countries in North Africa, such as Angola, Iraq, Bahrein, Oman, and Algeria, will experience significant stress in terms of depletion (Bortolotti and Fotak 2020).

7. For earlier writings on the use of remittances as a capitalization source of SWFs, see (Schena, Braunstein, and Ali 2018; Braunstein and Ali 2019).

8. For example, in March 2020, Germany's federal government created an Economic Stabilization Fund (Wirtschaftsstabilisierungsfonds), with €600 billion in assets, of which €100 billion is for equity investments, €400 billion for guarantees, and €100 billion for refinancing through Germany's state-owned development bank, the KfW Group.

9. In the same month (March 2020), the New Zealand government entered a debt-funding agreement with Air New Zealand worth NZ$0.9 billion, convertible to equity (IMF 2020). Also, Poland's government created on 8 April the Financial Shield, capitalized with $24 billion, providing loans and bonds as well as equity investment on market terms (PFR 2020). Italy's state owned investment bank, Cassa Depositi e Prestiti, created an emergency fund with an initial endowment of €4.5 billion for 2020 to make investments in private and listed Italian companies that have an annual turnover higher than €50 million (CDP n.d.). Recapitalization has also occurred at a subnational level. For example, Germany's state of Bavaria created the Bavarian Finance Agency (Bayfog) with €26 billion in order to stabi-

lize medium-size companies that are strategic for Bavaria through guarantees and equity investments (K&L Gates Hub 2020). Recapitalization has also occurred by channeling funds through exiting agencies. For example, the French Government tasked the French State Participation Agency with €20 billion in the recapitalization effort; the agency is allowed to take equity stakes in companies deemed vulnerable, including in the aeronautics and automotive sectors (BakerMcKenzie 2020).

10. For discussion on how domestic state society structures affected very different bailout policies of SWFs in Hong Kong and Singapore, see Braunstein 2017.

11. The "crowding out" argument associated with neoclassical economics emphasizes how government deficits affect interest rates—government borrowing to finance deficits causes interest rates to rise. Higher interest rates incentivize the private sector to save rather than invest, and thereby reduce or "crowd out" private investments.

Bibliography

Abdelal, R. 2009. "Sovereign Wealth in Abu Dhabi." *Geopolitics* 14, no. 2: 317–27.

Abu Dhabi Chamber of Commerce and Industry. 2013. *Annual Report*. Dubai: Abu Dhabi Chamber of Commerce and Industry. http://www.abudhabichamber.ae /PublicationsEnglish/Doc-19-8-2014-15455.pdf

Abu Dhabi Council. 2015a. "About Us: History." Abu Dhabi Council. Accessed 12 February 2015. http://www.adcouncil.ae/AboutUs/History/tabid/92/Defau lt.aspx

Abu Dhabi Council. 2015b. "Business Functions." Abu Dhabi Council. Accessed 12 February 2015. http://www.adcouncil.ae/BusinessFunctions/DirectInvestm ents/tabid/67/Default.aspx

ADCCI. 2015a. "Abu Dhabi Chamber of Commerce and Industry and Local Partners." ADCCI. Accessed 15 February 2015. http://www.abudhabichamber.ae /English/Partners/Pages/Partners.aspx?Type=2

ADCCI. 2015b. "Abu Dhabi Chamber of Commerce and Industry Council." Accessed 11 February 2015. https://www.abudhabi.ae/portal/public/en/depart ments/department_detail?docName=ADEGP_DF_14862_EN&_adf.ctrl-state=nhu7s7xc5_4&_afrLoop=5579396420938691

ADIA. *Annual Review*. 2009. Dubai: Abu Dhabi Investment Authority. http://www .adia.ae/en/pr/Annual_Review_Website2.pdf

ADIA. *Annual Review*. 2014. Abu Dhabi: Abu Dhabi Investment Authority. http:// www.adia.ae/En/pr/ADIA_Review_2014_Web.pdf

ADNOC. 2015. "The Supreme Petroleum Council." Abu Dhabi National Oil Company. Accessed 14 February 2015. http://www.adnoc.ae/Content.aspx?ne wid=24&mid=2

ADSG. 2015. "Abu Dhabi Chamber of Commerce." Abu Dhabi Sustainability Group. Accessed 15 February 2015. https://www.adsg.ae/membership/Pages /ADCCI.aspx

Advisory Committee on Diversification. 1979a. *Report of the Advisory Committee on Diversification—Sub Committee on Industrial Development.*

Advisory Committee on Diversification. 1979b. *Report of the Advisory Committee on Diversification.*

Ahmad, A. 2014. 'Re-run vote for Abu Dhabi Chamber of Commerce and Industry board candidates', *The National*, 12 June.

Aizenman, Joshua. 2007. *Large Hoarding of International Reserves and the Emerging Global Economic Architecture.* Cambridge, MA: National Bureau of Economic Research.

Aizenman, Joshua, and Reuven Glick. 2007. "Sovereign Wealth Funds: Stumbling Blocks or Stepping Stones to Financial Globalization?" Federal Reserve Bank of San Francisco, December 14. Accessed 31 July 2015. https://www.frbsf.org/economic-research/publications/economic-letter/2007/december/sovereign-wealth-funds-financial-globalization/

Aizenman, Joshua, and Reuven Glick. 2008. *Sovereign Wealth Funds: Stylized Facts about Their Determinants and Governance.* San Francisco, CA: Federal Reserve Bank of San Francisco.

Aizenman, Joshua, and Jaewoo Lee. 2005. *International Reserves: Precautionary vs. Mercantilist Views, Theory and Evidence.* Washington, DC: International Monetary Fund, Research Department.

Al-Atiqi. 2005. "Good Governance of the National Petrol Sector." Workshop, Chathamhouse. Accessed 15 July 2008. http://www.chathamhouse.org.uk/files/6387_ggkuwait.pdf/

Al-Dekhayel, Abdulkarim. 2000. *Kuwait: Oil, State and Political Legitimation.* Reading, UK: Ithaca Press.

Al-Hassan, Abdullah, Michael G. Papaioannou, Martin Skancke, and Cheng Chih Sung. 2013. *Sovereign Wealth Funds.* Washington, DC: International Monetary Fund.

Al-Kandari, Abdullah Ramadan A. 1982. "Industrial Development: A Case Study of Kuwait: Problems, Plans, Prospect, and Strategy." Master's thesis, University of Glasgow.

Allison, Graham T. 1971. *Essence of Decision; Explaining the Cuban Missile Crisis.* Boston: Little, Brown.

APF. 2015. "Transfer to Principal." 30 June, 1–4. http://www.akleg.gov/basis/get_documents.asp?session=29&docid=64075

Atkinson, Michael M., and William D. Coleman. 1989. "Strong States and Weak States: Sectoral Policy Networks in Advanced Capitalist Economies." *British Journal of Political Science* 19, no. 1: 47–67. doi:10.1017/s0007123400005317.

BAB. 2009. "Annual Report 2009." Bahrain Association of Banks, 1–30.

Bahgat, Gawdat. 2010. "The Kuwait Investment Authority—an Assessment." In *The Political Economy of Sovereign Wealth Funds.* Edited by Xu Yi-chong and Gawdat Bahgat, 72–87. Basingstoke: Palgrave Macmillan.

Bahrain Chamber. 2017. "About Us." Accessed 13 August 2017. https://www.bcci.bh/en

Baker, Philip. 1986. "Kuwait: The Taxation of International Commercial Transactions." *Arab Law Quarterly*: 141–57.

Barbary, Victoria, Bernardo, Bortolotti, Fotak, Veljko, and Miracky, William. 2010. "Sovereign Wealth Fund Investment Behavior." *Fondazione Eni Enrico Mattei.* Semi-Annual Report: January-June, 1–26.

Barr, Michael D. 2014. *The Ruling Elite of Singapore: Networks of Power and Influence.* London: I. B. Tauris.

Bazoobandi, Sara. 2013. *The Political Economy of the Gulf Sovereign Wealth Funds: A Case Study of Iran, Kuwait, Saudi Arabia, and the United Emirates.* Hoboken, NJ: Taylor and Francis.

Beck, Roland, and Michael Fidora. 2008. "The Impact of Sovereign Wealth Funds on Global Financial Markets." *Intereconomics* 43, no. 6: 349–58. doi:10.1007/s1 0272-008-0268-5.

Behrendt, Sven. 2008. "When Money Talks: Arab Sovereign Wealth Funds in the Global Public Policy Discourse." *Carnegie Middle East Center*, Carnegie Paper no. 12, 1–25.

Bernstein, Shai, Josh Lerner, and Antoinette Schoar. 2013. "The Investment Strategies of Sovereign Wealth Ffunds." *Journal of Economic Perspectives* 27, no. 2: 219–38.

Blundell-Wignall, Adrian, Yu-Wei Hu, and Juan Yermo. 2008. "Sovereign Wealth and Pension Fund Issues." *OECD Journal: Financial Market Trends*, no. 1: 117–32. doi:10.1787/fmt-v2008-art5-en.

Bocock, Peter W. 1970. "The Impact of Development: Progress for People through Industrial Revolution-Singapore." *Finance and Development* 7, no. 3: 26–35.

Bogaars, George. 1981. "The Public Service: A Retrospection." By Teo Hee Lian. Podcast audio. National Archives of Singapore, MSD 62.23D Vol. 2. 31 September 31.

Bortolotti, Bernardo, V. Fotak, V., William Megginson, and William Miracky. 2009. Sovereign Wealth Fund Investment Patterns and Performance. *Fondazione Eni Enrico Mattei*: Institutions and Markets no. 22, 1–58.

Börzel, Tanja A. 1998: "Organizing Babylon—on the Different Conceptions of Policy Networks." *Public Administration* 76, no. 2: 253–73. doi:10.1111/1467-9299.00100.

Bossart, Marco Kauffmann. 2017. "Staatskapitalismus Alla Turca." *Neue Zürcher Zeitung*, 9 June. Accessed 6 August 2018. https://www.nzz.ch/wirtschaft/ein-umstrittener-staatsfonds-fuer-die-tuerkei-staatskapitalismus-alla-turca-ld.1299995

Botterill, Linda C. 2005. "Policy Change and Network Termination: The Role of Farm Groups in Agricultural Policy Making in Australia." *Australian Journal of Political Science* 40, no. 2: 207–19. doi:10.1080/10361140500129982.

Boyd, R., 1987. "Government-Industry Relations in Japan: Access, Communication, and Competitive Collaboration." In *Comparative Government-Industry Relations: Western Europe, the United States, and Japan*, edited by Wilks, S. and Wright, M., 61–90. Oxford: Clarendon Press.

Braunstein, Juergen. 2013. "The Novelty of Sovereign Wealth Funds: The Emper-

or's New Clothes?" *Global Policy* 5, no. 2: 169–80. doi:10.1111/1758–5899 .12095.

Braunstein, Juergen. 2015. "Explaining Sovereign Wealth Fund Variation: The Role of Domestic Policies in Small Open Economies." Doctoral dissertation, The London School of Economics and Political Science (LSE).

Braunstein, Juergen. 2015a. *Different Twins and a Distant Cousin: Sovereign Wealth Funds in Hong Kong, Singapore, and South Korea*. Medford, MA: Tufts University. https://sites.tufts.edu/sovereignet/files/2017/08/Different-Twins-Distant-Cou sin.pdf

Braunstein, Juergen. 2015b. "Why Are SWFs Shy of African Investments?" *Financial Times*, 3 February. Accessed 29 July 2018. https://www.ft.com/content/d987 feab-72d9-300b-a558-e7bf43a46764

Braunstein, Juergen. 2017a. "Linking Financial Bailouts to Domestic Politics: How to Explain Different Bailouts in Hong Kong and Singapore." *Journal of Economic Policy Reform* 20, no. 1: 46–63. doi:10.1080/17487870.2016.1247705.

Braunstein, Juergen. 2017b. "The Domestic Drivers of State Finance Institutions: Evidence from Sovereign Wealth Funds." *Review of International Political Economy* 24, no. 6: 980–1003. doi:10.1080/09692290.2017.1382383.

Braunstein, Juergen. 2019. "Domestic Sources of Twenty-first-Century Geopolitics: Domestic Politics and Sovereign Wealth Funds in GCC Economies." *New Political Economy* 24, no. 2: 197–217. doi:10.1080/13563467.2018.1431619.

Braunstein, Juergen, and Arianne Caoili. 2016a. "Indonesia: The Vanguard of a New Wave of Sovereign Wealth Funds?" London School of Economics and Political Science, 30 August. Accessed 29 July 2018. http://blogs.lse.ac.uk/gov ernment/2016/08/30/indonesia-the-vanguard-of-a-new-wave-of-sovereign-wealth-funds/

Braunstein, Juergen, Marion Labouré, and Julius Sen. 2016b. "Windfall Revenues in Europe: What's Next?" London School of Economics and Political Science, 16 December. Accessed 29 July 2018. http://blogs.lse.ac.uk/eurocrisispress/20 16/12/16/windfall-revenues-in-europe-whats-next/

Braunstein, Juergen, and Mattia Tomba. 2017. "Building In-House Investment Capacity: The Early Case of GIC." In *Bocconi Sovereign Wealth Fund Annual Report*, Universita Bocconi – BAFFI CAREFIN Center, Sovereign Investment Lab, 63–69.

Braunstein, Juergen, and Mattia Tomba. 2018. "Sovereign Wealth Funds in Small Open Economies." NUS—Middle East Institute. Accessed 29 July 2018. https://mei.nus.edu.sg/publication/insight-182-sovereign-wealth-funds-in-sm all-open-economies/

Bremmer, Ian. 2009. "State Capitalism Comes of Age: The End of the Free Market?" *Foreign Affairs* 88, no. 3 (May/June): 40–55.

Brewer, Brian, and Stewart MacPherson. 1997. "Poverty and Social Security." In *Social Policy in Hong Kong*, edited by Wilding, Paul et al. Cheltenham, UK: Edward Elgar.

BRICS. 2017. "What Is BRICS?" BRICS, 26 January 26. Accessed 12 June 2017. https://www.brics2017.org/English/AboutBRICS/BRICS/

British Treasury. 1963. Confidential Conversation British Political Agent in Bahrain. 26 May, UK Treasury; T 317/495, Bahrain Budgets and Internal Finance (including Government Investment and Reserves and UK Aid).

Brookfield, Jonathan, Ravi Chaturvedi, and Patrick J. Schena. 2011. "Sovereign Wealth Funds and the Privatization of State Assets: Toward a Life-Cycle Framework." In *Braving the New World: Sovereign Wealth Fund Investment in the Uncertain Times of 2010*. The Monitor Group, 38–43.

Brooks, G. 1991. "Sheik Zayed Led Abu Dhabi to Riches and Remains a Hero—But BCCI Scandal Is a Cloud Over His Long Reign." *Wall Street Journal*, Eastern Edition, 19 July, p. 1.

Brown, W. C. L. 1981. "Industry Financial Assistance (1979–1983)." Speech, FHKI luncheon meeting, 17 February. Public Records Office Hong Kong, HKRS70-8-2255.

Brown, W. S., and C. S. Thomas. 1994. "The Alaska Permanent Fund: Good Sense or Political Expediency?" *Challenge* 37: 38–44.

Brunetti, Aymo. 2015. "Der irreführende Charme von Staatsfonds." *Finanz und Wirtschaft*, 6 June.

*The Bulletin. 1985. "The Hong Kong General Chamber of Commerce Magazine." *The Bulletin*, June. British Library Reference Collection P.511/5106.

Bundesrat. 2016. *Tiefzinsumfeld und Frankenstärke: Handlungsoptionen für die Schweiz*. Bericht des Bundesrates in Erfüllung des Postulats.

Carroll, Christopher, and Olivier Jeanne. 2009. *A Tractable Model of Precautionary Reserves, Net Foreign Assets, or Sovereign Wealth Funds*. National Bureau of Economic Research no. W15228. Cambridge, MA: NBER.

Chan, Cheuk-wah. 1998. *The Myth of Hong Kong's Laissez-Faire Economic Governance: 1960s and 1970s*. Shatin, New Territories, Hong Kong: Hong Kong Institute of Asia-Pacific Studies, Chinese University of Hong Kong.

Chen, Edward K. Y., and K. W. Li. 1991. "Hong Kong's Industrial Development." In *Industrial and Trade Development in Hong Kong*, edited by Edward K. Y. Chen, Mee-kau Nyaw, and Teresa Y. C. Wong, 2–49. Hong Kong: Centre of Asian Studies, University of Hong Kong, 1991.

Chen, Edward K. Y., Mee-kau Nyaw, and Teresa Y. C. Wong. 1991. *Industrial and Trade Development in Hong Kong*. Hong Kong: Centre of Asian Studies, University of Hong Kong.

Chen, Peter S. J. 1976. "The Power Elite in Singapore." In *Studies in ASEAN Sociology: Urban Society and Social Change*, edited by Peter S. J. Chen. Singapore: Chopmen Enterprises.

Chew, Emrys, and Chong Guan Kwa. 2012. *Goh Keng Swee: A Legacy of Public Service*. Singapore: World Scientific.

Chiu, Stephen Wing-kai. 1994. *The Politics of Laissez-Faire: Hong Kong's Strategy of Industrialization in Historical Perspective*. Shatin, New Territories, Hong Kong: Hong Kong Institute of Asia-Pacific Studies, Chinese University of Hong Kong.

Chiu, Stephen Wing-Kai, Kong-Chong Ho, and Tai-lok Lui. 1997. *City-States in the Global Economy: Industrial Restructuring in Hong Kong and Singapore.* Boulder, CO: Westview Press.

Choy Li, Chong. 1985. "Development Management in Singapore: Institutional Leadership in Development." *Southeast Asian Affairs 1985*, no. 1: 306–16. doi:10.1355/seaa85r.

Chwieroth, Jeffrey M. 2010. *Fashions and Fads in Finance: Contingent Emulation and the Political Economy of Sovereign Wealth Fund Creation.* Fashions and Fads in Finance. Working Paper, SSRN.

Chwieroth, Jeffrey M. 2014. "Fashions and Fads in Finance: The Political Foundations of Sovereign Wealth Fund Creation." *International Studies Quarterly* 58, no. 4: 752–63. doi:10.1111/isqu.12140.

*CIC. 2011. "Investments." China Investment Corporation. Accessed 11 March 2011. www.chininv.cn/cicen/investment/.html

Civil and Miscellaneous List, Hong Kong Government. 1968. "Hong Kong Colonial Secretariat." Hong Kong Government Printer, 1 April. Public Records Office Hong Kong, HKRS- X 1000860.

Civil and Miscellaneous List, Hong Kong Government. 1986. "Hong Kong Colonial Secretariat." Hong Kong Government Printer, 1 July. Public Records Office Hong Kong, HKRS- X 1000860.

Clark, G. L., and A. H. Monk. 2011. "Pension Reserve Funds: Aligning Form and Function." *Rotman International Journal of Pension Management* 4, no. 2.

Clark, G. L., and A. H. Monk. 2013. "The Scope of Financial Institutions: In-Sourcing, Outsourcing and Off-shoring." *Journal of Economic Geography* 13, no. 2: 279–98. doi:10.1093/jeg/lbs061.

Clark, Gordon L., Adam D. Dixon, and Ashby H. B. Monk. 2013. *Sovereign Wealth Funds: Legitimacy, Governance, and Global Power.* Princeton, NJ: Princeton University Press.

Coen, David. 1997. "The Evolution of the Large Firm as a Political Actor in the European Union." *Journal of European Public Policy* 4, no. 1: 91–108. doi:10.1080/135017697344253.

Cohen, Benjamin J. 2009. "Sovereign Wealth Funds and National Security: The Great Tradeoff." *International Affairs* 85, no. 4: 713–31. doi:10.1111/j.1468–2346.2009.00824.x.

Cohen, R. 1993. "Missing Millions—Kuwait's Bad Bet—A Special Report; Big Wallets and Little Supervision." *The New York Times*, 28 September, p. 20.

Congressional Research Services. 1992. *The BCCI Affair: A Report to the Committee on Foreign Relations United States Senate.* Available from: https://fas.org/irp/congress/1992_rpt/bcci/

Crystal, Jill. 1990. *Oil and Politics in the Gulf: Rulers and Merchants in Kuwait and Qatar.* Cambridge: Cambridge University Press.

Daugbjerg, Carsten. 1998a. "Linking Policy Networks and Environmental Policies: Nitrate Policy Making in Denmark and Sweden 1970–1995." *Public Administration* 76, no. 2: 275–94. doi:10.1111/1467-9299.00101.

Daugbjerg, Carsten. 1998b. "Similar Problems, Different Policies: Policy Networks and Environmental Policy in Swedish and Danish Agriculture." In *Comparing Policy Networks: Policy Networks in Theoretical and Comparative Perspective*, edited by D. Marsh, 75–89. Milton Keynes: Open University Press.

Davidson, Christopher M. 2009. *Abu Dhabi: Oil and Beyond*. London: Hurst.

Davies, S. N. G. 1977. "One Brand of Politics Rekindled." *Hong Kong Law Journal*, no. 7: 44–88.

Deyo, Frederic C. 1981. *Dependent Development and Industrial Order: An Asian Case Study*. New York: Praeger.

Diwan-Smith Diwan, Kristin. 2009. "Sovereign Dilemmas: Saudi Arabia and Sovereign Wealth Funds." *Geopolitics* 14, no. 2: 345–59.

Dixon, Adam. 2017. "The State as Institutional Investor: Unpacking the Geographical Political Economy of Sovereign Wealth Funds. In *Handbook on the Geographies of Money and Finance*, edited by R. Martin and J. Pollard, 279–98. Edward Elgar Publishing.

Doha News. 2013. "Ex-Prime Minister Loses Post as Chairman of Qatar Investment Authority." *Doha News*, 3 July.

Drake, Peter Joseph. 1969. *Financial Development in Malaya and Singapore*. Canberra: ANU Press.

Dunn, James A., and Anthony Perl. 1994. "Policy Networks and Industrial Revitalization: High Speed Rail Initiatives in France and Germany." *Journal of Public Policy* 14, no. 3: 311–43. doi:10.1017/s0143814x00007303.

Eastern Department. 1954. *Questions of Kuwait's Fabulous Revenues; Correspondence Letters*. Eastern Department. Accessed at National Archives, Kew.

Eaton, Sarah, and Zhang Ming. 2010. "A Principal–agent Analysis of China's Sovereign Wealth System: Byzantine by Design." *Review of International Political Economy* 17, no. 3: 481–506.

Eccleston, Richard. 2010. "The Political Economy of Australia's Future Fund: The Political Dimension." In *The Political Economy of Sovereign Wealth Funds*, edited by Xu Yi-chong and Gawdat Bahgat. Basingstoke: Palgrave Macmillan.

Eccleston, Richard. 2012. "Australia's Future Fund: A Future beyond the GFC." *Journal of the Asia Pacific Economy* 17, no. 2: 284–97. doi:10.1080/13547860.2012.668083.

EDB Annual Report. 1968. Economic Development Board, Singapore: EDB. Accessed at Singapore National Library, Special Collections.

EDB Hong Kong. 2012. *General Information on the Subsidized Schools Provident Funds*. Hong Kong: EDB. http://www.edb.gov.hk/attachment/en/sch-admin/admin/about-sch-staff/provident-fund/sspf_q&a_eng_nov12.pdf

Eichengreen, Barry J. 2004. *Capital Flows and Crises*. Cambridge: MIT Press.

EIU. 1962a. *Proposed Survey of Hong Kong's Industries 1961–1968*. Hong Kong: Economist Intelligence Unit.

EIU. 1962b. *Industry in Hong Kong: Report Prepared by the Economist Intelligence Unit Limited for the Federation of Hong Kong Industries*. Hong Kong: South China Morning Post.

EIU. 2008. *Country Profile UAE 2008*. Economist Intelligence Unit.

EIU. 2009a. *Country Profile Qatar 2009*. Economist Intelligence Unit.

EIU. 2009b. *Country Profile Bahrain 2009*. Economist Intelligence Unit.

EIU. 2013. *Country Profile Kuwait 2013*. Economist Intelligence Unit.

EIU Digital Solutions. 2013. "Israel Moves Closer to Setting Up Sovereign Wealth Fund." Economist Intelligence Unit. 16 April 16. Accessed 13 June 2014. http://country.eiu.com/article.aspx?articleid=423778426&Country=Israel&topic=Economy&oid=1123861296&flid=1110383495

El-Erian, Mohammed A. 2008. "Towards a Better Understanding of Sovereign Wealth Funds." In *Debating China's Exchange Policy*, edited by Morris Goldstein and Nicholas Lardy. Washington: Peterson Institute for International Economics.

El-Mallakh, R. 1979. *Qatar: Development of an Oil Economy*. London: Croom Helm.

Elson, Anthony. 2008. "The Sovereign Wealth Funds of Singapore." *World Economics* 9, no. 3: 73–95.

Elwell, Craig K. 2012. "The Depreciating Dollar: Economic Effects and Policy Response." Washington, DC: Congressional Research Service.

ESADEgeo. 2014. *Annual Sovereign Wealth Fund Report*. Madrid: ESADEgeo. http://itemsweb.esade.edu/wi/Prensa/SWF2014_ENG.pdf

ESADEgeo. 2015. "Fund Ranking." ESADEgeo. Accessed 4 May 4. http://www.esadegeo.com/global-economy

Executive Council Abu Dhabi. 2015. "Executive Council." Abu Dhabi Government. Accessed 30 July 30. https://www.ecouncil.ae/en/ADGovernment/Pages/ExecutiveCouncil.aspx

FedPrimeRate. 2015. "United States Prime Rate History." United States Prime Rate. Accessed 15 September 15. http://www.fedprimerate.com/wall_street_journal_prime_rate_history.htm

Fehrenbach, T. R. 1968. *Gnomes of Zurich: Inside Story of the Swiss Banks*. London: L. Frewin.

Feldstein, Martin. 1999. "A Self-Help Guide for Emerging Markets." *Foreign Affairs* 78, no. 2: 93–110. doi:10.2307/20049211.

Fernandez, David. 2008. *Sovereign Wealth Funds: A Bottom-Up Primer*. New York: JP Morgan. http://cama.anu.edu.au/Events/swf2008/swf2008_papers/Fernandez_SWF_paper.pdf

Fiechter, J. R. W. 2009. "The French Strategic Investment Fund: A Creative Approach to Complement SWF Regulation or Mere Protectionism?" Working Paper, 1–17.

Field, Michael. 1985. *The Merchants: The Big Business Families of Saudi Arabia and the Gulf States*. Woodstock NY: Overlook Press.

Fleischer, Victor. 2008. "A Theory of Taxing Sovereign Wealth" Draft for Columbia Law School Colloquium, 11 August. Available: https://www.law.columbia.edu/sites/default/files/microsites/tax-policy/files/2008/Fleischer_A%20Theory%20of%20Taxing%20Sovereign%20Wealth_Cover.pdf

Flood, Robert, and Nancy Marion. 2001. *Holding International Reserves in an Era of High Capital Mobility*. Brookings Trade Forum. Accessed 1 December 2018. https://www.dartmouth.edu/~nmarion/Papers/FM_Brookings.pdf

Foellmi, Reto. 2015. "Unvereinbar mit dem Auftrag der SNB." *Neue Zürcher Zeitung*. 3 August. Accessed 30 July 30. https://www.nzz.ch/meinung/debatte/unve reinbar-mit-dem-auftrag-der-snb-1.18589308

Fortescue, S. 2010. "Russia's SWFs: Controlled by a Domestic Agenda." In *The Political Economy of Sovereign Wealth Funds*, edited by Xu Yi-chong and Gawdat Bahgat. Basingstoke: Palgrave Macmillan.

Frankel, Jeffrey. 1992. "Measuring International Capital Mobility: A Review." *American Economic Review* 82, no. 2: 197–202.

Frankel, Jeffrey. 2011. *A Solution to Fiscal Procyclicality: The Structural Budget Institutions Pioneered by Chile*. Cambridge: Center for International Development at Harvard University.

Frieden, Jeffry A. 2014. *Currency Politics: The Political Economy of Exchange Rate Policy*. Princeton, NJ: Princeton University Press.

General Secretariat for Development Planning. 2008. "Qatar National Vision 2030." Doha: GSDP.

General Secretariat for Development Planning. 2011. "Qatar National Development Strategy 2011–2016." Doha: GSDP Doha.

George, Alexander L., and Andrew Bennett. 2005. *Case Studies and Theory Development in the Social Sciences*. Cambridge, MA: MIT Press.

GIC. 2015. "About-Corporate Governance." GIC. Accessed 24 August 2015. http://www.gic.com.sg/about/corporate- governance/overview-GAPP-7

GIC Report. 2012. "GIC Releases 'Report on the Management of the Government's Portfolio for the Year 2011/12'." GIC. 31 July. Accessed 24 June 2014. https://www.gic.com.sg/news-and-insights/gic-releases-report-on-the-manage ment-of-the-governments-portfolio-for-the-year-201112/

GIC Yearbook. 2001. Government of Singapore Investment Corporation Yearbook 2001. Accessed at the Monetary Authority Singapore Library.

Gilson, Ronald J., and Curtis J. Milhaupt. 2008. "Sovereign Wealth Funds and Corporate Governance: A Minimalist Response to the New Mercantilism." *Stanford Law Review* 60.

Glick, Reuven, and Ramon Moreno. 1994. *Capital Flows and Monetary Policy in East Asia*. San Francisco, CA: Center for Pacific Basin Monetary and Economic Studies, Economic Research Dept., Federal Reserve Bank of San Francisco.

Goh, K. S. 1958. "Entrepreneurship in a Plural Economy." *Malayan Economic Review* 3, no. 1: 1–7.

Goodstadt, Leo F. 2005. *Uneasy Partners: The Conflict between Public Interest and Private Profit in Hong Kong*. Hong Kong: Hong Kong University Press.

Goodstadt, Leo F. 2006. "Business Friendly and Politically Convenient—the History of Functional Constituencies." In *Functional Constituencies: A Unique Fea-*

ture of the Hong Kong Legislative Council, edited by Christine Loh, 41–44. Hong Kong: Hong Kong University Press.

Goodstadt, Leo F. 2007. *Profits, Politics and Panics: Hong Kong's Banks and the Making of a Miracle Economy, 1935–1985*. Hong Kong: Hong Kong University Press.

Gratcheva, Ekaterina, and Nikoloz Anasashvili. 2017. "Domestic Investment Practices of Sovereign Wealth Funds: Empirical Evidence to Inform Policy Debates." In *New Frontiers of Sovereign Investment*, edited by Malan Rietveld and Perrine Toledano, 101–23. La Vergne: Perseus Books (Ingram).

Griffith-Jones, Stephany, and José Antonio Ocampo. 2008. *Sovereign Wealth Funds: A Developing Country Perspective*. Working Paper. Accessed 15 January 2014. https://academiccommons.columbia.edu/doi/10.7916/D8S18853

Gulf News. 2014. "Abu Dhabi Executive Council Restructured." *Gulf News* (Dubai). Accessed 26 April 2015. https://gulfnews.com/news/uae/government/abu-dha bi-executive-council-restructured-1.1304536

Hall, Peter A. 1986. *Governing the Economy: The Politics of State Intervention in Britain and France*. New York: Oxford University Press.

Halland, Havard, Michel Noel, Silvana Tordo, and Jacob J. Kloper-Owens. 2016. *Strategic Investment Funds: Opportunities and Challenges*. Washington, DC: World Bank.

Hamilton-Hart, Natasha. 2003. *Asian States, Asian Bankers: Central Banking in Southeast Asia*. Singapore: Singapore University Press.

Hammer, Cornelia, Peter Kunzel, and Iva Petrova. 2008. *Sovereign Wealth Funds: Current Institutional and Operational Practices*. Washington, DC: International Monetary Fund, Monetary and Capital Markets Department.

Harris, Peter. 1988. *Hong Kong: A Study in Bureaucracy and Politics*. Hong Kong: Macmillan.

Helleiner, Eric. 2004. "The Evolution of the International Monetary and Financial System." In *Global Political Economy*, edited by John Ravenhill. Oxford: Oxford University Press.

Helleiner, Eric. 2009. "The Geopolitics of Sovereign Wealth Funds: An Introduction." *Geopolitics* 14, no. 2: 300–304. doi:10.1080/14650040902827740.

Helleiner, Eric, and Troy Lundblad. 2008. "States, Markets, and Sovereign Wealth Funds." *German Policy Studies* 4, no. 3: 59–82.

Herb, Michael. 2009. "A Nation of Bureaucrats: Political Participation and Economic Diversification in Kuwait and the United Arab Emirates." *International Journal of Middle East Studies* 41, no. 3: 375–95. doi:10.1017/s0020743809091119.

Herb, Michael. 2014. *The Wages of Oil Parliaments and Economic Development in Kuwait and the UAE*. Ithaca: Cornell University Press.

Herb, Ernst. 2016. "Bedenkliche Intransparenz von Asiens Staatsfonds." *Finanz und Wirtschaft*, 1 November. Accessed 2 July 2. https://www.fuw.ch/article/bedenkli che-intransparenz-von-asiens-staatsfonds

Hertog, Steffen. 2010. "Defying the Resource Curse: Explaining Successful State-Owned Enterprises in Rentier States." *World Politics* 62, no. 2: 261–301. doi:10.1017/s0043887110000055.

Hertog, Steffen. 2013. *The Private Sector and Reform in the Gulf Cooperation Council.* Research Papers 30. London: LSE Kuwait Programme. https://eprints.lse.ac.uk/54398/1/Hertog_2013.pdf

Hertog, Steffen, Giacomo Luciani, and Marc Valeri. 2013. *Business Politics in the Middle East.* London: Hurst & Company.

*HKGCC. 2014. "History: LegCo Representatives." Hong Kong General Chamber of Commerce. Accessed 24 April 2014. http://www.chamber.org.hk/en/about/hkgcc_history.aspx

Ho, K. K. 1977. "DBS/EDB Financing Scheme for Small Industries." In *Symposium on Small Industries in Singapore, 24–25 March 1977, Shangri-La Hotel Singapore.* Singapore.

Ho, Khai Leong. 2000. *The Politics of Policy-Making in Singapore.* Singapore: Oxford University Press.

Homeshaw, Judith. 1995. "Policy Community, Policy Networks and Science Policy in Australia." *Australian Journal of Public Administration* 54, no. 4: 520–32. doi:10.1111/j.1467–8500.1995.tb01165.x.

Hong Kong Commerce and Industry Department. 1964–70. *Quarterly Reports (23 Issues).* Hong Kong: Public Records Office Hong Kong, RID: X1000176.

Hong Kong General Chamber of Commerce. 1861–70. *Minutes of the General Meetings.* Hong Kong: Public Records Office Hong Kong, HKMS 147-1-2.

Hong Kong Greenpaper. 1977. *Help for Those Least Able to Help Themselves: A Programme of Social Security Development.* Hong Kong: The Branch, Public Records Office Hong Kong, BK002895.

Hong Kong Management Association. 1978. *Papers, Discussion of the Conference on Diversification of Hong Kong's Industries.* Hong Kong: Hong Kong Management Association and Federation of HK Industries.

Hong Kong Working Committee on Productivity. 1964. *Report of the Working Committee on Productivity.* Hong Kong: Government Printer.

Howlett, Michael. 2002. "Do Networks Matter? Linking Policy Network Structure to Policy Outcomes: Evidence from Four Canadian Policy Sectors 1990–2000." *Canadian Journal of Political Science/Revue canadienne de science politique* 35, no. 2. doi:10.1017/s0008423902778232.

Howlett, Michael, and Jeremy Rayner. 1995. "Do Ideas Matter? Policy Network Configurations and Resistance to Policy Change in the Canadian Forest Sector." *Canadian Public Administration/Administration publique du Canada* 38, no. 3: 382–410. doi:10.1111/j.1754–7121.1995.tb01055.x.

Hsieh, J. 1976. "The Chinese Community in Singapore: The Internal Structure and Its Basic Constituents." In *Studies in ASEAN Sociology: Urban Society and Social Change,* edited by Peter S. J. Chen. Singapore: Chopmen Enterprises.

Hufbauer, Gary Clyde, Y. Wong, and Ketki Sheth. 2006. *US-China Trade Disputes: Rising Tide, Rising Stakes.* Washington, DC: Institute for International Economics.

Hussein, A. K. 2004. "Banking Efficiency in Bahrain: Islamic Versus Conventional Banks." *Islamic Development Bank*, Research and Training Institute, Research Paper No. 68, 1–61.

Hussein, Bina. 2019. "Sovereign Investors: A Means for Economic Diversification?" *Atlantic Council Global Energy Center*, Research Paper, 1–36.

Hwang, P. Y. 2003. "The Public Service: Retrospection an Oral History." Podcast audio. Oral History Centre Singapore. 28 February. Accession Number: 002597/14.

Ibrahim, Ibrahim, and Frank Harrigan. 2012. "Qatar's Economy: Past, Present and Future." *QScience Connect* no. 9: 1–24. doi:10.5339/connect.2012.9.

IFSWF. 2018a. "Turkiye Wealth Fund." International Forum of Sovereign Wealth Funds. Accessed 6 August 2018. http://www.ifswf.org/members/turkiye-wealth -fund

IFSWF. 2018b. "CDP Equity SpA." International Forum of Sovereign Wealth Funds. Accessed 6 August 2018. http://www.ifswf.org/members/italy

IMF. 1983. "Staff Report for the 1982 Article IV Consultation." 2 April. International Monetary Fund Bahrain, Bahrain Economic Assessment, T439/126.

IMF. 1999. *Singapore: Selected Issues.* Washington, DC: IMF. https://www.imf.org/ex ternal/pubs/ft/scr/1999/cr9935.pdf

IMF. 2008. *Sovereign Wealth Funds—a Work Agenda.* Washington, DC: IMF. http:// www.imf.org/external/np/pp/eng/2008/022908.pdf

IMF. 2011. "IMF Survey: Assessing the Need for Foreign Currency Reserves." https://www.imf.org/en/News/Articles/2015/09/28/04/53/sopol040711b

Inderst, Georg. 2016. "Strategic Investment Funds: Different Animals to Deal With." *IPE*, June. https://www.ipe.com/investment/briefing-investment/strate gic-investment-funds-different-animals-to-deal-with/10014922.article

Industrial Bank Committee. 1959–66. *Industrial Bank Committee Proceedings; General Correspondence Files.* Hong Kong: Public Records Office Hong Kong, HKRS 163-1-2299.

Industrial Bank Committee. 1960. *Report of the Industrial Bank Committee.* Hong Kong: IBC. Public Records Office Hong Kong BK-000411.

InvestAD. 2015. "New Investment Horizons." 11 July. Accessed 29 July 2015. https://www.investopedia.com/terms/i/investment_horizon.asp

IPIC. 2105a. "About IPIC." International Petroleum Investment Corporation. Accessed 24 July 2015. http://www.ipic.ae/english/about-ipic/about-ipic-watch -video

IPIC. 2015b. "Board of Directors." International Petroleum Investment Corporation. Accessed 24 July 2015. http://www.ipic.ae/english/about-ipic/board-of-directors

Ishihara, M., and C. H. Kim. 1982. "Financial System of Singapore." In *Emerging Financial Centers Legal and Institutional Framework: Bahamas, Hong Kong, Ivory*

Coast, Kenya, Kuwait, Panama, Singapore, edited by Robert C. Effros, 913–33. Washington, DC: International Monetary Fund.

James, E. W. 1991. "Industrial and Trade Development in the Asia-Pacific: Implications for Hong Kong." In *Industrial and Trade Development in Hong Kong*, edited by Edward K. Y. Chen, Mee-kau Nyaw, and Teresa Y. C. Wong, 2–49. Hong Kong: Centre of Asian Studies.

Jao, Y. C. 1983. "Financing Hong Kong's Early Postwar Industrialization: The Role of the Hongkong and Shanghai Banking Corporation." In *Eastern Banking: Essays in the History of the Hongkong and Shanghai Banking Corporation*, edited by Frank H. H King, 554–58. London: Athlone.

Jao, Y. C. 2001. *The Asian Financial Crisis and the Ordeal of Hong Kong*. Westport, CT: Quorum Books.

Jeanne, Olivier. 2007. "International Reserves in Emerging Market Countries: Too Much of a Good Thing?" *Brookings Papers on Economic Activity* no. 1: 1–55.

Jen, S. 2007. "Sovereign Wealth Funds." *World Economics* 8, no. 4: 1–7. doi:10.7312/columbia/9780231158633.003.0058.

Jikon, Lai. 2012. "Khazanah Nasional: Malaysia's Treasure Trove." *Journal of the Asia Pacific Economy* 17, no. 2: 236–52. doi:10.1080/13547860.2012.668023.

Johns, R. 1976. 'Kuwait: Financial Times Survey.' *The Financial Times*, 25 February.

Josselin, D. 1995. "Domestic Policy Networks and the Making of EC Policy: The Case of Financial Services in France and the UK, 1987–1992." Master's thesis, London School of Economics and Political Science.

Jost, Gesine F., and Klaus Jacob. 2004. "The Climate Change Policy Network in Germany." *European Environment* 14, no. 1: 1–15. doi:10.1002/eet.337.

Katara Hospitality. 2015. "About Us." Accessed 15 September 2015. http://www.katarahospitality.com/about-us/

Katzenstein, Peter J. 1985. *Small States in World Markets: Industrial Policy in Europe*. Ithaca, NY: Cornell University Press.

Katzenstein, Peter J. 1987. *Corporatism and Change: Austria, Switzerland, and the Politics of Industry*. Ithaca, NY: Cornell University Press.

Kay, A. 2006. "Health Policy and Politics: Networks, Ideas and Power." *Australian Journal of Public Administration* 65, no. 4: 122–23.

Kéchichian, Joseph A. 2010. "Sovereign Wealth Funds in the United Arab Emirates." In *The Political Economy of Sovereign Wealth Funds*, edited by Xu Yi-chong and Gawdat Bahgat, 88–112. Basingstoke: Palgrave Macmillan.

Kemme, David. 2012. *Sovereign Wealth Fund Issues and the National Fund(S) of Kazakhstan*. Ann Arbor, MI: William Davidson Institute.

Khouja, Mohammad W., and Peter G. Sadler. 1979. *The Economy of Kuwait: Development and Role in International Finance*. London: Macmillan.

Kim, Woochan. 2012. "Korea Investment Corporation: Its Origin and Evolution." *Journal of the Asia Pacific Economy* 17, no. 2: 208–35. doi:10.1080/13547860.2012.668022.

Kimmitt, Robert M. 2008. "Public Footprints in Private Markets." *Foreign Affairs* 87, no. 1: 119–31.

Klingler-Vidra, R. 2014. "Politics Is Local: Sources of Variance in the Diffusion of Venture Capital Policies." PhD diss., London School of Economics and Political Science.

Koh, Ai Tee. 1987a. "Saving, Investment and Entrepreneurship." In *The Singapore Economy Reconsidered*, edited by Lawrence B. Krause, Ai Tee Koh, and Yuan Lee Tsao. Singapore: Institute of Southeast Asian Studies.

Koh, Ai Tee. 1987b. "Linkages and the International Environment." In *The Singapore Economy Reconsidered*, edited by Lawrence B. Krause, Ai Tee Koh, and Yuan Lee Tsao. Singapore: Institute of Southeast Asian Studies.

KOTC. 2015. "About Us: History." Kuwait Oil Tanker Company. Accessed 15 May 2015. http://www.kotc.com.kw/AboutUs/Pages/History.aspx

Krause, Lawrence B. 1988. "Hong Kong and Singapore: Twins or Kissing Cousins?" *Economic Development and Cultural Change* 36, no. S3: S45–S66. doi:10.10 86/edcc.36.s3.1566538.

Krause, Lawrence B., Ai Tee Koh, and Yuan Lee Tsao. 1987. *The Singapore Economy Reconsidered*. Singapore: Institute of Southeast Asian Studies.

Kumar, Anjali. 1992. *The State Holding Company: Issues and Options*. Washington: World Bank.

Kurlantzick, Joshua. 2016. *State Capitalism: How the Return of Statism Is Transforming the World*. New York: Oxford University Press.

Kuwait Airport. 2015. "History." Accessed 9 June 2015. www.kuwait-airport.com .kw/dgca/History_E.htm

Kuwait Banking Association. 2014. "Board Members." Accessed 3 November 2014. http://www.kba.com.kw/pages.aspx?page_ id=5

Kuwait Investment Authority. 2005. "Kuwait Investment Authority." http://www .kia.gov.kw/NR/exeres/73CF85E2-0C5A-4060-B94B-54E2D9EDA231.htm/

Kuwait Investment Authority. 2008. "Kuwait Investment Authority." Accessed 1 December. 2008. http://www.kia.gov.kw/NR/exeres/73CF85E2-0C5A-4060 -B94B-54E2D9EDA231.htm

Labour Advisory Board. 2000. *Report of the Labour Advisory Board 1999–2000*. Hong Kong: Hong Kong Government. http://www.labour.gov.hk/eng/public/dd/lab /report/99_00e.pdf

Labour Department Hong Kong. 2014. "About Us Hong Kong." Hong Kong Government. Accessed 14 September 2014. http://www.labour.gov.hk/eng/rbo/con tent1_1.htm

Landon, T. 2008. "Cash-Rich, Publicity-Shy, Abu Dhabi Fund Draws Scrutiny." *The New York Times*, 28 February.

Lansley, Stewart. 2016. *A Sharing Economy: How Social Wealth Funds Can Reduce Inequality and Help Balance the Books*. Bristol: Policy Press at the University of Bristol.

Lansley, Stewart. 2017. "Citizens' Wealth Funds." Progressive Economics Group, September. Accessed 30 July 2018. https://peg.primeeconomics.org/policybrie fs/citizens-wealth-funds

Laumann, Edward O., and David Knoke. 1987. *The Organizational State: Social Choice in National Policy Domains*. Madison, WI: University of Wisconsin Press.

Lawson, F. H. 1991. 'Managing Economic Crises: The Role of the State in Bahrain and Kuwait', Studies in Comparative International Development, 26 no. 1: 43–67.

Lawson, S., D. Heacock, and A. Stupnytska. 2007. "Beyond the BRICS: A Look at the 'Next 11.'" In *BRICS and Beyond*, edited by Goldman Sachs, 131–64. New York: Goldman Sachs. Accessed 13 December 2018. https://www.goldmansachs .com/insights/archive/archive-pdfs/brics-book/brics-chap-13.pdf

Lee, B. 2007. "Robust Portfolio Construction in a Sovereign Wealth Context." In *Sovereign Wealth Management*, edited by Jennifer Johnson-Calari and Malan Rietveld. London: Central Banking Publications.

Lee, C. L. Yvonne. 2010. "Between Principles and Politics: The Pragmatic Practice of Singapore's Sovereign Wealth Funds." In *The Political Economy of Sovereign Wealth Funds*, edited by Xu Yi-chong and Gawdat Bahgat, 47–71. Basingstoke: Palgrave Macmillan.

Lee, Jang-Yung. 1997. *Sterilizing Capital Inflows*. Washington, DC: International Monetary Fund.

Lee, John. 2012. "China's Geostrategic Search for Oil." *The Washington Quarterly* 35 no.3: 75–92.

Lee, J. P. 1976. "Small Industries' Contribution to the Hong Kong Economy." In *Seminar Proceedings: A Seminar Sponsored by the Japan External Trade Organisation (JETRO) in Cooperation with the Hong Kong General Chamber of Commerce at the Mandarin Hotel, Hong Kong, April 28 1976*. Hong Kong: JETRO.

Lee, Kuan Yew. 2006. "Keynote Address by Minister Mentor Lee Kuan Yew, Chairman, GIC, at the GIC 25th Anniversary Dinner." Government Investment Corporation. 11 July. Accessed 22 July 2018. www.gic.com.sg/newsroom?id= 365&Itemid=159

Lee, Sheng-Yi. 1974. *The Monetary and Banking Development of Malaysia and Singapore*. Singapore: Singapore National University Press.

Lee, Sheng-Yi. 1976. "Business Elites in Singapore." In *Studies in ASEAN Sociology: Urban Society and Social Change*, edited by Peter S. J. Chen. Singapore: Chopmen Enterprises.

Lee, Sheng-Yi. 1978. "Business Elites in Singapore." In *Studies in ASEAN Sociology: Urban Society and Social Change*, edited by Peter S. J. Chen. Singapore: Chopmen Enterprises.

Lee, Sheng-Yi. 1981. "Ownership and Control of Local Banks." *Singapore Yearbook of Banking and Finance 1980–1. Singapore: Institute of Banking and Finance*, 109–17.

Lee, Sheng-Yi. 1984. "Financial Institutions and Markets in Singapore." In *Financial Institutions and Markets in Southeast Asia*, edited by Michael T. Skully. London: Palgrave Macmillan.

Lee Tsao, Yuan. 1987. "The Government in the Labour Market." In *The Singapore Economy Reconsidered*, edited by Lawrence B. Krause, Ai Tee Koh, and Yuan Lee Tsao, 176–218. Singapore: Institute of Southeast Asian Studies.

Lee Tsao, Yuan, and Linda Low. 1990. *Local Entrepreneurship in Singapore: Private &* *State*. Singapore: Institute of Policy Studies.

Leung, Benjamin K. P. 1990. "Power and Politics: A Critical Analysis'." In *Social Issues in Hong Kong*, edited by Benjamin K. P. Leung and G. H. Blowers, 13–26. Hong Kong: Oxford University Press.

Li, M. K. Y. 1988. "Interest Groups and the Debate on the Establishment of a Central Provident Fund in Hong Kong." Master's thesis, Hong Kong University.

Li, Raymond. 1999. *Banking Problems: Hong Kong's Experience in the 1980s*. Bank of International Settlements. https://www.bis.org/publ/plcy06d.pdf

Liew, Leong H., and Liping He. 2012. "Operating in an Inharmonious World: China Investment Corporation." *Journal of the Asia Pacific Economy* 17, no. 2: 253–67. doi:10.1080/13547860.2012.668027.

Lim, Linda, and Eng Fong Pang. 1986. *Trade, Employment, and Industrialisation in Singapore*. Geneva: International Labour Office.

Lim, Siong Guan. 2006. "Interview by Lim Siam Kim." Oral History Centre. Accession Number: 003060/13. 14 September 2006.

Liu, Hong, and Sin Kiong Wong. 2004. *Singapore Chinese Society in Transition: Business, Politics, and Socio-Economic Change, 1945–1965*. New York: Lang.

López, Diego. 2015. *The Major Role of Sovereign Investors in the Global Economy*. PWC. https://www.pwc.com/gx/en/sovereign-wealth-investment-funds/pub lications/assets/major-role-of-sovereign-investors-in-the-global-economy.pdf

Low, Linda. 2001. "The Singapore Developmental State in the New Economy and Polity." *The Pacific Review* 14[3], 411–41.

Low, Linda. 2005. *The Political Economy of a City-State Revisited*. Singapore: Marshall Cavendish Academic.

Lyle, F. J. 1959. "An Industrial Development Programme." *Singapore Legislative Assembly*.

Lyons, Gerard. 2007. "State Capitalism: The Rise of Sovereign Wealth Funds." *Journal of Management Research* 7, no. 3: 119–46.

MacInnes, I. "Policy Networks within the Department of Energy and Energy Policy." *Essex Papers in Politics and Government* 82.

Mahbubani, Kishore. 2008. *The New Asian Hemisphere: The Irresistible Shift of Global Power to the East*. New York: Public Affairs.

Mallakh El, Ragaei, and Dorothea H. El Mallakh. 1982. "Saudi Arabia: Energy, Developmental Planning, and Industrialization." https://www.osti.gov/biblio /5333977

Martin, Michael F. 2008. "China's Sovereign Wealth Fund." Congressional Research Service, Library of Congress.

MAS Commemoration. 2011. "Sustaining Stability: Serving Singapore, Monetary Authority of Singapore 40th Anniversary." Monetary Authority of Singapore.

MAS Economic Explorer. 2014. *Inflation, Economic Explorer Series 3*. Singapore: Monetary Authority of Singapore.

McCarthy, I. 1982. "Financial System of Hong Kong." In *Emerging Financial Centres: Legal and Institutional Framework*, edited by Effros, 95–140. Washington, DC: International Monetary Fund.

Mazzucato, Mariana. 2013. *The Entrepreneurial State: Debunking Public vs. Private Sector Myths*. London: Anthem Press.

McConnell, Allan. 1993. *Parliamentarism, Policy Networks and the Poll Tax*. Glasgow: Department of Government, University of Strathclyde.

Mehran, Kamrava. 2013. *Qatar: Small State, Big Politics*. Ithaca: Cornell University Press.

Meier, Henri B., John E Marthinsen, and Pascal A. Gantenbein. 2012. *Swiss Finance: Capital Markets, Banking, and the Swiss Value Chain*. Hoboken: John Wiley & Sons.

Memorandum GIC. 1981. *Memorandum and Articles of Association, 22 May 1981*. Accessed at the Monetary Authority of Singapore Library. Singapore: Government Investment Corporation.

Milhench, Claire. 2017a. "A New Breed of Sovereign Wealth Fund—without the Wealth." Reuters (London), 20 March. https://www.reuters.com/article/us-emerging-swf-investment/a-new-breed-of-sovereign-wealth-fund-without-the-wealth-idUSKBN16R0QY

Milhench, Claire. 2017b. "Home-grown African Wealth Funds Seeking Foreign Partners to Fix Infrastructure Gap." Reuters (London), 25 January. https://www.reuters.com/article/us-africa-economy-infrastructure/home-grown-african-wealth-funds-seeking-foreign-partners-to-fix-infrastructure-gap-idUSKBN1591F5

Ministry of Information. 1985. "Development and Progress in the State of Qatar." Qatar News Agency (Doha), 1–48.

Mok, H. 1986. *Provident Fund for Social Welfare Agencies*. Hong Kong: Hong Kong Social Workers General Union.

Monk, Ashby H. 2010. "Sovereignty in the Era of Global Capitalism: The Rise of Sovereign Wealth Funds and the Power of Finance." *Environment and Planning A* 43, no. 8: 1813–32. doi:10.1068/a43326.

Monks, Sarah. 2010. *Toy Town: How a Hong Kong Industry Played a Global Game*. Hong Kong: Toys Manufacturers' Association of Hong Kong.

Montpetit, Éric. 2002. "Policy Networks, Federal Arrangements, and the Development of Environmental Regulations: A Comparison of the Canadian and American Agricultural Sectors." *Governance* 15, no. 1: 1–20. doi:10.1111/1468-0491.00177.

Montpetit, Éric. 2005. "A Policy Network Explanation of Biotechnology Policy Differences between the United States and Canada." *Journal of Public Policy* 25, no. 3: 339–66. doi:10.1017/s0143814x05000358.

Moore, Pete W. 2002. "Rentier Fiscal Crisis and Regime Stability: Business-State Relations in the Gulf." *Studies in Comparative International Development* 37, no. 1: 34–56. doi:10.1007/bf02686337.

Moreno, R. 2012. "Exchange Rates and Monetary Policy in Singapore and Hong Kong." In *Monetary Policy in Pacific Basin Countries: Papers Presented at a Conference Sponsored by the Federal Reserve Bank of San Francisco*, edited by Hang-sheng Cheng, 173–201. Boston: Kluwer Academic Publishers.

Moser, C. 2008. "NLSC: Leaders of National Life [Track 14, Session 5]." By J. Wingate. Podcast audio. British Library. 18 March.

Moser, D., and T. Stuck. 2007. "The National Bank's Investment Policy." In *The Swiss National Bank: 1907–2007*, edited by Werner Abegg and Ernst Baltensperger, 439–51. Zurich: Neue Zuercher Zeitung.

Mubadala. 2014. "About Mubadala." Mubadala. Accessed 12 February 2014. http://www.mubadala.ae/

Mubadala. 2015. "Board of Directors." Mubadala. Accessed 12 February 2015. https://www.mubadala.com/en/who-we-are/board-of-directors/mahmood-ebr aheem-al-mahmood

Mumtalakat. 2017. "Investment Philosophy." Mumtalakat. Accessed 13 February 2017. http://www.bmhc.bh/en/17.aspx

Musacchio, A., and Lazzarini, S.G., 2014. *Reinventing state capitalism*. Harvard University Press.

National Bank of Abu Dhabi. 2015. "Board of Directors." Accessed 18 May 2015. https://www.nbad.com/en-ae/about-nbad/overview/board-of-directors.html

National Bank of Kuwait. 2015. "History." Accessed 18 May 2015. http://www.nbk .com/aboutnbk/profile/history_en_gb.aspx

Ngiam, Tong Dow, and Simon Tay. 2006. *A Mandarin and the Making of Public Policy: Reflections*. Singapore: National University of Singapore Press.

Ngo, T. W. 1996. "The East Asian Anomaly Revisited: The Politics of Laissez-Faire in Hong Kong 1945–1985." PhD diss., School of Oriental and African Studies.

Nguyen, Duc-Tho, Tran-Phuc Nguyen, and Jeremy DK Nguyen. 2012. "Vietnam's SCIC: A Gradualist Approach to Sovereign Wealth Funds." *Journal of the Asia Pacific Economy* 17, no. 2: 268–83.

NIIF India. 2017. "NIIF and Abu Dhabi Investment Authority Finalise Investment Agreement Worth US$1 Billion." 16 October. Accessed 14 July 2018. http://www.lightsandbox.com/pressreleases/niifindia/

NIIF India. 2018. "Who We Are." Accessed 13 July 2018. http://niifindia.com/Str ucture-Fund.html

Norges Bank. 2018. "About the Fund." Norges Bank Investment Management. Accessed 6 August 2018. https://www.nbim.no/en/the-fund/about-the -fund/

Nyaw, Mee-Kau. 1991. "The Experiences of Industrial Growth in Hong Kong and Singapore: A Comparative Study." In *Industrial and Trade Development in Hong Kong*, edited by Edward K. Y. Chen, Mee-Kau Nyaw, and Teresa Y. C. Wong, 185–222. Hong Kong: Centre of Asian Studies.

OECD. 2011. "OECD Guidance on Sovereign Wealth Funds." Accessed 20 March 2011. http://www.oecd.org/document/19/0,3746,en_2649_34887_41807059 _1_1_1_1,00.htm

OECD. 2015. *Policy Framework for Investment, 2015 Edition*. Washington, DC: Organisation for Economic Co-operation and Development.

OMELCO. 1986. *OMELCO Annual Report*. Hong Kong: Office of the Members of the Executive and Legislative Councils.

OMELCO. 1987. *The Legislative Council: Behind the Scenes*. Hong Kong: Hong Kong Government Printer.

O'Neill, Jim. 2001. *Building Better Global Economic BRICs*. New York: Goldman Sachs. https://www.goldmansachs.com/our-thinking/archive/archive-pdfs/bui ld-better-brics.pdf

Orji, Uche, and Stella Ojekwe-Onyejeli. 2017. "The Role of the Nigeria Sovereign Investment Authority in a New Era of Fiscal Responsibility." In *New Frontiers of Sovereign Investment*, edited by Malan Rietveld and Perrine Toledano, 168–82. La Vergne: Perseus Books (Ingram).

Orr, Adrian. 2017. "Sovereign Wealth Funds as Long-Term Investors: Taking Advantage of Unique Endowments." In *New Frontiers of Sovereign Investment*, edited by Malan Rietveld and Perrine Toledano, 26–43. La Vergne: Perseus Books (Ingram).

Paulson, Anna L. 2009. "Raising Capital: The Role of Sovereign Wealth Funds." *Chicago Fed Letter* 258 (January).

Pekkanen, Saadia M., and Kellee S. Tsai. 2011. "The Politics of Ambiguity in Asia's Sovereign Wealth Funds." *Business and Politics* 13, no. 2: 1–44. doi:10.2202/146 9-3569.1344.

Penrose, T. Edith. 1968. *The Large International Firm in Developing Countries*. London: George Allen and Unwin.

Petras, James F., Morris Morley, and Steven Smith. 1977. *Nationalization of Venezuelan Oil*. New York: Praeger.

Pillay, J. Y. 2006. "Economic Development of Singapore." By Shashi Jayakumar. Podcast audio. Oral History Centre Singapore. 22 May. Accession Number: 003056/2.

Prequin. 2015. *Global Private Equity and Venture Capital Report*. https://www.preq in.com/docs/reports/2015-Preqin-Global-Private-Equity-and-Venture-Capi tal-Report-Sample-Pages.pdf

Prokesch, S. 1991. "Abu Dhabi Drops BCCI Revival in Britain." *The New York Times*, 4 October, p. 12.

Public Sector Divestment Committee. 1987. *Report of the Public Sector Divestment Committee*. Singapore: Singapore National Printers.

Qatar Diar. 2014. "Who We Are." Accessed 29 October 2014. http://www.qatarid iar.com/English/

Qatar Holding. 2013. "About Us." Accessed 12 March 2013. http://www.qatarhold ing.qa/Pages/Home.aspx

Qatar Investment Authority. 2014. "Frequently Asked Questions." Accessed 18 November 2014. http://www.qia.qa/faq.html

Qatar Islamic Bank. 2015. "Board of Directors." Accessed 27 June 2015. http://www .qib.com.qa/en/footer/about-us/board-of-directors.aspx

Qatar Monetary Agency. 1985. *The Banking and Financial System in Qatar*. London: LSE Government Publications.

Qatar National Bank. 2015. "Board of Directors." Accessed 28 June 2015. http:// www.qnb.com.qa/cs/Satellite/QNBQatar/en_QA/AboutQNB/enBoardofDire ctors

Quah, Danny. 2010. *The Shifting Distribution of Global Economic Activity*. London: London School of Economics. http://citeseerx.ist.psu.edu/viewdoc/download ?doi=10.1.1.182.4046&rep=rep1&type=pdf

Quah, Danny. 2011. "The Global Economy's Shifting Centre of Gravity." *Global Policy* 2, no. 1: 3–9. doi:10.1111/j.1758–5899.2010.00066.x.

Raab, Charles D. 1992. "Taking Networks Seriously: Education Policy in Britain." *European Journal of Political Research* 21, nos. 1–2: 69–90. doi:10.1111/j.1475–6 765.1992.tb00289.x.

Ramirez, Carlos, and Tan Ling Hui. 2003. *Singapore, Inc. versus the Private Sector: Are Government-Linked Companies Different?* Washington, DC: International Monetary Fund.

Raphaeli, N., and B. Gersten. 2008. "Sovereign Wealth Funds: Investment Vehicles for the Persian Gulf Countries." *Middle East Quarterly* 15, no. 2: 45–53.

Rear, J. 1971. "One Brand of Politics." In *Hong Kong, the Industrial Colony: A Political, Social and Economic Survey*, edited by Keith Hopkins, 55–139. Hong Kong: Oxford University Press.

Reinsberg, Bernhard. 2009. "Sovereign Wealth-no Fund: The Decisive Role of Domestic Veto Players." Arbeitsstelle Internationale Politische Ökonomie, Freie Universität Berlin. (No. 1/2009). PIPE-Papers on International Political Economy, 1–22.

Report of the Economic Committee. 1986. *The Singapore Economy: New Directions*. Singapore: Ministry of Trade and Industry; Singapore National Library, Special Collections.

Rhodes, R. A. W., and G. Wistow, eds. 1988. *The Core Executive and Policy Networks: Caring for Mentally Handicapped*. Colchester: University of Essex Department of Government.

Riedel, James. 1974. *The Industrialization of Hong-Kong*. Tübingen: J. C. B. Mohr (Paul Siebeck).

Rietveld, Malan, and Perrine Toledano, eds. 2017. *New Frontiers of Sovereign Investment*. New York: Columbia University Press.

Roberts, D. 2011. "Kuwait." In *Power and Politics in the Persian Gulf Monarchies*, edited by Christopher M. Davidson, 89–113. New York: Columbia University Press.

Rodan, Garry. 1989. *The Political Economy of Singapore's Industrialization: National State and International Capital*. Basingstoke: Macmillan.

Rodrik, Dani. 2004. *Industrial Policy for the Twenty-First Century*. Cambridge, MA: John F. Kennedy School of Government, Harvard University.

Rose, Paul. 2008. "Sovereign Wealth Funds: Active or Passive Investors?" *Yale Law Journal Pocket Part* 118 (November): 104–8. Accessed 1 December 2018. https://www.yalelawjournal.org/pdf/725_wbyy6ecq.pdf

Rose, Paul. 2011. *American Sovereign Wealth*. Ohio State Public Law Working Paper no. 161.

Rose, Paul. 2012. "Sovereign Investing and Corporate Governance: Evidence and Policy." *Fordham Journal of Corporate & Finance Law*, no. 18: 913–62. doi:10.21 39/ssrn.2220222.

Rose, Paul. 2014. "The Foreign Investment and National Security Act of 2007: An Assessment of Its Impact on Sovereign Wealth Funds and State-Owned Enterprises." In *Research Handbook on Sovereign Wealth Funds and International Investment Law*, 145–77. doi:10.4337/9781781955208.00017.

Rozanov, Andrew. 2005. "Who Holds the Wealth of Nations?" *Central Banking Journal* 15, no. 4: 52–57.

Said Zahlan, Rosemarie. 1989. *The Making of the Modern Gulf States*. London: Unwin Hyman.

Sally, Razeen. 2013. *States and Firms: Multinational Enterprises in Institutional Competition*. London: Routledge.

SBR Harbour Department of Social Services. 1974–76. *Confidential Report: Central Provident Fund Scheme Visit to Singapore and Malaysia*. Hong Kong: SBR. Public Records Office Hong Kong, HKRS 163-9-1080.

*SCCC. 2014. "Online Directory." Singapore Chinese Chamber of Commerce and Industry. Accessed 1 January 2015. http://english.sccci.org.sg/index.cfm?GPID=388

Schaffer, J. 2003. "Overdetermining Causes." *Philosophical Studies* 114, no. 1: 23–45.

Schein, Edgar H. 1996. *Strategic Pragmatism: The Culture of Singapore's Economic Development Board*. Cambridge, MA: MIT Press.

Schena, Patrick J. 2012. *The China Investment Corporation at 4 Years: An Evolving Legacy of Capitalization and Control*. Medford, MA: Sovereign Wealth Fund Initiative. https://sites.tufts.edu/sovereignet/files/2017/08/Archives-The-China-Investment-Corporation-at-4-Years-An-evolving-legacy-of-capitalization-and-control.pdf

Schena, Patrick J. 2017. "When States Invest at Home: The Development Role of Sovereign Wealth Funds in Public Finance." *Wake Forest Law Review* 52, no. 4: 917–48.

Schena, Patrick J., and Asim Ali. 2017. "Sovereign Wealth Fund Investment in Economic Transformation: Toward an Institutional Framework." *World Economics Journal*, 18, no. 1: 123–44.

Schena, Patrick J., Juergen Braunstein, and Asim Ali. 2018. "The Case for Economic Development through Sovereign Investment: A Paradox of Scarcity?" *Global Policy* 9, no. 3: 365–76. doi:10.1111/1758-5899.12549.

Schena, Patrick J., and Ravi Shankar Chaturvedi. 2011. *Sovereign Wealth Funds, Debt Issuances, and the Development of Capital Markets*. Medford, MA: Sovereign Wealth Fund Initiative. https://sites.tufts.edu/sovereignet/files/2011/11/Archives-Sovereign-Wealth-Funds-Debt-Issuances-and-the-Development-of-Capital-Markets.pdf

Schulze, David L. 1990. *Domestic Financial Institutions in Singapore: Public Sector Competition*. Singapore: Centre for Advanced Studies, National University of Singapore.

Scott, Ian. 2010. *The Public Sector in Hong Kong*. Hong Kong: Hong Kong University Press.

Seng, Y. P., and L. Chong-Yah. 1971. *The Singapore Economy*. Singapore: Eastern University Press.

Senner, Richard, and Didier Sornette. 2017. *The 'New Normal' of the Swiss Balance of Payments in a Global Perspective: Central Bank Intervention, Global Imbalances and the Rise of Sovereign Wealth Funds.* Geneva: University of Geneva.

Setser, Brad W. 2008. *Sovereign Wealth and Sovereign Power.* Council on Foreign Relations Special Report No. 37, September. https://www.cfr.org/report/sov ereign-wealth-and-sovereign-power

Seznec, Jean-Francois. 2008. "The Gulf Sovereign Wealth Funds: Myths and Reality." *Middle East Policy* 15, no. 1: 97–111.

Sheikh Mohammed. 2014. "History: Bani Yas." His Highness Sheikh Mohammed bin Rashid Al Maktoum. Accessed 13 December 2014. https://sheikhmohamm ed.ae/ar-ae/Pages/home.aspx

Shih, Victor. 2009. "Tools of Survival: Sovereign Wealth Funds in Singapore and China." *Geopolitics* 14, no. 2: 328–44.

Singapore Government Press Releases. 1980. "Statement from the Prime Minister's Office." National Archive, No: 1230-1980-08-01.

Singapore Infopedia. 2015. "J. Y. Pillay." National Library Board Singapore. Accessed 4 June 2015. http://eresources.nlb.gov.sg/infopedia/art06.html

Skancke, Martin. 2003. "Fiscal Policy and Petroleum Fund Management in Norway." In *Fiscal Policy Formulation and Implementation in Oil-Producing Countries*, edited by Jeffrey M. Davis, Rolando Ossowski, and Annalisa Fedelino, 316–38. Washington, DC: International Monetary Fund.

Skully, Michael T. 1984. *Financial Institutions and Markets in Southeast Asia.* London: Palgrave Macmillan.

Skully, Michael T, and G. J. Viksnins. 1987. *Financing East Asia's Success.* London: Palgrave Macmillan.

Slovenian Sovereign Holdings. 2018. "Company Details." SDH—Domov. Accessed 6 August 2018. http://www.sdh.si/en-gb/about-ssh/company-details

SMA. *Championing Manufacturing: Partner in Nation Building.* 2012. Singapore: Singapore Manufacturing Federation.

SNB. 2017. "About Us." *Swiss National Bank.* Accessed 15 December 2017. https://www.snb.ch/en/ifor/public/qas/id/qas_unternehmen#t5

Sornette, D. 2015. "Ein Schweizer Souveraenitatetsfond." *Schweizer Monat*, October.

Srinivasan, Krishna, Julie Kozack, and Doug Laxton. 2008. "The Macroeconomic Impact of Sovereign Wealth Funds." In *Economics of Sovereign Wealth Funds: Issues for Policymakers*, edited by Adnan Mazarei, Udaibir S. Das, and Hans Van der Hoorn. Washington, DC: International Monetary Fund.

State of Singapore First Development Plan, 1961–1964: Review of Progress for the Three Years 1961–1963. 1961. Singapore: Economic Planning Unit, Prime Minister's Office.

Stiglitz, Joseph E., Justin Yifu Lin, and Ebrahim Patel. 2013. *The Industrial Policy Revolution.* New York: Palgrave Macmillan.

Strange, Susan. 1988. *States and Markets: An Introduction to Political Economy.* London, Pinter.

Sung, Yun-wing, and Lee Ming-kwan. 1991. *The Other Hong Kong Report 1991*. Hong Kong: Chinese University Press.

Sovereign Wealth Fund Institute. 2015. "Fund Rankings." Accessed 6 February 2015. http://www.swfinstitute.org/fund-rankings/

Sovereign Wealth Fund Institute. 2017. "Fund Ranking." 2017. Accessed 26 August 2017. http://www.swfinstitute.org/fund-rankings/

Summers, Lawrence. 2007. "Funds That Shake Capitalistic Logic." *Financial Times*, 29 July. Accessed 28 September 2010. https://www.ft.com/content/bb8f50b8 -3dcc-11dc-8f6a-0000779fd2ac

Swiss Bankers Association. 2008. *Sovereign Wealth Funds—a Position Paper by the Swiss Bankers Association*. http://shop.sba.ch/999978_e.pdf

Szczepanik, Edward F. 1958. *The Economic Growth of Hong Kong*. London: Oxford University Press.

Szczepanik, Edward F. 1986. *The Economic Growth of Hong Kong*. Westport, CT: Greenwood Press.

Tan Jake, Hooi, ed. 1972. *Urbanization Planning and National Development Planning in Singapore*. New York: Southeast Asia Development Advisory Group of the Asia Society.

Tan Yew Lee, Kevin. 2011. *Constitutional Law in Singapore*. Alphen aan den Rijn, The Netherlands: Kluwer Law International.

Temasek. 1982. *Directory of Subsidiaries and Related Companies of Temasek Holdings (Pte) Ltd., Sheng-Li Holding Co. Pte. Ltd., MND Holdings (Pte) Ltd.* Singapore: Temasek Holdings.

Temasek. 2011. "Our Portfolio." Temasek corporate website. Accessed 7 March 2011. http://www.temasek.com.sg/our_portfolio.htm

Teo, Chee Hean. 1993. *Interim Report of the Committee to Promote Enterprise Overseas*. Singapore: SNP Publishers.

Tetreault, Mary Ann. 1991. "Autonomy, Necessity, and the Small State: Ruling Kuwait in the Twentieth Century." *International Organization* 45, no. 4: 565–91.

Tetreault, Mary Ann. 1995. *The Kuwait Petroleum Corporation and the Economics of the New World Order*. Westport, CT: Greenwood, 1995.

Thatcher, Mark. 1998. "The Development of Policy Network Analyses." *Journal of Theoretical Politics* 10, no. 4: 389–416. doi:10.1177/0951692898010004002.

Thatcher, Mark, and Braunstein, Juergen. 2015. "Issue Networks: Iron Triangles, Subgovernments, Policy Communities, Policy Networks." *International Encyclopedia of the Social & Behavioral Sciences*, 2nd ed. 769–73. doi: 10.1016/B978-0-08-097086-8.75025-2.

Thatcher, Mark, and Tim Vlandas. 2016. "Overseas State Outsiders as New Sources of Patient Capital: Government Policies to Welcome Sovereign Wealth Fund Investment in France and Germany." *Socio-Economic Review* 14, no. 4: 647–68. doi:10.1093/ser/mwwo28.

Toke, David. 2000. "Policy Network Creation: The Case of Energy Efficiency." *Public Administration* 78, no. 4: 835–54. doi:10.1111/1467-9299.00233.

Topley, T. 1964. "Capital, Saving and Credit among Indigenous Rice Farmers and Immigrant Vegetable Farmers in Hong Kong's New Territories." In *Capital, Saving and Credit in Peasant Societies*, 157–86. London: Allen & Unwin.

Trade and Industry Department. 2014. "Trade and Industry Advisory Board." 23 April. Accessed 28 August 2014. http://www.tid.gov.hk/english/aboutusl

Tranøy, Bent Sofus. 2010. "Norway: The Accidental Role Model." In *The Political Economy of Sovereign Wealth Funds*, edited by Xu Yi-chong and Gawdat Bahgat, 177–201. Basingstoke: Palgrave Macmillan.

Truman, Edwin M. 2007. "Sovereign Wealth funds: The Need for Greater Transparency and Accountability." No. PB07-6. Washington, 1–9. DC: Peterson Institute for International Economics.

Truman, Edwin M. 2008. "A Blueprint for Sovereign Wealth Fund Best Practices." PIIE. 29 April. Accessed 28 July 2018. https://piie.com/publications/policy-bri efs/blueprint-sovereign-wealth-fund-best-practices

Truman, Edwin M. 2010a. *Sovereign Wealth Funds Threat or Salvation?* Washington, DC: Peterson Institute for International Economics.

Truman, Edwin M. 2010b. "The Case for an Indian Sovereign Wealth Fund." Peterson Institute for International Economics. 23 September. Accessed 28 July 2018. https://piie.com/commentary/op-eds/case-indian-sovereign-wealth -fund

Tsim, T. L. 1989. *The Other Hong Kong Report*. Hong Kong: Chinese University Press.

Tugwell, Franklin. 1975. *The Politics of Oil in Venezuela*. Stanford, CA: Stanford University Press.

Udaibir Das, Yinqiu Lu, Mulder, Christian, Amadou Sy. 2009. *Setting Up a Sovereign Wealth Fund: Some Policy and Operational Considerations*. Washington, DC: International Monetary Fund.

UNDP. 1972. *Singapore Country Programme Background Paper for United Nations Development Assistance 1973–1975*. Kuala Lumpur: United Nations Development Programme.

UNIDO. 2016. "Unlocking Domestic Investment for Industrial Development." Inclusive and Sustainable Industrial Development Working Paper Series WP12, 1–55.

Urban Council Annual Conventional Debate. 1975. *Files Relating to Urban Council 1974–1982*. Urban Council Annual Conventional Debates. Public Records Office Hong Kong, HKRS 1074-1-4

Velasco, Andrés, and Eric Parrado. 2012. *The Political Economy of Fiscal Policy: The Experience of Chile*. Oxford University Press.

Vennewald, Werner. 1994. *Technocrats in the State Enterprise System of Singapore*. Murdoch, Western Australia: Asia Research Centre, Murdoch University.

Visscher, Sikko. 2007. *The Business of Politics and Ethnicity: A History of the Singapore Chinese Chamber of Commerce and Industry*. Singapore: NUS Press.

Wade, Robert H. 2012. "Return of Industrial Policy?" *International Review of Applied Economics* 262, no. 2: 223–39. doi:10.1080/02692171.2011.640312.

Walter, Andrew. *World Power and World Money: The Role of Hegemony and International Monetary Order*. New York: Harvester Wheatsheaf, 1991.

Wang, D. 1991. "The Economic Relations between China and Hong Kong: Prospects and Principles." In *Industrial and Trade Development in Hong Kong*, edited by Edward K. Y. Chen, Mee-kau Nyaw, and Teresa Y. C. Wong, 447–63. Hong Kong: Centre of Asian Studies, University of Hong Kong.

Wang, Di, and Quan Li. 2016. "Democracy, Veto Player, and Institutionalization of Sovereign Wealth Funds." *International Interactions* 42, no. 3: 377–400.

Watson Wyatt. 2006. "The World's 300 Largest Pension Funds." *The P&ll Watson Wyatt Global 300 Ranking.* 1–31. Accessed 12 January 2010. http://www.agingso ciety.org/agingsociety/publications/public_policy/300largest.pdf

Weiss, John. 2015. *Taxonomy of Industrial Policy. UNIDO Research, Statistics and Industrial Policy Branch Working Paper 8/2015*. Vienna: UNIDO.

Wilks, S., and Wright, M. 1987. *Comparative Government-Industry Relations: Western Europe, the United States, and Japan*. Vol. 1. Oxford: Clarendon Press.

Winsemius, Albert. 1982a. "Economic Development of Singapore." By Tan Kay Chee. Podcast audio. Oral History Centre Singapore. No: 000246/12. 31 August 1982.

Winsemius, Albert. 1982b. "Economic Development of Singapore." By Tan Kay Chee. Podcast audio. Oral History Centre Singapore. No 000246/17. 3 September.

Winsemius, Albert. 1982c. "Economic Development of Singapore." By Tan Kay Chee. Podcast audio. Oral History Centre Singapore. No: 000246/9. 31 August 31.

Winsemius, Albert. 1982d. "Economic Development of Singapore." By Tan Kay Chee. Podcast audio. Oral History Centre Singapore. No: 000246/2. 30 August.

Wong, K. A. 1991. "The Hong Kong Stock Market." In *The Hong Kong Financial System: A New Age*, edited by Simon S. M. Ho, Robert Haney Scott, and Kie Ann Wong, 215–34. New York: Oxford University Press.

Wong, Siu-lun. 1988. *Emigrant Entrepreneurs: Shanghai Industrialists in Hong Kong*. Hong Kong: Oxford University Press.

World Bank. 2015. "Gross Savings (% of GDP)." World Bank Open Data. Accessed 6 February 2015. http://data.worldbank.org/indicator/NY

World Bank Database. 2017. World Bank Open Data. Accessed 6 November 2017. https://data.worldbank.org

Wright, M. 1990. "The Comparative Analysis of Industrial Policies: Policy Networks and Sectoral Governance Structures in Britain and France." *Staatswissenschaften und Staatspraxis* 1: 503–33.

Wu, Friedrich, Christine Goh, and Ruchi Hajela. 2012. "Transformation of China's Sovereign Wealth Fund since the 2008–2009 Global Crisis." *Thunderbird International Business Review* 54, no. 3: 347–59. doi:10.1002/tie.21466.

Yeung, Chak-sze. "A Strategic Study of the General Insurance Industry in Hong Kong." PhD diss., University of Hong Kong, 1990.

Yeung, Henry W. 1999. "Regulating Investment Abroad: The Political Economy of the Regionalization of Singaporean Firms." *Antipode* 31, no. 3: 245–73. doi:10 .1111/1467–8330.00103.

Yeung, Henry W. 2004. "Strategic Governance and Economic Diplomacy in China: The Political Economy of Government-Linked Companies from Singapore." *East Asia* 21, no. 1: 40–64. doi:10.1007/s12140-004-0009-8.

Yeung, Henry W. 2011. "From National Development to Economic Diplomacy? Governing Singapore's Sovereign Wealth Funds." *The Pacific Review* 24, no. 5: 625–52.

Yeung, Henry W. 2014. "Governing the Market in a Globalizing Era: Developmental States, Global Production Networks and Inter-Firm Dynamics in East Asia." *Review of International Political Economy* 21, no. 1: 70–101. doi:10.1080/09 692290.2012.756415.

Yeung, K. Y. 1991. "The Role of the Hong Kong Government in Industrial Development." In *Industrial and Trade Development in Hong Kong*, edited by Edward K. Y. Chen, Mee-Kau Nyaw, and Teresa Y. C. Wong, 48–56. Hong Kong: Centre of Asian Studies.

Yi-Chong, Xu, and Gawdat, Bahgat. 2010. *The Political Economy of Sovereign Wealth Funds*. London: Palgrave Macmillan.

Yoshihara, Kunio. 1975. *Foreign Investment and Domestic Response: A Study of Singapore's Industrialization*. Singapore: Eastern Universities Press.

Young, Arthur Nichols. 1983. *Saudi Arabia, the Making of a Financial Giant*. New York: New York University Press.

Youngson, A. J. 1982. *Hong Kong, Economic Growth and Policy*. Hong Kong: Oxford University Press.

Zonescorp. 2010. "New Members to Join Abu Dhabi's Economic Board." Accessed 26 January 2015. http://www.zonescorp.com/En/News/Pages/Nepx

Zysman, John. 1983. *Governments, Markets, and Growth Financial Systems and Politics of Industrial Change*. Ithaca: Cornell University Press.

NEWSPAPERS

Accessed via Factiva.com; Eresources.nlb.gov.sg; Press clippings of the Public Records Office (Hong Kong); Press Clippings of the Monetary Authority of Singapore Library; Press Clippings of the Hong Kong University Library; Press Clippings of the National University of Singapore Library; Press Clippings of the National Archives of Singapore.

HANSARDS

All of the cited Hong Kong Hansard references can be accessed online via http://www.legco.gov.hk/yr97–98/english/former/lc_sitg.htm

All of the cited Singapore Hansard references can be accessed online via http://www.parliament.gov.sg/publications-singapore-parliament-reports

Index

regression analysis, 4, 155; multinomial,
151
regulation, improved, 101
relationship, 23, 32, 69, 92, 115, 151,
156; close, 116; indirect, 120; state's,
102; state-society, 33, 139
Rentier States, 111
representation, 33, 46, 131, 139; direct,
109; exclusive, 158; institutional, 69;
private interest, 118; strong banking,
54
representatives: appointing, 69; employee, 99; employer, 99; union, 99
research, 5, 26, 58, 96, 98, 140; economic, 12
reserves, 3, 22, 53, 79, 95, 108, 116, 121,
125, 128, 133–34; foreign, 53, 82;
large, 23, 94; massive, 2, 129; official,
121
resources, 2, 19, 28, 30, 34, 45, 103, 112,
125, 136, 149; financial, 56; fiscal,
126; hydro-carbon, 87; limited, 136;
natural, 44, 104, 112; nonrenewable,
127; single finite, 12
responsibility, 90–92, 94
restraints, regulatory, 70
revenues, 12, 103, 108, 127, 130, 145;
budget, 19; enlarged state, 11; governmental, 11, 127; hydrocarbon, 103–4;
petroleum, 131; rent-based, 132;
surplus oil, 12; tax, 127
review: fundamental, 91; informal, 58,
64, 67
risk profile, 132
risks, 30, 91, 100, 152; financial, 100
role, 1, 4–6, 22, 28–30, 34, 44, 53, 62, 71,
119, 123–24, 132–33, 138, 142, 147;
central, 6, 30, 34, 130, 139, 149, 159;
competitive, 31; entrepreneurial, 37;
government's, 52, 59; important, 9,
19–20, 23, 29, 36, 76; key, 116; significant, 5; strong, 131
royalties, 132; oil/gas, 105
Russia, 4, 30, 128, 133, 151

Sarkozy, Nicolas (President), 2
Saudi Arabia, 11–12, 17, 121, 156
savings, 3, 5, 16–17, 19–20, 22–23, 26–
27, 30–31, 80–82, 86–87, 90–91, 101–

2, 122, 128–29, 140–41, 156; country's
excess, 27, 34, 139; high, 87; large, 82;
long-term, 10; national, 1; private, 81–
82, 91; public, 91; sizable, 79
SCCCI (Singapore Chinese Chamber
of Commerce and Industry), 48–49,
70–72, 157
sectors, 5–6, 31, 34, 72, 97, 114, 117, 120,
137; clothing, 59; commercial, 101;
communication, 77; finance/com-
merce, 57; health, 34; housing, 159;
labor-intensive, 64; life insurance, 101;
life science, 9; material supply, 148;
merchant, 104, 145; nonstrategic, 72;
pearl fishing, 105; private domestic,
73, 110, 120; private domestic insurance, 92; private pension fund, 102;
provident fund, 96; public, 41, 76, 118,
126; short-term, 90; strategic, 13, 76;
tourism, 13; transport, 42; transport/
logistics, 148
securities, 62–63, 86, 95; old-age, 86, 101
segments: fastest growing, 37; mobilized,
122; narrow, 50; particular, 33
Senegal, 13, 37
Shanghai, 9, 47–48
Silicon Valley, 9
Singapore, 7–10, 21, 28, 37–46, 48–51,
64–71, 73–78, 80–82, 84–88, 90–95,
102, 139–42, 144, 148–49, 156–60
Slovenia, 126, 128
SMA (Singapore Manufacturing Association), 48–49, 157–58
social security benefits, 101
socioeconomic actors, 3, 5–6, 26, 30–31,
35, 37, 73, 78, 80, 88–90, 102, 109,
139, 146, 149
South Africa, 133, 135
Southeast Asia, 65, 69, 81
South Korea, 28, 39, 44, 56, 134–35, 144,
157
sovereign wealth funds. *See* SWFs
stabilization, 3, 16–17, 19–20, 22, 148,
153, 156; fiscal, 19
stakes: direct, 142; included, 114; large,
9; majority/controlling, 43; minority,
10, 20; significant, 65
state actors, 30, 35, 46, 67, 78, 89, 139,
145; enabled, 78, 102

Printed and bound by CPI Group (UK) Ltd, Croydon, CR0 4YY

09/06/2025